# Radical Conservatism

# RADICAL

# CONSERVATISM

## The Right's

## Political Religion

**Robert Brent Toplin**

University Press of Kansas

Published by the University Press of
Kansas (Lawrence, Kansas 66045), which
was organized by the Kansas Board of
Regents and is operated and funded by
Emporia State University, Fort Hays State
University, Kansas State University,
Pittsburg State University, the University of
Kansas, and Wichita State University

Library of Congress Cataloging-in-
Publication Data

Toplin, Robert Brent, 1940–
   Radical conservatism : the right's political
religion / Robert Brent
Toplin.
      p.   cm.
Includes bibliographical references and
index.
ISBN 0–7006–1487–7 (cloth : alk. paper)
1. Conservatism—United States.
2. Right-wing extremists—United States.
3. Radicalism—United States. I. Title.
JC573.2.U6T66 2006
320.520973—dc22    2006013439

British Library Cataloguing-in-Publication
Data is available.

Printed in the United States of America

10 9 8 7 6 5 4 3 2 1

The paper used in this publication meets
the minimum requirements of the
American National Standard for
Permanence of Paper for Printed Library
Materials Z39.48-1992.

# CONTENTS

# Radical Conservatism

On November 7, 2005, when I was putting the final touches on this book, I attended a luncheon in my community sponsored by the John Locke Foundation, a conservative organization known for its strong opposition to government regulation and taxes. I was not a member of the group, but I was pleased to attend the event so that I could hear the comments of the foundation's invited speaker, Fred Barnes, a prominent figure in right-oriented journalism and television commentary. I was especially interested in hearing Fred Barnes's speech because of his position with one of the right's most distinguished publications about politics and ideas. Barnes is executive editor of the *Weekly Standard*. The authors of a recent study of conservatism call the *Weekly Standard* "perhaps the most influential weekly magazine in George W. Bush's Washington."[1] Another prominent commentator on political affairs observes that the magazine was George W. Bush's "most influential journalistic champion" and claims the *Weekly Standard* enjoys "the same privileged relationship that the *New Republic* had with Woodrow Wilson when he brought America into the First World War."[2] Over the years, this neoconservative publication has featured commentaries by many of the right's heavy hitters, including the magazine's founder, William Kristol, senior editor David Brooks, and foreign policy specialist Robert Kagan. During the time George W. Bush has been in the White House, the president's top aides as well as Republican members of Congress have considered the magazine "must" reading.

When driving to the luncheon, I turned on the car radio to see if the day's political commentary might show some resemblance to Barnes's presentation at the luncheon. Neil Boortz, a popular libertarian radio host, was on the air late that morning. His theme was the Iraq War and debates about weapons of mass destruction (WMDs). Vigorously defending George W. Bush's decision to call for an attack on Iraq in 2003, Boortz insisted that plenty of circumstantial evidence had come to light showing that WMDs were present in Iraq. Boortz's broadcast occurred two and a half years after U.S. troops attacked the Middle Eastern country. Long before, several investigators had reported that Saddam Hussein's government lacked the dangerous weapons that had been frighteningly described by proponents of war in the Bush administration. Yet Neil Boortz insisted on claiming that evidence clearly supported his contention that Saddam's military had stockpiled plenty of WMDs.

Later, at the luncheon, Fred Barnes recited some favorite political jokes that were appropriate for the roast beef circuit and then led off the serious part of his talk with remarks about the Iraq War. His message: "We are winning in Iraq." Barnes considered the various Iraqi elections and votes on a constitution encouraging, because they attracted many eligible voters. He claimed that Americans were helping the Iraqi army to turn into an effective fighting force. The speaker suggested that Americans did not recognize the progress being made in Iraq because influential figures in the mainstream media were reluctant to tell the public about improvements. He singled out the *New York Times* for particular criticism.

Like Boortz's interpretation of the debates over WMDs, Fred Barnes's commentary on America's situation in Iraq on November 7, 2005, was far from conventional wisdom at the time. U.S. deaths in the country had just surpassed the 2,000 mark, and more than 16,000 Americans had been injured. Iraqi society was in a shambles. Many public services were not functioning, and electrical power came intermittently at best. Americans (and pro-American Iraqis) could not safely walk or drive through Baghdad. At the time an informal civil war appeared to be in the making as Sunnis, Shiites, and Kurds grew increasingly suspicious and violent toward each other. If only Barnes's confident words about progress in Iraq had been true! Barnes's upbeat commentary on recent events were evidently designed to defend the policies of President George W. Bush (a position he took in a book published a few months later)—even in the face of an enormous body of evidence that deeply undermined his arguments.[3]

After the luncheon, I returned to my car, turned on talk radio again and listened to Rush Limbaugh. Questions about the Iraq War emerged in his program, too. Limbaugh delivered messages that were fundamentally similar to Barnes's. He spoke in ways that indirectly defended the president against intense public criticism. Limbaugh pointed to an article in the *Washington Post* that described the U.S. military's effort to recruit soldiers for duty in Iraq from among young people in America's poor rural areas. The *Post*'s account indicated that economically deprived people with limited formal education often joined the armed services because they lacked good employment opportunities in their communities. This news story represented an insult to the troops, barked Limbaugh. It was a product of the liberal media and was "all about destroying Bush."

Whether the subject of discussion was Iraq or various details about foreign, social, or economic policies, the messages I heard from the speakers that day were broadly similar. Each commentator recited homilies from the conservative prayer book rather than engaging their listeners in thoughtful, open-minded inquiries into political issues of the day. Each assumed that Truth was simple, one-sided, and not subject to much questioning or negotiation. Each viewed people who doubted their conclusions with suspicion and contempt. Barnes used an acronym that many other conservatives employ when referring to journalists who do not agree with their outlooks on the news: MSM (the right's term for mainstream media or the liberal media). Boortz, Barnes, and Limbaugh made MSM a familiar target in their remarks about the *New York Times,* the *Washington Post,* and the *Los Angeles Times.*

The hard-core approaches of Boortz and Limbaugh were not surprising, since radio listeners expect to hear sharply partisan diatribes from their favorite right-wing broadcasters. A basic similarity of Barnes's speech to the radio commentaries is more intriguing, however, since Fred Barnes manages the dissemination of opinion from one of the neoconservatives' most distinguished intellectual organs. His remarks were similar in message if not in style.[4] When listening to Barnes, I was reminded of the comment of Hans Blix, the chief of UN weapons inspections in Iraq, who offered a biting summary of the Bush administration's claims about WMDs. After reviewing an appalling lack of evidence to support the administration's hyped-up claims about weapons of mass destruction, Blix expressed dismay. "They said this was the best intelligence we have," reported Blix, "and I said, if this is their best, what is the rest?"[5] Indeed, if one example of the right's "best" on issues of the time was evidenced by the one-sided, unquestioning approach to issues offered that November day by the editor of the *Weekly Standard,* what does that say about "the rest" of conservative political thought?[6]

My negative impression of Fred Barnes's performance related to his promotion of ideology, not to his personal characteristics. Barnes was a skilled speaker who effectively entertained the crowd while also provoking his listeners to think. His show of intellect and good humor gave strong evidence of the attractions that made him a popular figure on Fox's Special Report with Brit Hume and other television shows. Barnes appeared to be a good-natured, amiable fellow, too. Charming and welcoming to each stranger who approached him, he seemed like the kind of individual one would enjoy spending time with as a friend. There was, in short, nothing personal in my critical reaction to Fred Barnes's speech. It was the message, not the man, that gave me pause.

After listening to hard-right comments on the radio and at the luncheon, I sought a more sophisticated treatment of current issues by perusing the latest books on display at a local bookstore. At the front table I came upon Jimmy Carter's publication, *Our Endangered Values: America's Moral Crisis*. I noticed that in the opening chapters of the book Carter discusses "a disturbing trend toward fundamentalism" in the United States. The former president is speaking about religion, not politics, but his remarks sound relevant to the perspectives I had heard expressed that day by Boortz, Barnes, and Limbaugh. Fundamentalists, says Carter, "draw clear distinctions between themselves as true believers, and others." They are convinced "that they are right and that anyone who contradicts them is ignorant and possibly evil." Fundamentalists take militant stands when dealing with challenges to their beliefs, Carter notes. They resist negotiation and compromise. In their eyes, efforts to resolve differences look like "signs of weakness."[7] The former president is describing religious zealots who close their minds to different ways of thinking about controversial issues, but he could just as well use these words to describe devotees on the right of a militant ideological perspective.

Jimmy Carter did not intend to use his criticism of fundamentalist zealotry as a means to attack religious belief. He identifies himself as a deeply spiritual, born-again evangelical Christian. Carter's personal religious faith is intense and sincere, he tells readers, but he characterizes it as very different from the militant religious fundamentalism that is becoming increasingly prominent in American life. Jimmy Carter maintains that his personal religious precepts emphasize open-mindedness, tolerance, and compassion. He objects primarily to the radical and doctrinaire character of fundamentalist expressions and to the contemptuous treatment of fellow Americans who do not accept the fundamentalists' worldview. In a similar manner critics of today's *political* fundamentalism say that their objections to the right's mentality do not imply a blanket rejection of conservative ideas. Those critics acknowledge that broad-minded, moderate, and responsible expressions

of conservative perspectives are useful and valuable in any consideration of political choices. The problem is with militant, close-minded
expressions.

My discovery of Jimmy Carter's book that November day did not constitute one of those eureka moments—I had already established political
fundamentalism as the basic working concept for my interpretation of
the radical right's outlook. Carter's message about a need to understand
the problematic character of religious zealotry did strike me, however, as
a valuable example for many Americans as they struggle to make sense
of the formidable challenges presented by militant conservatism. Those
liberal Democrats, moderate Republicans, and practical-minded independents often look in puzzlement at millions of Americans who approach political issues as if there is only one truth—the orthodox political
doctrine preached to them by dogmatic gurus of the right. Why, these
critics ask, do so many partisans take unquestioning stands and resist
compromise? Some answers to this question can be found in similarities
between the right's political "faith" and the mentality of religious fundamentalists in America and the world.

I have adopted the term "radcon" as a succinct reference to these ultraconservatives of modern times who judge controversial political issues
primarily on the basis of the preconceptions honored by their radical
"faith" rather than in terms of open-minded analysis of conflicting evidence. Radcons filter information selectively, privileging details that confirm their prejudices and dismissing evidence that does not support their
assumptions. Robert Reich, a progressive commentator on economic issues and secretary of labor in the Clinton administration, deserves credit
for giving the term its strongest promotion. He criticizes radical conservatives who act as if they have a monopoly on truth. "What defines a Radcon
is not openness to the case for them," he writes, "but fervent certainty that
they're correct and necessary, and disdain for those who disagree."[8] When
describing conservative devotees of the free market, for instance, Reich
employs language that is relevant to this study. He detects the mentality
of a "fundamentalist." Reich notes that such individuals believe "the free
market has the same intoxicating quality that religion has to born-again
Christians. Facts aren't especially relevant. The perfection of the market
has to be accepted as a matter of faith."[9]

Radical conservatives have been around for a long time. Some were
ultra-enthusiasts of laissez-faire in the late nineteenth century. During

the early and mid-twentieth century various radcons championed isolationism (as opposed to internationalism), spoke anxiously about modernity, or criticized cosmopolitan life in the United States. Conservatives who lived in the Midwest sometimes expressed suspicion about Americans who lived in the Eastern United States (these Midwesterners considered Easterners, especially the rich ones, to be snobbish, effete, European-oriented, and dangerously powerful). Americans with radically conservative sentiments sometimes joined extremist organizations such at the Ku Klux Klan in the 1920s or the John Birch Society in 1960s. Some hard-core conservatives expressed support for Joseph McCarthy's reckless charges during the Red Scare of the 1950s. These outbursts by radical conservatives were significant but generally sporadic. They tended not to leave a long-lasting impact.

In recent decades, however, a broader-based conservative "faith" has emerged that has a stronger image of respectability and greater staying power. The radcons' influence has expanded in starts and stops, yet their progress in exciting the hearts and minds of the American electorate has been impressive over the last forty years. Generously funded by wealthy benefactors and vigorously supported by eloquent pundits of the press, radio, TV, and the Internet, radical conservatives have emerged as muscular participants in American political life. The radcons now dominate the Republican Party, and their outlook finds abundant expression in the GOP leaders' commentaries about economic, social, and international issues. Millions of Americans now recite homilies of a radcon faith, supporting simplistic, hard-line, uncompromising positions on complex political matters. They invoke doctrinaire preachments of their favorite ideological gurus, enthusiastically reciting arguments they have heard articulated on radio and television by well-known communicators of radical ideas.

Commentators on American politics frequently note the difficulties faced by Republican leaders who try to carve out a place for moderate positions. They recall the failed efforts of President Dwight D. Eisenhower to build a modern form of Republicanism. During the 1950s, Eisenhower sought to take members of the GOP beyond their isolationist tendencies, contempt for the New Deal's reforms, suspicion of the "Eastern Establishment," and xenophobic resistance to negotiations with Communists. Eisenhower wanted to turn his party in the direction of mainstream politics rather than radical politics. During the time of his presidency, other prominent figures in the GOP supported moderate stands as well, including Prescott Bush, a Republican senator from Connecticut and the father and grandfather of two future presidents.

By the early twenty-first century, however, moderate conservatism and moderate Republicanism had been pushed aside. Right-wing ultras had succeeded in dominating the political scene. These militants provided the strongest voices in defining right-wing thought through their newspaper and journal commentaries and appearances on the radio and television. Occasionally GOP moderates complained about this situation, as in the case of the former New Jersey governor and EPA administrator in George W. Bush's administration, Christine Todd Whitman. Her book, *It's My Party, Too: Taking Back the Republican Party . . . And Bringing the Country Together Again,* communicated a sense of frustration felt by Americans who were conservatively oriented but uncomfortable with the influence of the radcons. Whitman and her supporters faced difficult challenges, for conservatism had become largely synonymous with ideas of the radical right. Despite the complaints of Whitman and others, an ultra perspective characterized the viewpoint of the right's principal activists, from its celebrity intellectuals and talk show hosts to its politicians and the numerous grassroots champions among the American public.

Observers of this radical conservative mentality find its ideas about America and the world scattered in so many different directions that, at first glance, the radcon persuasion seems deeply layered, complex, and often contradictory. Lots of Americans who think of themselves as "conservatives" disagree intensely with each other about priorities, principles, and policies. Nevertheless, a broadly encompassing view from above this complicated landscape reveals large and striking patterns. Today's partisans on the right cluster primarily around three salient interests. Their principal concerns relate to economic, cultural, and international issues. Furthermore, an arresting characteristic is generally evident in the rhetoric of conservatives who champion each of these interests. The promoters of these outlooks tend to view controversial issues in the manner of religious fundamentalists. They view political enemies as dangerous threats to their basic values and sanction a missionary-like crusade to purify American society of the supposedly corrupt influences. Radcons warn that pernicious liberal ideas have seriously undermined the nation at home and abroad. They counsel strong challenges to liberal concepts in every aspect of political life.

Not surprisingly, people who view politics in this manner do not usually sanction negotiation or compromise. Nor do they welcome pointed questions about their political assumptions. They approach controversies in the fashion of True Believers, exhibiting a mentality that can best be described as a form of political faith.

# CHAPTER ONE

# Politics as Religion

In *What's the Matter with Kansas?*, a funny and brilliantly critical book about conservative thought, Thomas Frank occasionally employs religious metaphors to characterize right-wing outlooks. More specifically, Frank's references sound like descriptions of the thinking of religious *fundamentalists*. The author speaks of "true believers" who are driven by hate for the supposedly powerful and wicked representatives of liberalism in America.[1] When these conservatives seek support for their ideology, says Frank, they proselytize "one convert at a time."[2] As new rightists join the conservative movement, they frequently describe an intense emotional happening that convinced them to join the cause. "Conservatives often speak of a conversion experience, a quasi-religious revelation," notes Frank.[3] Once inside the movement, these rightists promote a worldview that seems to provide all-inclusive answers to life's problems. When describing right-wing economic perspectives, Frank says, "Everything fits together; everything has its place . . . The god of the market may not have much to offer you personally, but that doesn't change its divinity, or blur the awesome clarity of the conservative vision."[4] Frank also points out that some advocates of this quasi-religious vision engage in angry grudges about doctrine and try to "excommunicate" individuals in their movement who seem guilty of "this or that bit of heresy or thought-error."[5]

Thomas Frank has done more than most observers of conservatism to draw attention to the partisans' quasi-religious vision (as was evident in the title of his previous publication, *One Market under God*), but he has not offered a broad examination of this connection. Frank's books do not trace the resemblance of militant right-wing thinking to religious thought in modern America, especially a resemblance to the perspectives of religious fundamentalists. In fact, the comments identified above represent just about all of the religious metaphors that appear in *What's the Matter with Kansas?*

Like Thomas Frank, other commentators on conservatism tend to mention the likeness to religious thinking briefly and fleetingly. They employ religious analogies when describing right-wingers' thinking but then move quickly to other matters. For example, Michael Lind, a prolific writer who worked inside the conservative movement before abandoning it, notes that rightists often promote an extreme philosophy of laissez-faire. They treat this concept as the Holy Word passed down from the heavens. "American conservatives have adopted free-market fundamentalism, in its crudest forms, as their political religion," reports Lind.[6] David Brock, another commentator who worked on the right before abandoning (and attacking) the conservative movement, employs related language when describing the conservatives who loathed Bill Clinton. Those critics displayed "a religious-like faith and fervor" when blasting the Democratic president, says Brock.[7] Regarding another realm of right-wing thought, journalists Daniel J. Balz and Ronald Brownstein observe that hatred toward federal power is an "article of faith" for many people on the right. A contemptuous attitude toward the state is central to "the new conservative catechism," they report.[8] Sidney Blumenthal, a journalist and later adviser to President Clinton, points out that the conservatives' battles over interpretations of political doctrine sound very much like disputes between religious factions that splinter over interpretations of their canon. Each group acts like a "sect mobilized around its own internally consistent theoretical system," he says.[9] A religious analogy also appears in Fareed Zakaria's analysis of the way conservative architects of America's war with Iraq refused to abandon their ideological assumptions. "Foreign policy is not theology," Zakaria warns. Facts on the ground in the Middle East suggested that the ideological and theoretical beliefs of many conservatives in the White House and the Pentagon were incorrect (as well as the beliefs of their supporters in the Republican Party). Nevertheless, the Bush administration's planners (and the party faithful) remained committed to a "theology." Beliefs trumped realities.[10]

These are just a few of the many uses of religious metaphors that appear in publications about American conservatism. Typically, analysts offer only passing mention of the way right-wing political outlooks resemble religious perspectives. The idea behind these abundant references deserves extensive analysis, because a religious perspective, particularly a *fundamentalist* viewpoint, is strongly evident in the thought of many hard-right partisans in America.

Proponents of the radical conservative *political* faith demonstrate a tenacious commitment to preconceived ideas, the teachings of their creed. Like religious fundamentalists, they point to a respected canon. They praise specific books that served as primary guides for their thought (these publications look to them like scriptures). Partisans of the ultra-right speak deferentially of those who write about or interpret the tenets—political wise men and women who serve very much like priests, pastors, rabbis, or mullahs for their faith. Those authorities receive tremendous respect from the adherents. Citing the guru's ideas as enduring truths, fundamentalist partisans have little difficulty discerning right from wrong. They proffer firm opinions when dealing with complex problems, because the political sermons of adored interpreters of their creed seem to deliver clear guides for judgment.

This fundamentalist-style commitment has contributed to the polarization of politics in the United States. Americans who adopt the militant right-wing perspective tend to address issues in abrasive ways. They express contempt for "liberals" in the manner that conservatives reserved years ago for communists. Militant right-wingers frequently describe their political opponents as followers of a dangerous ideology. They portray struggles with liberals as fights-to-the-finish, take-no-prisoners clashes for high stakes. The course of American values and civilization appears to hang in the balance. This rhetoric is stunningly apocalyptic. Vanquishing liberals appears justified in view of the horrible ideas the radical right associates with the despised "left."

Fareed Zakaria, the noted commentator on world affairs who warned about the danger of a theological perspective on foreign policy, has also pointed out the danger of treating politics as some religious zealots approach faith. Zakaria is sometimes identified as a conservative, yet he exhibits critical judgment in ways that separate him from the radcons. Describing conditions in the modern Middle East, Zakaria observes that political opponents of regimes in Islamic countries often make their case by employing the language of religion, with its claims about fundamental, unquestionable truths. "This combination of religion and politics has proven to be combustible," he notes. "Religion, at least the religion of the Abrahamic traditions (Judaism, Christianity, and Islam), stresses moral absolutes." But politics, says Zakaria, "is all about compromise." The consequence of a religionlike approach to debates about governance in the Middle East "has been a ruthless, winner-take-all attitude toward political life."[11] Zakaria's conclusion is relevant to the political scene in the United States. Journalists often bemoan the savage tone of partisan political squabbling in the United States and blame both liberals and conservatives for contributing to the descent into polemics and viciousness. A more honest examination of the sources of ferociously partisan debate in America should draw greater attention to the radical right's attraction to a quasi-religious, politically fundamentalist approach to controversial issues.

The term "fundamentalist" is presented here to provide a framework for examining the outlook referenced by Thomas Frank and many other commentators on conservatism in America. Political fundamentalism represents a construct that helps to make *some* sense of significant patterns in right-wing thinking that have caught the passing attention of commentators on American politics. In the following chapters I suggest that the connection between militant right-wing thought and fundamentalist religious thought is impressive. Although *all* conservatism does *not* fit the mold, evidence presented in these chapters indicates that a quasi-religious, fundamentalist-style perspective on diverse issues is characteristic of *a good deal* of right-wing thought. This outlook is especially present in the language of partisans identified with strong adjectives: the hard-right, the militant right, ultraconservatives—the radical right. When thinking of the radical right, many Americans conjure up images of strident radio and television personalities that appeal emotionally to the frustrations of angry white males. Names such as Rush Limbaugh, Sean Hannity, Ann Coulter, and Bill O'Reilly readily come to mind. Yet radical conservatism has been promoted not only by those shrill partisans but also by individuals with distinguished academic credentials and impressive publication records, including many who have held high public office. It can be detected in the writings and speeches of leading editors (as I found in the case of Fred Barnes). It is evident, as we shall see, in the ideas expressed by office holders such as William J. Bennett (a prominent academic who found posts at the top of Republican administrations in Washington, D.C.), Robert Bork (a law professor and judge nominated unsuccessfully to the U.S. Supreme Court), Richard Armey (a top figure in the Republicans' congressional leadership), and William E. Simon (an influential cabinet official in Republican administrations and head of an important conservatively oriented foundation). The "ultra" mentality is visible, too, in the thought of pioneering neoconservative intellectuals such as Irving Kristol and Norman Podhoretz, and it is evident in the publications of respected gurus of conservative philosophy such as William F. Buckley and Milton Friedman. Prolific right-oriented authors such as George Will, and Dinesh D'Souza also communicate this militant perspective when dealing with controversial issues of the day.

This study focuses especially on *books* written by these and other ardently conservative pundits and intellectuals. It seeks a broader understanding of the right's framework than can be found in a glimpse at brief commentaries concerning diverse political issues that appear on op-ed pages and in right-wing news stories and commentaries. A study of these conservatives' treatment of large topics regarding history, economics, culture, foreign policy, and other subjects is more revealing when it deals with lengthy tomes rather than sporadic strikes at a particular issue. The framework of right-wing analysis—ergo, the fundamentalist perspective—becomes more evident when the source for examination is a comprehensive judgment that cuts across diverse themes. Book-length publications often betray a tendency of the writers to apply fundamentalist-style doctrines to many different political topics. The shape of their faith appears in clearer form when they approach subjects in the manner described briefly by Thomas Frank—as a "worldview" of "breathtaking beauty" in which, it seems that "everything fits together."[12]

This interpretation takes issue with the familiar assumption mentioned previously—that evangelicals and other "enthusiastic religionists" are primarily, indeed, almost solely responsible for the fundamentalist-style mentality of conservative attitudes.[13] Critics of the right often express discomfort with the way various evangelical groups seem to be locked into one-minded positions on the great "social" and "moral" issues of the day. These people, they complain, act like religious extremists when taking inflexible positions on hot-button topics such as the place of abortion, gays, or religion in American life. Yet a fundamentalist mentality affects a much broader spectrum of conservative attitudes and ideas. Right-wing fundamentalist politics is prevalent in the thinking of dyed-in-the-wool market radicals, too. These ideologues exhibit a religionlike enthusiasm for laissez-faire. In many respects their hard-line opinions in opposition to government regulation and taxation qualify them as libertarians, a group that favors seemingly doctrinaire stands on many controversial topics. These market radicals are basically fundamentalist in outlook, yet the object of their worship is quite different from that of social conservatives who display a nostalgic longing for the family values they believe were prevalent in America back in the 1950s. A closer look at conservative thought reveals, as well, that many Americans of the radical right are quasi-religious in their attitudes about foreign policy. Once they choose a doctrine to frame their understanding of international issues, it is difficult for them to break free from their ideological assumptions. Exposure to unpleasant facts does not usually lead them to question fundamental beliefs. As Fareed Zakaria notes, they are reluctant to challenge or revise their "theology," despite evidence to its contrary.

In this respect, critics of the right often fail to appreciate the breadth of the radcon faith. They find the social radicals' participation in culture wars so appalling that they focus on that group's highly controversial statements and give much less attention to the doctrinaire thinking of different "sects" on the right. Culture Warriors look, at first glance, like much more irritating and dangerous ideologues than spokespersons for other right-wing groups. Militants involved in the cultural battles appear determined to press their views of morality on all Americans. Many of them want to challenge the teaching of evolution in the public schools, to break down the constitutional separation of church and state, to overturn *Roe v. Wade,* deny rights to homosexuals, or censor mass entertainment (from music to the movies). Often, they sound like they want to reverse the general course of modernization in American life. Culture Warriors look like the nation's most troublesome True Believers. Yet modern-day radical conservatism is also represented by other problematic strains of militant ideology that involve powerful allegiances to dogma. America's market extremists and foreign policy hawks reveal a fundamentalist approach to political issues that is as uncompromising as the approach of the culture-minded rightists who frequently join them in a quasi-united front at the time of elections.

## A Triad of Interests

I have mentioned these three major branches of radcon thought—the economic, cultural, and international outlooks—because they are the particularly salient divisions with respect to special interests. Each group rallies around particular goals that may not be shared by other members of the basic political triad. Often these interests are in conflict. In view of the significant differences, it seems remarkable that partisans on the right manage to champion common causes and march together into political battles against Democrats and liberals.

Some constructs provide a useful framework for the discussion. This study advances a three-part breakdown of radcon interests. As in the case of my description of a "fundamentalist" mentality, this employment of labels does not imply insistence on a rigid application of distinctions. Obviously, not all radically minded conservatives fall squarely into the three suggested categories. Individuals overlap, too, demonstrating interests in two or all three major branches. Yet the tripartite breakdown helps to clarify an important point addressed earlier. It demonstrates that many people on the right who exhibit a quasi-religious political attitude are not exclusively driven by the so-called cultural issues (and, in fact, some of them are not especially inclined toward involvement in the spiritual affairs of religious groups). Their expressions of a fundamentalist mentality may be directed especially to economic or foreign affairs.

Proponents of the three perspectives are identified in the following pages as Stealth Libertarians, Culture Warriors, and Hawkish Nationalists. These terms serve as conceptual tools for interpreting major clusters of interests. Just as other general labels employed in familiar discussions about conservatism facilitate a consideration of distinctions (terms such as "neoconservative" and "paleoconservative"), these labels identify important differences. They facilitate an investigation, for instance, of why some libertarians rejected George W. Bush's war in Iraq but cheered his tax policies. They help us to understand why many Culture Warriors demanded attention to "values" but showed little interest in the ideas of the libertarian champions of "free markets" (and sometimes expressed suspicion toward these ideas, as well).

As mentioned previously, most individuals do not line up completely and separately as advocates of just one perspective. In fact, many partisans on the right have demonstrated a strong interest in supporting all three themes. William F. Buckley, Frank S. Meyer, and some of their associates at the *National Review* made notable attempts in the 1950s to "fuse" the three interests and bring largely separated partisans together under a common right-wing banner (the principal international issue that interested them in those days was anticommunism). Most important, Buckley and his associates tried to combine the long-antagonistic camps of business-oriented and culture-oriented conservatism. In later years Irving Kristol, sometimes called the "father" or "godfather" of neoconservatism, connected economic, social, and defense issues in his many articles and books. Intellectuals on the right have tried, at times, to fuse specific themes, as Michael Novak, a Catholic neoconservative, attempted when he advanced moral and religious arguments in defense of capitalism. These efforts to connect themes from radical conservatism have continued into recent times. President George W. Bush and his key adviser, Karl Rove, were among the leading modern strategists for a program of fusion. They worked arduously to bring champions of the three principal themes together, lining them up for an impressive march behind the GOP banner during George W. Bush's first term in the White House.

Stealth Libertarians are enthusiasts of laissez-faire, the notion of leaving business enterprise free from government interference and regulation. They maintain that markets provide their own correctives for economic problems and produce a better life for all when left alone. These advocates of largely unfettered markets usually describe the "state" in sharply negative terms. They describe the federal government as a cumbersome and inefficient organization, claiming that Washington-based bureaucrats who interfere in the society and economy usually create more problems than they solve. "Unintended consequences" almost always result, they claim. Ultraenthusiasts of markets, like many other partisans of the radical conservative faith, show a penchant for extreme views. On economic issues many of them sound like libertarians at heart. They are severe critics of the state who desire a hugely reduced role for government in the lives of the American people and in the affairs of business.[14] Of course, these figures cherry-pick the economic concepts of libertarian philosophy and turn their backs on other important elements of that outlook. They seldom identify openly with libertarianism, because they wish to make their viewpoints appear to be in the mainstream, not the radical fringes. Stealth Libertarians do not want to alienate colleagues on the right who take issue with elements of libertarianism (church-oriented partisans of the right are especially suspicious of libertarian ideas).

Culture Warriors often express concern about the course of American "civilization." They frequently look back to a supposedly better and happier era. Many of them express nostalgia for the 1950s, seen as a golden period before the troubling social disruptions of the late 1960s. Others detect a finer quality of life in earlier periods of American and European history. Many culture-minded militants on the right sound pessimistic about the direction that U.S. society has been moving in recent decades. They cite disturbing evidence about a decline of the nuclear family, sexual promiscuity, growing crime and violence, and other societal problems that appear to be more severe today than in earlier years. They claim that a breakdown in values is at the foundation of modern problems and identify university professors, intellectuals, journalists, media personalities, Hollywood figures, and others (whom they call the liberal "elite" or the "New Class") as purveyors of ideas that contributed significantly to a decline in morality and culture.[15]

Hawkish Nationalists promote a hard line on U.S. foreign policy. They usually advocate tough stands when dealing with America's adversaries. During the Cold War, many of them defended America's military engagement in Vietnam, while others recognized some of the mistakes associated with U.S. intervention, but they devoted much of their intellectual energy to chastising radical critics of American policies in Southeast Asia. These nationalists spoke warily about negotiating with communists in the Soviet Union, China, Vietnam, and elsewhere during the Cold War years, claiming that agreements signed by the venal enemy could not be trusted. When contemplating reasons for communism's demise, Hawkish Nationalists usually emphasize military factors. They believe that tough language against communism and large defense budgets helped the United States to rally the free world, establish American military superiority, and force a communist surrender. In other international confrontations, as well, these partisans tend to think in terms of military reactions and solutions. Many of them were enthusiastic supporters of U.S. armed intervention in the Persian Gulf in 1991 and the attack on Saddam Hussein's Iraq in 2003. Today, quite a few Hawkish Nationalists advocate wide-ranging U.S. intervention in the affairs of developing nations in order to support the fight against terrorism. These individuals often claim that Americans need to look after their own interests first and place concerns expressed by the international community in a distinctly secondary position. They are wary of U.S. participation in global organizations such as the United Nations. Many of them express concern about American sovereignty, fearing that cooperation with global institutions—including an international criminal court—will undermine national interests.

## Diversity and Unity

When observing the different backgrounds of these radcons, it seems that conservatives should face tremendous difficulties presenting a unified case before the American public. Their movement often appears to be on the edge of splintering, since it appeals to people of very different socioeconomic roots. The ranks of the militant right include millions of lower- and middle-class Americans who thrill to the strident rhetoric of media-based verbal warriors such as Rush Limbaugh and Michael Savage. Those ranks are also composed of small business owners, white-collar workers, managers, and executives who avidly read the editorial pages of the *Wall Street Journal*. Some of today's radically inclined conservatives are affiliated with the U.S. military or associated with veterans groups such as the American Legion or the Veterans of Foreign Wars. Others are drawn to the right because of their activities in churches, especially evangelical and Pentecostal congregations. The hard right includes Americans who think of themselves as "libertarians" and wish to reduce the role of government drastically. Some of these libertarians show little interest in practicing religion or promoting religious viewpoints. Other enthusiasts of conservative causes join the movement principally because of their opposition to gun laws.

Radical conservatism provides a home for Americans of diverse religious, ethnic, racial, and sectional backgrounds. There are Jews and Catholics in its leadership ranks as well as a large contingent of Protestants. Radical conservatism welcomes some blacks as well, including noted professors, politicians, and judges. There are plenty of Ivy Leaguers, Northeastern intellectuals, and Establishment types in the movement and a substantial contingent of right-wing intellectuals who work in the high-rent districts of New York City and Washington, D.C. Yet conservative causes also attract a huge following in the South and West, and the dress, speech, and attitude of those right-wingers often seem quite different from the fashions of their Northeastern comrades. In fact, some southerners and westerners see themselves as populists of the New Right and resent the authority and prestige of old wealth and the pedigree of academic credentials exhibited by some of the Eastern partisans. In view of these numerous differences, it seems difficult to speak of a focused and relatively coherent radical "faith."

It would seem, too, that right-wing partisans should face difficulty supporting common causes because of their divergent stands on issues. Some on the right, such as the advocates of laissez-faire in economic matters, seek a drastic reduction in government's role in American society. Others who emphasize "family values," morals, and religion seek a strong role for the federal government to promote their vision of a good society. The libertarian branch emphasizes unrestrained freedom, and many of its enthusiasts want to remove legal penalties for crimes they consider victimless. Quite a few of them view engagement with drugs, pornography, or a gay lifestyle as personal choices, yet many religiously oriented conservatives are alarmed by these behaviors and wish to regulate them. Today's ultras are divided on issues concerning abortion and illegal immigration (on abortion, for instance, conservatives living in the Northeast tend to be less agitated than evangelicals living in the South). Some traditionalists in the ultra-right's camp, called paleoconservatives, have participated in angry fights with later arrivals in the movement, called neoconservatives. There are partisans on the right who want free trade, and others who seek protectionism. Quite a few representatives of the hard right advocate U.S. military intervention in foreign affairs, but others call for restraint. Some sound like isolationists who fear international commitments. Even so, many conservatives speak as internationalists, advocating a large global role for the United States, including commitments to nation-building and democracy-building. The militant right looks, then, like it brings together a hodgepodge of different causes. In this respect the movement does not appear to operate with a common core of ideas.[16]

Because of these divisions, political observers, including commentators on the right, sometimes report that a conservative "crack-up" is in the making. With the possible exception of splits during the 1992 presidential election, this expected splintering never amounts to very much. It usually lacks nationwide political significance. Even though some issues cannot be resolved easily among partisans on the right, as in the case of immigration reform, these matters do not wreck the conservatives' hopes for broader cooperation. Though right-wing partisans often disagree with each other or care little about the interests of other conservatives, they tend to display impressive unity when making their case in America's political arena. Two factors, especially, contribute to the right's general success in demonstrating a united front (especially at election time) despite the many internal differences.

First, radical conservatives appreciate the value of subordinating their principal differences to achieve general goals. Enthusiasts of the distinctive clusters of interests tolerate opinions of their right-wing confederates, even though the particular opinions are not appealing or may be irritating. They go along to get along, and keep their eyes on the prize. Stealth Libertarians, Culture Warriors, and Hawkish Nationalists do not wish to undermine the conservatives' progress in American politics. When they argue with each other, it is often behind closed doors, and they usually do not reveal those disagreements once the doors fling open. Most Americans are not familiar with their intense intramural disputes. Ultras tend to conceal their doctrinal clashes in publications designed for the faithful and in meetings and conventions attended by fellow partisans. When radical conservatism goes public, through commentaries in the mass media and in GOP politics, it often appears to reflect consensus.[17]

Second, these militant right-wingers with distinctive and often conflicting interests find unity by concentrating on a particular enemy. Liberals, the supposed advocates of alien ideas, are their favorite political targets. Partisans from all three groups view liberals as worshipers of pagan beliefs such as relativism, secular humanism, socialism, governmental interventionism, and multiculturalism. The libertarian types rail about advocates of Big Government, High Taxes, and Bureaucracy. Some accuse liberals of pacifism in international relations and claim they promote anti-American attitudes through their severe criticisms of U.S. policies. In the militants' political rhetoric liberals appear to be destroyers of values, promoters of lethargy, advocates of appeasement, and defenders of weakness. Stealth Libertarians, Culture Warriors, and Hawkish Nationalists often join together in denouncing the supposed common enemy, the liberal.

Militants level these indictments against liberals by fudging distinctions and thereby providing a grossly distorted picture of the meaning of liberalism. They frequently mix references to "liberal" and "left" indiscriminately. Often they cite the extreme statements and actions of individuals who advocate radical causes of the far left, combining those examples loosely with abundant citations of ideas and activities of mainstream liberals. In this grossly simplistic fashion, advocates of market, culture, or nationalist causes act as if there is virtually no difference between liberals and leftist radicals.

"Liberal" serves as a catch-all phrase in this rhetoric that summarizes diverse problems that deeply trouble radcons. The battle against liberalism is not defined simply as a dispute about small political matters. It looks, instead, like a titanic struggle between the forces of right and wrong. Political fundamentalists (as well as religious fundamentalists) favor highly dramatic descriptions of their struggles. They employ emotion-laden imagery, speaking of clashes between good and evil, light and darkness. This language, evoking impressions of a crusade for Truth and a war against the liberal Satan, makes the stakes in political battles seem enormous. Just as fundamentalist religious fervor sometimes promotes notions of a "culture war" in American society, fundamentalist-style political rhetoric about despised liberals has contributed substantially to the nasty character of current politics.

## Political Faith Distinguished from Religious Faith

Attention to the way conservative political thought sometimes resembles the thinking of religious fundamentalists does not imply hostility to religious faith. Religion plays an important and significant role in American society. It is of central importance in the spiritual and emotional lives of millions of Americans, liberals as well as conservatives. Religious belief—indeed, religious "faith"—properly commands respect, as Jimmy Carter argues in *Our Endangered Values*. Faith becomes problematic, however, when it is applied to *political* ideas. Once these political notions take on the character of orthodoxy—of accepted and unquestioned truths—supporters of the faith often fail to exhibit the kind of critical mentality that is essential for the working of a vibrant and effective democracy. Enthusiasts of a political faith serve as malleable followers who can easily be directed by their leaders.

Just as an examination of the radical conservatives' "faith" does not imply hostility to religious beliefs, it does not suggest a specific criticism of pious individuals known as fundamentalists. Troubles associated with *political* orthodoxy and intolerance cannot be traced simply to the activities of those individuals. Obviously, religious convictions sometimes foster unquestioning and uncompromising stands on important political issues that fundamentalists associate with "morality," but an attempt to blame these church-based groups for all right-wing political orthodoxy is mistaken. Fundamentalist-style politics is not the exclusive possession of evangelicals or Pentecostals (nor, as we will see, is religious fundamentalism the exclusive domain of Protestant religious groups—it is evident in the activities of some Muslims, Jews, and Hindus as well). Furthermore, the votes of America's evangelicals and Pentecostals are not devoted fully to one political camp. Presently, they tend to vote Republican, and many call themselves conservatives, yet millions of these Christians vote Democratic and do not think of themselves as conservatives. Evangelicals and Pentecostals represent only a portion of the large and diverse American population that stands on the right. Some militant conservatives are not particularly spiritual or orthodox in their religious practices, and quite a few of these secular types rank among the nation's most prominent voices on the right. Several are agnostics or atheists. Other hard-line conservatives *claim* to be religious but rarely visit a house of worship. Some prominent conservative intellectuals who call themselves Straussians (because of their enthusiasm for the ideas of the political philosopher Leo Strauss) consider religious beliefs beneath themselves, but they recognize religion's usefulness in providing a moral structure for the masses. In short, fundamentalist *religious* attitudes are not prerequisites for engaging in fundamentalist-style conservative thought or political action. The ranks of the fundamentalist *political* right include both religious and nonreligious people.

## Do Ideas Serve Mainly as a Cover for Selfish Interests?

The evidence presented here about a radcon "faith" suggests that ideas have power. People's beliefs can influence their political behavior in significant ways. Nevertheless, it would be naïve to assume that militant conservatives approach politics *only* on the basis of their ideological notions about what is right or wrong for U.S. society and the world. Selfish and practical interests provide motivation for their thought and behavior, too. Political leaders often say one thing but do another. When holding elective office, they compromise on principals in order to achieve limited political goals. Right-wing partisans often make bold promises to win elections and then conveniently overlook those pledges once in office. Quite a few prominent radcon leaders are guilty of hypocrisy. They eagerly preach high ideals to their followers, but they fail to live up to the impressive standards in their private lives.

Although this interpretation advances a case for the influence of ideas on political behavior, obviously, any discussion of thought must be grounded on a realistic understanding of the many ways that political principles are violated in political practice. The following brief discussion addresses some of the most familiar situations in which political behavior frequently contradicts politicians' high-sounding statements. This analysis acknowledges the importance of selfish interests in framing political thought, but it nevertheless maintains that ideas give considerable energy to political action—especially when they appear in the form of hard-core, fundamentalist-style perspectives on controversial economic, social, and international issues.

Conservative leaders are often driven by a selfish interest in grabbing the spoils of politics rather than honoring commitments to ideals. They espouse high principles to get elected, but then violate those tenets in practice. Early in the Bush administration, for instance, many Republican enthusiasts of the conservative "faith" readily abandoned a cherished traditional goal of the right—the commitment to hold limits on federal spending and balance the budget. When Republicans saw opportunities to legislate large tax cuts that especially benefited the rich, they seized them, contributing to the growth of a huge deficit. They also spent lavishly on a war in Iraq, supported expensive drug-benefit programs favored by large pharmaceutical companies, and voted to bring expensive and often wasteful "pork" to their communities. These actions expanded the role of the federal government greatly and violated old conservative principles of fiscal discipline. Republican practices left the impression that much of the rhetoric conservatives articulated about honoring cherished ideals served to conceal their more basic interest in riches and power.

Ideas also seem to have limited importance in view of the way specific conservative politicians contradict them when holding elective office. Ronald Reagan's behavior is a good case in point. Reagan often expressed strong right-wing convictions, but he surprised his critics by compromising with liberals. As governor of California, Reagan agreed to significant increases in state spending, and he pumped large funds into the state's university system even though he had severely criticized college administrators and students.[18] As president of the United States Reagan spoke forcefully against welfare programs but displayed little inclination to participate in the political battles that were necessary to bring substantial reductions in the welfare rolls. Reagan sounded like a political fundamentalist when invoking high-sounding conservative principles, but on various occasions he acted like a practical politician and negotiated with his opponents.

The power of ideas also seems limited in view of the abundant evidence of conservatives' hypocrisy. Right-wingers often preach a strict form of morality but fail to honor their preachments in practice. Many of the right's most famous promoters of virtue have been embarrassed in recent years. These prominent rightists built impressive careers in the national media complaining about the moral lapses of others, yet news reports eventually revealed their serious personal failings. Evidently, these self-righteous conservatives needed lessons in humility.

Rush Limbaugh's hypocrisy became evident when he came under investigation on charges of buying thousands of addictive painkillers from a black-market drug ring. His housekeeper in Palm Beach made the claim in a story reported in the *National Enquirer*. She said the famous radio host was consuming as many as thirty OxyContin pills a day. Investigators wondered how Limbaugh obtained so many drugs, asking if he had been "doctor shopping" by ordering the same medicines at various pharmacies through multiple prescriptions (an illegal activity in Florida).[19] When the story of Limbaugh's dependence on drugs broke, the radio host acknowledged an addiction to the pills, saying, "I was a drug addict from about 1996, 1995 or whatever to just five weeks ago."[20] He then checked himself into a treatment center in Arizona and remained there for several weeks. Critics in the news media observed a conflict between Limbaugh's talk and action. They noted that Limbaugh had complained earlier that too many people were "getting away" with drug abuse, and in 1995 he said the country was being destroyed by people's dependence on illegal drugs. It was time to "find the ones who are getting away with it, convict them, and send them up the river."[21] Limbaugh was not eager to deal harshly with alleged drug abuse in his own case, however.

Americans were also surprised to discover that William Bennett, author and editor of books about morality and decency, suffered from a severe gambling habit that led to his loss of millions of dollars. Bennett had served in Republican administrations as the director of the National Endowment for the Humanities, as secretary of education, and as the chief administrator responsible for leading the nation's war on drugs. He also achieved fame as a sort of self-appointed cultural commissar. Bennett published a best-seller called *The Book of Virtues* and gave numerous speeches around the country in which he promoted conservative social values. He pulled in $50,000 a lecture, and when news appeared revealing his gambling habits, the public learned where much of those earnings had been directed. Bennett was a preferred customer at casinos in Las Vegas and Atlantic City, and he had a line of credit of $200,000 in each locale. This preacher of virtues who had complained about "unrestricted personal liberty" frequently pulled the slot machines for $500 to $1,000 a tug. In all, Bennett had lost over $8 million in gambling activities over several years.[22]

The news media also revealed that Ralph Reed, a former leader of the Christian Coalition and author of a book about expressions of religious commitment through political action called *Active Faith,* had especially demonstrated faith in the power of money. Reed enjoyed a national reputation as an energetic defender of moral values. He had been identified on the cover of *Time* magazine in 1995 as "The Right Hand of God." Reed promoted his Christian upbringing when trying to arouse interest in his candidacy for lieutenant governor of Georgia. He told a group of about fifty citizens, "Growing up in Georgia is when I was inoculated with the values of faith and freedom that I've carried with me my entire life."[23] Because of his effectiveness in reaching out to religious groups, Reed had been appointed southeastern United States director of the Bush-Cheney campaign.

Reed had characterized gambling as a "cancer" on the U.S. body politic. Yet the revelations that aroused public concern involved dollars from gambling. Reed's public relations firm had received at least $4.2 million from Jack Abramoff, who became embroiled in a large-scale lobbying scandal in Washington, D.C. Ralph Reed and Abramoff had been close friends back in the 1980s, when they were leaders in the College Republicans.[24] Abramoff provided millions to Reed's organization so that Reed could mobilize Christian voters to oppose Indian casinos that might compete with the casinos of Abramoff's clients. When reports about this conflict of interest reached the news media, Reed claimed that he did not believe the money his organization received from Abramoff was associated with gambling interests. Some of Reed's e-mails came to light at the time and proved embarrassing. One from Reed to Abramoff in late 1998 said, "I need to start humping in corporate accounts! . . . I'm counting on you to help me with some contacts." In another message, Reed sent Abramoff a bill of $120,000 for his services and indicated that he would ask for as much as $300,000 in additional funds. Eventually, the lobbyist became disgusted with Reed's repeated demands of hefty fees for political influence. Abramoff recommended that his people stop dishing out money to Reed.[25]

The problem with conservative hypocrisy extends beyond questions about drugs, gambling, and money applied to questionable lobbying activities. It relates also to the right's preachments about family values. When news about Bill Clinton's affair in the White House with Monica Lewinsky reached the public, many Republican leaders in Congress sensed the president's political vulnerability. They recommended that Clinton leave office because of his immoral activity with a young intern and because he lied about it. After Clinton demonstrated his determination to hold on to his position despite the embarrassment, Republicans called for his impeachment. They expressed outrage over Clinton's adultery and his failure to acknowledge it, insisting that a national leader should set an example for the nation through a strong personal commitment to his wife and family.

In the midst of Clinton's crisis, information surfaced revealing that some of Congress's supposed defenders of moral virtue had been tainted by their own sexual adventures. The American public learned that Henry Hyde, the Republican House Judiciary Committee chairman who was leading efforts to bring forward impeachment charges, had been involved in an adulterous affair years before. Hyde was disturbed by the appearance of news reports about his amorous activities but defended himself, saying, "The statute of limitations has long since passed on my youthful indiscretions."[26] Hyde had been forty-one years old when he established a lengthy relationship with a hair stylist and mother of three children. He was married at the time and the father of four boys.

Another eager enthusiast for Clinton's dismissal from the White House was Helen Chenoweth, a Republican congresswoman from Idaho. She criticized Clinton severely for his "sordid spectacle."[27] Attempting to take advantage of the anger over Clinton's affair, Chenoweth put out a campaign ad in which she announced (in poor English), "I believe personal conduct and integrity does matter."[28] Then the public learned that Chenoweth had been involved in a long-term romance with a married man. She claimed that she achieved a pardon from the highest source. "I've asked for God's forgiveness," she told the public, "and I've received it."[29]

Dan Burton, Republican congressman and another advocate of Clinton's impeachment, had referred to the president as a "scumbag." Then news appeared indicating that Burton had been involved in an adulterous affair, too. Burton had fathered a child out of wedlock in the early 1980s.[30]

More revelations seemed likely after the publisher of *Hustler,* Larry Flynt, offered a substantial bounty to anyone who could prove that they had an affair with a high-ranking government official.[31] Flint's appeal helped to snare Louisiana's Bob Livingston, who had just become Republican speaker of the U.S. House of Representatives. Larry Flynt reported that Livingston had been involved in relationships with several women while he was married. Quickly Livingston resigned from his leadership post as well as his congressional seat.[32] His action was distinctive, for most Republicans who faced embarrassment associated with drug addiction, gambling, influence peddling, and adultery continued working to advance their political careers.

These and other examples of hypocrisy on the part of prominent figures on the right suggest that conservative rhetoric is often honored in the breach. Republican politicians of the militant right speak strongly about morality, virtue, and family values. They proclaim a deep personal faith in religion. When a leader in the Democratic Party falls from grace, as in the case of Bill Clinton, they often display a harsh reaction, demanding that the individual tarnished by scandal quickly exit from the political stage. Yet when news of their own transgression surfaces, they brush it off as a mistake and promise not to err again. These glaring contradictions between stated principles and actual behavior suggest that it is more useful to observe what conservatives do rather than what they say.

Interest in focusing attention on right-wingers' *real* purposes as opposed to their stated goals has been prominent in recent publications about conservatism. That curiosity was central in Thomas Frank's eye-opening book, *What's the Matter with Kansas?,* which threw light on the

phony concentration of many right-wing politicians on cultural issues
when they waged election campaigns. Before getting elected those Republican candidates talked excitedly about busing, un-Christian art,
prayer in the schools, and gay marriage. They exploited what Frank calls
the "Great Backlash," a view that hard-working grassroots Americans
needed to challenge the contemptuous attitudes of wealthy, secular-
minded liberal snobs who looked down on them. Once those Republican
candidates got into office, said Frank, they tended to forget their
speeches about cultural tensions. Instead, these right-wing politicians devoted most of their energy to advancing the interests of big business.
They promoted laissez-faire policies that, ironically, harmed rather than
helped the poor and middle-class citizens who had voted them into office. In a broad sense, then, Republican politicians *used* ideas as tools for
gaining leverage against Democrats. The true object of the conservatives'
emotion-laden appeals, argues Frank, was not to honor cherished concepts in practice but to gain political power and to deliver benefits to
powerful groups in American life.

All of these approaches to dealing with rhetoric bring much-needed
political savvy into discussions about the role of conservative ideas, and
particularly radcon ideas, in American life. Observers profit from an
understanding of the tendency of conservatives to compromise when in
office (as in the case of Ronald Reagan). It is useful to recognize the questionable personal behavior of supposedly self-righteous conservatives (as
in the discussions about Limbaugh, Bennett, Hyde, Chenoweth, and others). A student of conservative ideas is better informed after taking into
account the contrast between stated goals and actual legislative initiatives (which Thomas Frank does). These varied approaches contribute to
a more realistic assessment of the actual role of conservative thought in
political affairs.

Nevertheless, this "functionalist" or "instrumentalist" view of the
place of ideas in politics (to use language that academics sometimes
apply to self-interested and manipulative behavior) does not completely
satisfy. While many political leaders and popular pundits on the right
probably do not actually *believe* all that they say, it is evident that millions of their eager listeners and readers consider their arguments quite
seriously. Appreciative conservative audiences read op-ed pieces written
by right-oriented columnists. They purchase many books that promote
conservative ideas or eagerly vote for individuals who deliver strong,

idealistic arguments about conservative values. Clearly, ideas resonate among conservative partisans. With considerable interest, these enthusiasts read articles in the *National Review,* the *Weekly Standard,* and *Commentary*. They consult newspaper columns written by influential radcon figures such as Charles Krauthammer and George Will. Many listen with fascination to conservative discourse presented on talk radio and the Fox News Channel. They eagerly consult conservative blogs.

Representatives of the right frequently insist that they speak for an insightful philosophy. They claim proudly that they are champions of "new ideas." Radcons point to the many concepts advanced by their leaders in recent decades and look contemptuously upon liberals, declaring that they lack fresh ideas. The political literature of radical conservatives is replete with essays championing supposedly bold and insightful new research and interpretations of the right.

Richard M. Weaver, a traditional intellectual on the right who favored quirky analyses, communicated this notion in a way that many of today's conservatives appreciate. The title of Weaver's most famous book was *Ideas Have Consequences*. His treatise appeared in 1948, and since then many authors on the right have cited his title as an inspiring example. They affirm that there *is* a robust conservative intellectual tradition in America and believe the precepts that defined this tradition have made a significant impact on American life. When Russell Kirk published his influential book, *The Conservative Mind,* in 1953, rightists gained additional confidence, praising Kirk for tracing the origins of their esteemed philosophical legacy. In later years conservatives praised figures such as William F. Buckley and George Nash for documenting the evolution of those ideas in the United States.[33]

George Packer, author of *Assassins' Gate: America in Iraq,* observes that many of the neoconservatives who influenced George W. Bush's decisions to go to war and occupy Iraq thought of themselves as men of ideas. Some of those early neoconservative leaders, such as Irving Kristol and Norman Podhoretz, demonstrated "that ideas could lead to power, and that power required ideas." The neocons who eventually played a major role in advancing rationales for America's engagement in Iraq after the 9/11 tragedy viewed intellectual combat as an extension of political combat. Ideas served as weapons for clashes over policies.[34] Robert Kagan and William Kristol, prominent intellectuals, thought ambitiously about the potential influence of neocon concepts. "Their first goal was to ensure that their vision became dominant in the Republican Party," says Packer. Later these neoconservatives moved on to influencing the nation and the world. "This is the lesson that the American right has fully absorbed and put into practice ever since the 1960s," writes Packer: "Ideas matter."[35]

While these efforts brought conservative thought to prominence among the well-educated and the well-heeled, a much larger outpouring of books and articles dealing with radcon ideas eventually reached a broader audience. Those publications were written for readers from less privileged backgrounds. As conservatism gained momentum late in the twentieth century and began attracting support from the masses in the cities as well as in suburbia and exurbia, a huge market became available for the promotion of right-oriented perspectives. Bookstores across the United States featured publications that reached out to the right's diverse public, and today these idea-oriented publications are abundantly evident on their shelves. Some of these books offer compendiums of conservative thought, as in the case of Irwin Stelzer's *The Neoconservative Reader* (2004). Many of the books outline conservative values, such as Senator Rick Santorum's *It Takes a Family: Conservatism and the Common Good* (2005). There are, of course, lots of publications that identify conservative values by contrasting them invidiously with liberal ones. Robert H. Bork's *Slouching towards Gomorrah* (1996) is a notable example. The anti-liberal genre is enormously popular with right-oriented readers, who enjoy seeing conservative values contrasted with supposedly nefarious liberal values.

The ideas that appear in these volumes—from arguments presented by subtle and sophisticated opinion-makers to viewpoints expressed by the more strident and flamboyant right-wing debaters—carry considerable weight in today's political exchanges and deserve a closer look. This analysis suggests that important patterns are discernible in a good deal of the radical right's modern rhetoric. These patterns may be characterized most basically in terms of the three principal themes associated with Stealth Libertarians, Culture Warriors, and Hawkish Nationalists. In each of these outlooks partisans have articulated hard-nosed concepts. Their views often have the appearance of firm, strongly revered ideas that do not receive much internal challenge. Even though the libertarian, cultural, and nationalist varieties of modern conservatism are very different with regard to the issues that arouse partisan interest, there is a common denominator that connects all three.

Many years ago a talented historian searched for that common characteristic when he observed that an extreme and militant form of right-wing thought was beginning to attract a strong following in some sectors of American life. In *The Paranoid Style in American Politics* (1964) Richard Hofstadter tried to make sense of a phenomenon that observers today call "radical conservatism." The author was especially curious about people who expressed a conspiracy-minded version of right-wing thought that at the time was associated with McCarthyism and the John Birch Society. Hofstadter invoked some early concepts of social psychology when analyzing this phenomenon. He spoke of a "paranoid style" and status anxiety when speculating about the motivations and fears that animated some conservatives. Yet Hofstadter also wrote about intellectually sophisticated individuals who got caught up in a "spiritual wrestling match between good and evil."[36] His description of the way these figures approached issues suggested another means of interpreting right-wing thought, one based on the analogy of a religious impulse. Hofstadter observed the thinking of many ex-communist intellectuals in the conservative movement of the 1950s and 1960s—people who moved rapidly from left to right, "clinging all the while to the fundamentally Manichaean psychology . . . Such authorities on communism remind one of those ancient converts from paganism to Christianity of whom it is told that upon conversion they did not entirely cease to believe in their old gods but converted them into demons."[37]

Conservatism has expanded and morphed in many ways since Richard Hofstadter attempted to make sense of its mid-twentieth-century forms. Yet the language he used in 1964 is still relevant for an analysis of the way militant right-wingers view the world around them. The "spiritual wrestling" between "good" and "evil" continues. A Manichaean perspective remains strongly evident. Partisans who declare enthusiasm for conservative ideology often demonstrate loyalty to their cause with the passion of religious converts who have discovered the true light. Many of them express a view of demons that resembles the fears of those frightened people of Hofstadter's time. Today those partisans on the right loosely refer to the evil ones—their demons—as "liberals."

In Hofstadter's time this syndrome, which is essentially political fundamentalism, was articulated in the rhetoric of small extremist groups that spoke often about conspiracies. Today the syndrome is evident across a much broader spectrum of conservative groups. Political fundamentalism has gone "mainstream." Embellished with the jargon of erudition, fortified with the riches of right-wing moguls, bolstered by the productivity of intellectuals working at conservative think tanks, and publicized by a supportive national media, it has reached out to huge audiences in the United States. Right-wing fundamentalism now looks respectable and sophisticated, hip and relevant. When examined in terms of its religionlike structure, however, that syndrome looks problematic.

## CHAPTER TWO

# Fundamentalism

In recent years many radcons have displayed powerful convictions in their approaches to diverse national problems. Whether dealing with the economy, social issues, or foreign policy, right-wing partisans have demonstrated intense commitment to the teachings of their ideology. Their perspective resembles the framework of a fundamentalist political faith. That outlook places strong emphasis on absolute truths and looks for clues to them in the words of various prophets and seemingly sacred documents. As with fundamentalist religious groups, the militant conservatives' firm notions about verities often lead them to worry about challenges from people standing outside their fold. Nonbelievers (the liberals) seem ever threatening. Beating off the liberals' challenge requires constant vigilance. Leaders on the right often warn the faithful that some among them are inadequately committed to their group's principles and may be vulnerable to the enemy's appeal. These tainted followers must be rooted out. Worship on the right is only for the saved.

George M. Marsden, a prominent historian of fundamentalist religious movements in the United States, offers an "offhand" definition of the fundamentalist as "an evangelical who is angry about something." That anger is usually directed against "modern liberal theologies and to some aspects of secularism in modern culture."[1] There is a parallel in political circles evident in the radcons' militant resistance to the liberal view of a progressive, modern society. In many respects, when today's militant conservatives rail against liberal politics they sound like angry religious fundamentalists criticizing liberal theology and lifestyles.

The concept of religious fundamentalism implied here is not limited to the beliefs of Protestant groups in the United States. Recent scholarship has drawn attention to similarities between fundamentalist religions in diverse cultures. In 1992 Martin E. Marty and R. Scott Appleby traced these international parallels in *The Glory and the Power: The Fundamentalist Challenge to the Modern World*. Their book summarized the findings of more than 100 scholars who examined fundamentalist religious movements in three cultures: Protestant evangelicals and Pentecostals in the United States, Orthodox Jews in Israel, and Islamic fundamentalists in Egypt. Karen Armstrong, author of many books about religious history, provided a popular version of these comparative findings (that included her own insights) in a 2000 best-seller, *The Battle for God*. Later, R. Scott Appleby joined Gabriel A. Almond and Emmanuel Sivan to release a study of even broader scope. Their book, *Strong Religion: The Rise of Fundamentalisms around the World* (2003), examined the ideas and attitudes of Protestants, Christians, and Muslims and added groups such as Hindus and Buddhists to the global view of fundamentalism.[2]

Although some scholars of American religious history like to slice definitions and point out that fundamentalists were only one group within a larger evangelical movement, this analysis promotes a broader and more universal application of the term "fundamentalism" favored by Karen Armstrong as well as various contributors to *The Glory and the Power* and *Strong Religion*. As Armstrong notes, "The term [fundamentalist] is not perfect, but it is a useful label for movements that, despite their differences, bear a strong family resemblance."[3] The views of various political conservatives, although different in interests and goals, also bear a strong, underlying family resemblance. Like the traditional and evangelical religious groups, America's radical conservatives have long been divided over details associated with their beliefs and practices. It seems remarkable that their distinctive leaders and organizations can achieve coherence in view of their many disagreements and lively clashes about doctrines and policies. Yet, as in the case of fundamentalist religious groups, America's radcons often manage to come together for their principal struggle against liberals. They find opportunities to unite on the basis of ideas they intensely oppose.

Religious fundamentalists have described their enemy as modernists, secularists, secular humanists, and liberals (particularly liberal theologians), and in recent years they have settled primarily on the term "liberal" to succinctly identify the kind of individual they consider most troubling. Fundamentalists of the political right have evolved in a roughly similar way. Years ago they spoke anxiously about threats from the communists, socialists, the "left," and the liberals. In the twenty-first century, references to communists have largely disappeared, and comments about socialists turn up mostly in brief and sweeping accusations rather than in serious commentaries about political conditions in the United States. References to the "left" remain popular, but militant conservatives now most consistently identify the target of their criticisms simply as the "liberal."

What do the studies of religion in America and the world reveal about the perspectives of fundamentalists, and how do these notions resemble the mentality of militant *political* conservatives in the United States? Five characteristics of religious fundamentalists are especially relevant to an examination of the outlook of right-wing ultras in the United States:

1. They promote a Manichaean (dualistic) view of clashes with a strong and dangerous liberal enemy.
2. They call for uncompromising commitment to the faith.
3. They show great respect for their canon and the leaders who interpret it.
4. They divide among themselves over specific doctrines but show unity when confronting liberals.
5. They seek to restore the past by using the technology of the present.

Following is a fuller discussion of those characteristics.

*Fundamentalists Promote a Manichaean View of*
*Clashes with a Strong and Dangerous Liberal Enemy*

As Karen Armstrong observes, religious fundamentalists see their fight against liberal ideas as a "cosmic war between the forces of good and evil."[4] Fundamentalists view the world as divided into two camps: the immoral and the moral, the right and the wrong, the forces of light and the forces of darkness, the interests of God and the interests of Satan.[5]

Scholars often call this perspective a "dualistic" or Manichaean world-view, one that favors a white/black perspective on issues of deep concern to the groups. Fundamentalists argue that liberalism's powerful attraction must be fought off with great energy. They describe their struggle against liberal, secular influences as a daunting challenge, because liberals control many of society's major organizations, including the mass media, the leading educational institutions, and the major cultural centers. Since the liberals are well-connected in society, effective resistance to their influence requires tenacious efforts.[6] Religious beliefs must be strong, say fundamentalists, or they will not succeed against the strong enemy. A militant counterestablishment should be created to challenge the powerful rivals. Sometimes Protestant evangelicals describe that opposition as believers in an alternative religion, secular humanism (this notion of a counterreligion suggests that the threat is quite serious, since it involves a different philosophy about the basic meaning of life).[7]

There are obvious parallels in the *politics* of the militant right. Often, America's radical conservatives invoke sharply negative imagery when describing liberals. They, too, favor a Manichaean perspective. Militant rightists claim they are engaged in an important battle to free U.S. society of pernicious liberal influences. Like religious fundamentalists, they describe their opponents as a deeply entrenched elite that commands enormous prestige and power. Liberals, they claim, dominate the universities, Hollywood, the news media, and other centers that affect the economic, cultural, and political ideas of the American people. Some conservatives have talked about the growing power of a "New Class" in the United States made up of influential liberals in public institutions as well as various private foundations. Like the religious fundamentalists, radcons justify their militant ideology and tactics as necessary remedies for dealing with a powerful and pervasive liberal establishment.

In the manner of religious fundamentalists, militants on the right tend to describe political clashes as significant, principled conflicts. They say disagreements with liberals involve much more than just small disputes about the details of governing and living. These disputes concern fundamental ideological disagreements. They involve very different attitudes about ways to realize the good life, argue these conservatives. Market-oriented commentators describe liberals as basically unsympathetic to their ideals of a free enterprise system. Culture Warriors claim liberals do not share their fundamental moral values. Hawkish Nationalists charge liberals with viewing America's role in the world in a manner that greatly compromises and undermines the nation's self-interests. To be sure, various radcons use different words and imagery to communicate messages about the liberal threat. Attack dogs of the mass media, such as Sean Hannity, are much more given to issuing wild accusations against liberals than erudite figures such as George Will. Yet both the populist and elite-sounding commentators adhere to a basic framework: they treat the philosophical ideals of conservatism as fundamentally correct and the philosophical ideals of liberalism as basically wrong. For political fundamentalists on the right, liberalism looks like a competing religion or, in a sense, an atheistic rejection of the true conservative faith.

*Fundamentalists Show Great Respect for Their Canon and*
*the Leaders Responsible for Interpreting It*

Religious fundamentalists point respectfully to sacred documents, books, and speeches, identifying them as especially truthful and insightful. Protestant evangelicals point often to messages in the Bible. Orthodox Jews draw attention to the Torah or the interpretations in the Talmud. Muslims focus on the words of the Koran, treating the words of Muhammad as divinely inspired.[8] Since fundamentalists view their principles as fixed, they are anxious about the presence of individuals in their camps that seem insufficiently committed to the group's ideals. Those who raise questions about the absolute virtues of the sacred words are denounced as "relativists." Fundamentalists claim the relativists are too willing to negotiate with representatives of the prevailing liberal theology. These wavering souls must be rooted out of the movement. The fundamentalist camp should not tolerate frequent questioning of the faith's ideals. "God's word is pure, not pluralist," they say.[9] There is one principal Truth on the great questions, not many.

Religious leaders are responsible for interpreting the sacred canon, and they receive tremendous respect. Pastors, rabbis, and mullahs of the fundamentalist faiths are responsible for identifying ideas from the scriptures, doctrines, and laws to which followers can turn with absolute confidence. The authority of these charismatic, guru-like leaders is formidable, since these leaders enjoy special status as the "elect" or "chosen" people who are uniquely familiar with tenets of the theology.[10]

Political radcons are not likely to attribute divine qualities to their leaders and their ideas in the manner of religious followers, but their attitudes do, nevertheless, resemble the perspective of religious fundamentalists in some intriguing ways. Militant rightists often point to books they consider unusually insightful, claiming those writings opened their eyes to fundamental truths. They sound reverential, too, when talking about the U.S. Constitution, treating it like a sacred document that should not be reinterpreted loosely by liberals. Supreme Court judges should stick to the Founding Fathers' original meaning when dealing with the document's provisions, these rightists counsel; justices should not try to read modern messages into the words of the Founders and attempt to "legislate from the bench." Interestingly, constitutional scholar Cass R. Sunstein employs the term "fundamentalist" to identify extreme judicial conservatives who believe the Constitution should be interpreted according to an "original understanding." He notes that "'Strict construction' of the Constitution finds a parallel in literal interpretation of the Koran or the Bible. Some [judicial] fundamentalists seem to approach the Constitution as if were inspired directly by God."[11]

Many conservatives are enamored of favored gurus, identifying them as brilliant figures that demonstrate unusual expertise in revealing universal truths. Enthusiasts of militant conservatism often turn to radio gurus for insight and inspiration, listening carefully to the messages of figures such as Rush Limbaugh, James Dobson, Bill O'Reilly, or Sean Hannity. These listeners often refer to insights delivered to them by the media gurus when they engage in political conversations with friends and acquaintances. Highly educated champions of conservatism are more likely to seek wisdom about ideological precepts from more erudite-sounding commentators, such as George Will and David Brooks. Others on the right revere the concepts of philosophically inclined dead white male interpreters of conservative ideals. They comment glowingly about the theories of figures such as Edmund Burke, Friedrich Hayek, or Leo Strauss. In the years since Ronald Reagan's death, militant conservatives have put aside many of the reservations they had expressed earlier about the compromises Reagan made during his presidency. Now they identify the former president as a genuine conservative "hero" and quote him frequently. Jacob S. Hacker and Paul Pierson observe that since Reagan left the White House, conservatives have been identifying him as their "patron saint." For many on the right, Reagan has emerged as a godlike figure of uncommon, down-to-earth conservative wisdom.[12]

*Fundamentalists Divide among Themselves over*
*Specific Doctrines but Show Unity When Confronting Liberals*

Religious fundamentalists tend to engage in intense disputes about their view of the true faith. Quite often they express disagreement about specific doctrines and practices by breaking away from established groups and forming new sects devoted to their own particular expressions of the faith. The presence of charismatic leaders in fundamentalist religious movements contributes to this splintering. Headstrong leaders often insist on pursuing a particular reading of the canon. They readily form new organizations to achieve their devotional goals.[13] Among American Protestants, this tendency to split into numerous competing groups has proven to be a source of strength, not weakness. Evangelicals, Pentecostals, Mormons, and other spiritual groups have created abundant innovations in belief and practice by setting up their own places of worship. Their efforts to mobilize subgroups of enthusiastic religionists have contributed to a vast expansion of grassroots religious activity in the United States.

Despite numerous divisions within, fundamentalists manage to display impressive unity when confronting supposedly powerful forces from without. They share a common disdain for secular and modernist influences in the larger society. When dealing with the target of their anger—a threat characterized generally as liberalism—these fundamentalists tend to set aside their differences and join forces for common battle.

Similar characteristics are evident among the strong-minded partisans of American conservatism. Within the ranks of the right there is considerable fractiousness. Individuals and groups view issues differently and split over details when defining their interests and their ideology. Libertarians engage in numerous disputes with each other about interpretations of their philosophy, and they often take issue with other conservatives. Libertarians, who are generally distrustful of government, look askance at the efforts of cultural conservatives to use the powers of the federal government to "legislate morality." Paleoconservatives and neoconservatives have often cast aspersions at each other. Some on the right want to promote their religious objections to abortion, the teaching of evolution, and gay marriage. Others on the right are embarrassed by these campaigns, which they associate with "culture war," and wish that Republicans would devote greater attention to substantive questions about economics and foreign policy. There are conservatives who want the United States to play a huge role in world affairs as the dominant superpower, and others on the right who are deeply suspicious of the country's international commitments. In the 1990s members of the Christian Coalition and the Cato Institute expressed dramatically different political concerns, yet on essential questions about opposing "liberal" influences in the United States (as they defined them), these individuals rallied around a common cause. Conservative partisans, whatever their interest, tend to set aside their differences during political campaigns and work together in support of favored candidates that vigorously attack liberalism.

*Fundamentalists Seek to Restore the Past by*
*Using the Technology of the Present*

Fundamentalist groups frequently emphasize a restoration theme, arguing that the values and practices of earlier years were quite admirable but mainstream society has gone astray in modern times by adopting liberal, secularist theories and practices. These religionists say they do not seek revolutionary change but, rather, a return to time-tested virtues of the past.[14] This interpretation proves enormously appealing with individuals who are troubled by the many new developments in their fast-changing societies. Supporters of the faith feel like they have lost their mooring and have been cast adrift in a strange new modern society. It is comforting, then, to be told that the old verities still apply but that liberal modernists turned away from them and substituted a relativist, secularist lifestyle in which "anything goes." Fundamentalists seek to redeem their culture by challenging the supposedly flawed mentality and restoring traditional values.

Although fundamentalist religious leaders often rail against liberalism, secularism, and modernism, they are willing to employ the instruments of a modern liberal and secular society to communicate their messages to followers and to reach larger audiences among the general public. Fundamentalists frequently imitate techniques of the seculars and try to improve upon them as well. For instance, religious fundamentalists understand the importance of creating an image of authenticity and respectability for their teachings. They attempt to counter the popularity of liberal ideas by establishing their own outlets for faith-based learning and scholarship. Their supporters provide abundant financial support for organizations that promote a fundamentalist theology.[15] They pour money into seminaries and educational institutions so that the graduates of these programs can move on to leadership positions within the faith. Then the licensed graduates, carrying degrees and honors from fundamentalist organizations, are well positioned to disseminate the theology to a larger public.[16]

The authors of *The Glory and the Power* note that fundamentalists in the United States, Israel, and Egypt have become avid students of modern mass communications. Often, these religionists create their own media outlets for the faithful, delivering radio and television programming that is effective both as entertainment and education. Through these efforts, fundamentalists expand opportunities for listeners and viewers to hear The True Word uncontaminated by liberal error. They try to establish an active presence in the mainstream media as well. Fundamentalists position graduates of their institutions in secular programming on radio and television, promoting individuals who have been honored by their organizations as legitimate and insightful commentators on issues of the day.

There are, of course, roughly parallel examples of this mentality and practice among radcons in the United States. A restoration theme remains prominent in the militant right's political rhetoric.

The mindset is most obviously present in the thinking of Culture Warriors who object to liberal, secular, and modernist attitudes and lifestyles. These Warriors often point to the 1960s, arguing that relativist values became dominant during that tumultuous decade. The 1960s ushered in sexual permissiveness, political correctness in the universities, excessive emphasis on "multiculturalism," and disdain for religion, they complain. Culture Warriors seek to return U.S. society to the family values that they believe were dominant in the 1950s.

Market-oriented radcons (the Stealth Libertarians) argue frequently that the United States lost its attachment to sound economic principles during the Great Depression. They report that liberals tried to legitimize alien notions in the 1930s that favored Big Government. Liberals gained prominence in the universities during and after the New Deal period, they complain. Franklin D. Roosevelt's programs in the 1930s and Lyndon Johnson's Great Society programs of the 1960s led America down a mistaken path toward creation of a bureaucratic welfare state. Laissez-faire–minded fundamentalists of the right seek to return the nation to supposedly sound economic principles of the "pre-statist" New Deal years.

Hawkish Nationalists also look nostalgically to an earlier time. They claim the United States could pursue its interests unfettered by the heavy influences of international organizations back in the nineteenth century and in the early twentieth century. Many Hawkish Nationalists are suspicious of Europeans (especially the French) and of the United Nations. They are uncomfortable, too, with international pressures placed on the United States to cooperate with the world criminal court or to sign disarmament treaties. Hawkish Nationalists object to international pressures that force the United States to engage in military action only after obtaining support in the United Nations. They recall an earlier time in American history, noting that before World War II the United States often took bold and sometimes unilateral action in defense of its goals. Many of these conservatives promote the idea of "American Exceptionalism," a notion that suggests the United States had a felicitous origin as a new nation because its people enjoyed basic freedoms long before they became available to citizens of other nations. Consequently, say these Nationalists, the Americans are in a unique position to lead the world toward a better future. Americans are best equipped to advance democratic values around the world.

Obviously, these conservatives have demonstrated impressive skills in using modern technology to promote their messages about the importance of traditional verities. Back in the 1960s, for example, intellectuals on the right attracted little respect in the major cultural centers of the nation. Since then, militant right-wingers have sponsored numerous outlets for advancing their ideology. They have fortified the intellectual development of bright young conservatives by giving them scholarships for university study and fellowships at well-endowed conservative think tanks. Right-wing policy wonks have learned to use the mass media with stunning effect. They have served as articulate and persuasive commentators on national affairs over radio and television and have rushed into the Internet age with gusto, creating many entertaining and influential blogs. Radcons have also shown that they are excellent students of the modern techniques of mobilization. In the 1960s and 1970s, they mastered techniques of mass mailing and succeeded in mobilizing millions of voters behind GOP candidates, and presently they employ newer techniques very effectively to get out the vote. Like religious fundamentalists, hard-core rightists have been eager users of current technology to spread their messages about the virtues of the past.

## New Evangelists in Religion and Politics

Scholarly discussions about religious fundamentalism in the United States have stressed an important distinction that applies in a general way as well to analyses of militant political conservatism. Students of fundamentalist religious movements in the United States have noted that tradition-minded religionists tended to take a separatist tack during much of the early twentieth century. Over the second half of the century, however, new strategies emerged that proved much more successful in reaching a larger public and making a significant impact on mainstream religious beliefs and practices. In a related way conservative politics took a separatist tack in the first half of the century and proved unappealing to the wider public. Especially after the defeat of Barry Goldwater's presidential candidacy in 1964, conservatism adopted new outlooks and techniques that gave it a much broader reach in mainstream American politics.

George M. Marsden, a prolific scholar of American Protestantism, has thrown light on this distinction among religious fundamentalists. Marsden argues that the "fundamentalist" identification relates particularly to one strain of Protestant religious activity within the larger theme of evangelism. Unlike Armstrong, Almond, Appleby, and Sivan, who make fundamentalism the principal generic term for discussing this mentality, Marsden sees evangelism as the broader theme and treats fundamentalists as a subgroup of the evangelistic movements. Marsden focuses on conditions in the United States, in contrast to the other authors, who are interested in identifying wide-ranging characteristics of a fundamentalist mentality that apply internationally across several different religions and cultures. The more generic models provided by Armstrong, Almond, Appleby, and Sivan work better for considering the resemblance of militant politics to militant religion, but Marsden's analysis does, nevertheless, offer some intriguing insights about religious trends that can be useful for thinking about changes in right-wing political styles.

Marsden notes that the term "fundamentalist" became familiar in the American vocabulary when people interested in promoting the Bible as the literal truth tried to break away from the supposedly corrupt mainstream churches and mainstream American society in the 1910s and 1920s. The fundamentalists' reputation was damaged by the famous Scopes "Monkey" Trial of 1925, which made them look like close-minded opponents of modern science, especially the teaching of evolution in the

public schools. The fundamentalists' attachment to a strictly literal interpretation of the Bible undermined their national appeal.

However, a "new evangelism" gained ground beginning in the 1950s,
observes Marsden. Its leaders were no longer preoccupied with
defensive-sounding debates about Biblical literalness. They showed
greater interest in projecting a sunny, optimistic outlook. The new evangelicals offered a more emotionally appealing message to the masses.
Billy Graham was particularly skilled in this regard. He called for open
expressions of spirituality and greater engagement of Protestant groups
with mainstream American life. Graham also sounded more hopeful
about the possibilities for redeeming American culture than did the old-
time fundamentalists. He was willing to seek recruits for his cause
through appeals directed to the mainline churches and in broadcasts
over radio and television. Many evangelical pastors followed Billy
Graham's example, promoting diverse new forms of spiritually expres-
sive religious faith. Their efforts excited interest in established Protestant
churches as well as among newly formed "charismatic" congregations.
Eventually, enthusiasts of the new evangelical style gained much
broader influence in American society.[17]

This distinction between old and new forms of evangelism bears directly on a consideration of radcon politics in the United States. During
the first half of the twentieth century, prominent American conservatives resembled the traditional religious fundamentalists. Their messages often sounded pessimistic. Looking suspiciously at the modernization, urbanization, and secularization of the United States, they tended to
retreat into snarling expressions of disgust. Some displayed considerable
doubt about the progressive course of Western civilization and, in particular, of American civilization. These tradition-minded right-wingers
talked of protecting a "remnant of sanity" amidst the disarray, hoping to
gather together a few supposedly wise men for leadership who demonstrated respect for the old values. There were separatists among the old
conservatives who wanted to protect their group from the contaminating
forces of mainstream liberal society (much like separatists among religious fundamentalists in the 1920s, 1930s, and 1940s). Some of the traditional political conservatives were isolationists regarding foreign policy.
They distrusted connections and alliances with the troubled world beyond the borders of the United States. The old advocates of laissez-faire
sometimes offered strongly negative assessments of American progress,

too. Many of them presented dire warnings about creeping socialism when they crafted a rationale for laissez-faire (this defensiveness turned particularly acute during the Great Depression).

The old fundamentalists of political conservatism are especially represented today by people commonly identified as "paleoconservatives." Today paleos have only limited appeal among militants on the right. During the first half of the twentieth century, they appeared old-fashioned, surly, and politically inept. Comments from some paleos smacked of anti-Catholicism and anti-Semitism. Those bigots displayed transparent animus toward individuals who did not come from Anglo-Saxon or Nordic ancestry. They left Americans from other ethnic backgrounds strongly suspicious of their motives. Furthermore, some paleos sounded elitist. They wrote about hierarchy and looked suspiciously at America's newly rich or newly middle class. A few appeared uneasy about capitalism itself. They associated it with a crass, materialistic civilization that lacked moral norms.

At midcentury, when varieties of paleoconservatism seemed to dominate mentalities on the right, some of America's leading intellectuals offered contemptuous remarks about the lack of a viable conservative tradition in the United States. These commentators characterized thinkers and politicians on the right as standing far from the country's political mainstream. One of the most influential and oft-quoted characterizations appeared in 1950 in a publication by Lionel Trilling, a prominent intellectual at Columbia University. Liberals like to cite his observation as evidence of the powerful legacy of the New Deal in the 1950s, a time when liberalism appeared triumphant and conservatism seemed to have been routed. Conservatives often cite the statement as evidence of the pompous condescension of liberals at the time, and they note with pride that figures such as Russell Kirk and William F. Buckley helped to revive the conservative intellectual tradition just a few years after Trilling published the harsh words. At the beginning of a book called *The Liberal Imagination* (1951) Trilling said:

> In the United States at this time liberalism is not only the
> dominant but even the sole intellectual tradition. For it is the plain
> fact that nowadays there are no conservative or reactionary ideas
> in general circulation. This does not mean, of course, that there is
> no impulse to conservatism, or to reaction. Such impulses are

certainly very strong, perhaps even stronger than most of us know. But the conservative impulse and the reactionary impulse do not, with some isolated and some ecclesiastical exceptions, express themselves in ideas but only in action or in irritable mental gestures which seek to resemble ideas."[18]

Radical conservatism took on a new character in the second half of the twentieth century, one that is somewhat analogous to the changes Marsden detected in the evolving evangelist movement. The new right-wingers, like the new evangelicals, became increasingly prominent in the ranks of American conservatism after the 1960s. These individuals were not as likely to turn their backs on mainstream American society as traditional conservatives did. In fact, they worked quite effectively to infiltrate the American social and political establishment, and they hoped to dominate it eventually. The newer groups projected a more positive attitude toward capitalism, often describing it as essentially "moral." They were much more comfortable engaging and praising the nouveau riche. Conservatism's newer groups welcomed Americans into their fold from diverse ethnic, religious, racial, and national backgrounds. These "new evangelicals" of the right tended to look down, too, on isolationist sentiments and sometimes argued for bold new initiatives by the United States on the international front.

To accomplish their goals, conservatism's new political groups copied techniques of an establishment that they portrayed as liberal. Modern-minded radcons sponsored think tanks to honor their "scholars." They funded the advanced education of young believers so that these individuals, carrying supposedly impressive credentials, could participate actively in debates about the nation's political future. Conservatism's "new evangelicals" understood how to use radio and television to great effect. They wanted to give their movement intellectual *gravitas* that it lacked in the old days when it was dominated by the paleoconservatives. Some of the emerging figures became known as neoconservatives, an erudite group that proved especially successful in placing its advocates in prominent positions in the national government and the mass media. Other conservative leaders combined elements of both the old and new appeals as they sought to evangelize American society by promoting their ideals.

## Political Fundamentalism in Practice

Does the model of religious fundamentalism laid out by students of international religious trends, such as Armstrong, Almond, Appleby, and Sivan, apply to an examination of militant right-wing mentalities in the United States? Does the pattern of traditional and modern strategies observed by Marsden in connection with evangelical activities resemble changing patterns in *political* thought and activities as well? To explore the relevance of these interpretations it is useful to examine the attitudes of individuals who have been recognized and celebrated as leading communicators of modern American conservatism. The names appearing in the following chapters certainly do not represent an all-inclusive list of influential radcons. Rather, they have been selected because these individuals' ideas strongly reflect major elements of the three principal themes in conservative rhetoric: their comments express the spirit of a Stealth Libertarian's perspective on economics, a Culture Warrior's outlook on social change, and a Hawkish Nationalist's viewpoint on the nation's changing role in international affairs. As mentioned previously, the primary focus here is on book-length expositions written by radcons. The goal is not just to examine right-wing arguments about specific issues but to detect broad patterns of thought that resemble the mental framework of religious fundamentalists.

## CHAPTER THREE

# Right-Wing Fundamentalists

Examples of the fundamentalist political persuasion can be seen in the outlooks of two very prominent radcon figures, Ronald Reagan and Irving Kristol. These conservative leaders did not establish a perfect profile of right-wing fundamentalism, because each had to deal with the complex realities of American politics when attempting to apply their ideas. Reagan compromised on many issues during his years as governor of California and president of the United States. When necessary, Reagan could look like a practical (and often successful) politician. Irving Kristol, a bright and informed commentator on national affairs who became known as the "godfather" of neoconservatism, had to tailor his remarks, as well, to the realities of a constantly changing political situation. Kristol understood that he could not always get what he wanted, and his remarks in numerous publications over several decades reflected an appreciation of limitations. Yet both individuals exhibited a fundamentalist mentality as they dealt with broad political issues. When describing their vision, they turned to religious-style imagery. The ideological evolution of Reagan and Kristol is significant. It reflects a pattern seen in the lives of several other radcons who became influential in right-wing politics during the second half of the twentieth century. Both Reagan and Kristol began their political evolution by taking strong positions on the left, and each completed his transformation by promoting hard-line perspectives of the right.

Ronald Reagan moved swiftly and emphatically from left to right in the late 1940s and into the 1950s. The intensity of Reagan's liberalism in his younger years was impressive. His father, a Democrat, was an enthusiast of Franklin D. Roosevelt and his New Deal programs. Ronald Reagan became a solid Democrat, too. After World War II, when Reagan was a nationally recognized movie star, he campaigned for President Harry S. Truman. Ronald Reagan also mobilized the film community behind a liberal Democrat, Hubert Humphrey. Reagan supported Helen Gahagan Douglas (wife of his friend, the actor Melvyn Douglas) in a congressional race against the Republican Richard Nixon. He joined the American Veterans' Committee, which opposed colonialism and racial discrimination. Often he warned about the danger of "neo-Fascism" in the United States. Reagan hated the Ku Klux Klan, an attitude he picked up from his father, who was disgusted with the Klan's revival of racial and religious bigotry in the 1920s. Ronald Reagan's role in the movie *Storm Warning* (1951), an anti-Klan story, was genuine. Like the character in the film, he considered the activities of those white-robed Americans appalling. Interestingly, Reagan seemed too liberal for some Democrats at this time. Members of the Los Angeles Democratic Central Committee declined to recommend him in 1952 as a candidate for an open seat in Congress because they thought his reputation as a Hollywood leftist might undermine his candidacy.[1]

In his two autobiographies Reagan employs suggestive language to describe the intensity of his commitment to the Democrats and liberalism. He reports that he was a "very emotional New Dealer" and a "New Dealer to the Core" and that he "idolized" FDR and followed him "blindly." At another point Reagan writes, "I was a near hopeless hemophilic liberal. I bled for 'causes.'" In his 1965 book the future president notes that after World War II he "blindly" joined just about every available international-minded organization.[2] "Thus," he writes, "my first evangelism came in the form of saving the world from neo-Fascism."[3]

When describing his turn away from liberalism, Reagan again sounds like a man determined to think like a True Believer in political causes. Recalling his break from liberalism, Reagan spoke about the experience as if he were coming out of a trance. "Light was dawning in some obscure region of my head," he reported. "I was beginning to see the seamy side of liberalism." He claimed that liberals displayed an inability to recognize communism as it truly was. Liberals suffered from "ideological myopia," Reagan charged.[4] He claimed that some people in the liberal/Democratic camp were excessively tolerant of communists and suggested that their naïveté damned the entire political group. From Reagan's perspective, liberals had become tainted by too much tolerance for Marxism; they were not redeemable. In his eyes, the Democrats looked insufficiently pure.

Of course with similar emotion and intensity of commitment, Ronald Reagan soon demonstrated faithfulness to causes of the right. For a time, he acted like an anticommunist moderate liberal, but he then moved swiftly and strongly toward conservatism, though he did not change his registration to Republican until 1962. By 1964 Reagan was publicly endorsing Barry Goldwater for president, and two years later he ran for governor of California on an avowedly conservative platform.

Several factors drove Reagan to the right. Troubles with communists in the movie industry gave him difficulties when he emerged as a leader of the acting community in the late 1940s. In letters and in his first autobiography, Ronald Reagan pointed to those confrontations as the most important factor in his decision to switch parties and political philosophy. Other matters evidently affected his turn as well. Reagan's marriage to actress Jane Wyman fell apart, after which he married Nancy Davis, stepdaughter of a wealthy and conservative neurosurgeon. Nancy became his most trusted adviser. A trip to socialist-minded England in the late 1940s to film *The Hasty Heart* aroused Reagan's disgust over the weighty bureaucracy of the welfare state. He also began to complain loudly about the high tax rates that affected his take-home pay as well as that of many other wealthy entertainers. When Reagan became a spokesman for General Electric after his film career slipped, he made Big Government a principal target of his criticism. All of these developments came within a relatively short period of his life, a time when Reagan turned away dramatically from the politics of his father and his early adulthood.

Ronald Reagan changed parties and philosophies, but he never strayed far from a fundamentalist outlook on politics. In his early years he was a True Believer in liberal and Democratic causes. He did not demonstrate an inclination to question those traditions seriously, as he admitted in his autobiography. When developments of the late 1940s and early 1950s led him to switch allegiance, he did so with full heart and soul. Unlike many liberals who sought to save their movement from difficulties posed by members of the far left, particularly communists and communist sympathizers, Reagan abandoned liberals and the Democrats. He called people of those political sentiments "weak-willed" and "excessively tolerant of dangerous radicals." Reagan concluded that the left had been naïve in dealing with communists and in resisting collectivist trends in the United States. By the 1960s he was defending ultra versions of laissez-faire, railing against Big Government and Washington bureaucracy, disparaging liberalism like a Culture Warrior, and acting like a Hawkish Nationalist when speaking about U.S. relations with the Soviet Union. Reagan had become a fundamentalist of the right much like he had been a fundamentalist of the left in earlier years. He unintentionally acknowledged his earlier liberal fundamentalism when he reported happily that a turn toward conservatism helped him to break out of his "early white-eyed liberal daze."[5]

Edmund Morris, the biographer tapped by Reagan aides to get close to the president during his time in the White House and to write a definitive biography, observed this religionlike mentality, although he did not employ the term *fundamentalism* when describing the condition. Morris's book has been subject to sharp criticism, because the author mixed fiction with fact at various points in his analysis, but the author does, nevertheless, offer some intriguing insights. One such example appears in the language Morris chooses to characterize Reagan after watching him at length. In Morris's words, the president seemed to reflect a fundamentalist mentality. Reagan "listened [to contrary opinions] but would not hear, or looked at figures and did not see," says the biographer. "It was not obstinacy so much as an inability to comprehend the reason that challenges faith." Morris points out that the president "*believed* [italics in the original] the way a child believes—ardently and absolutely."[6] Later Edmund Morris writes about "the fundamentally childlike, bipolar quality of the President's mind, its tendency to see all moral questions in terms of opposites. Like a magnet among iron filings, it either concentrated acceptable facts in a tight cluster, or repelled them and kept itself clean."[7]

A related proclivity for strong belief can be detected in the life story of another prominent radcon, Irving Kristol. He became neoconservatism's "godfather" and emerged as one of its leading voices for many years. Kristol also viewed political issues with a religionlike perspective. In the manner of Ronald Reagan, he began on the left—in fact, he started his political maturation at a much more extreme location. Kristol confesses to making dramatic switches over his intellectual career from left to right.[8] As a student at the City College of New York, Irving Kristol and his friends gathered at a library alcove with Trotskyists (Stalinists established a meeting place in a different, nearby alcove). Kristol recalls that he engaged in "a Marxist scholasticism that was as rigorous and learned, in its way, as the Jesuit scholasticism it so strikingly paralleled."[9] He also served in the Young People's Socialist League, but during graduate studies at Harvard he discovered the writings of Leo Strauss and began his personal movement to the ideological right. Kristol became managing editor of *Commentary* after World War II, cofounded and edited the British publication *Encounter* (which received secret funding from the CIA), served as an executive with Basic Books, and taught at New York University before becoming a fellow at the American Enterprise Institute.[10]

Irving Kristol provides some revealing commentaries about his philosophical and political journey in a notable book, *Neoconservatism: The Autobiography of an Idea* (1995). He begins with stories about a search for direction in youth and as a young adult. The language Kristol employs to explain his personal transformation from left to right reveals a yearning for certitude. He was a strong believer in religious values, ideologies, and politics, but he switched back and forth in his early years as he considered the intellectual choices before him. Despite these switches, Kristol identifies a basic consistency in the search. He says he was essentially "theotropic," suggesting that his interest in religious ideals remained strong even though his family did not practice Orthodox Judaism in his early years.[11]

In his opening remarks Kristol wonders if there is such a thing as a "neo" gene, for if there is, he apparently has it. Over the course of his many personal political explorations, Kristol was notably "neo. "I have been a neo-Marxist, a neo-Trotskyist, a neosocialist, a neoliberal, and finally a neoconservative," he reports. In his own interpretation of this long record of intellectual movement, Kristol suggests the changes reflect the work of an inquiring mind. A different characterization appears more appropriate, however, for he seems to have displayed a strong attraction to firm-minded political perspectives throughout his life. Kristol adored muscular ideologies, but for many years the ones he embraced did not serve his interests adequately. Marxism, Trotskyism, and socialism proved easy to reject in the early Cold War years. His "neoliberal" years were not as truly liberal as Kristol portrays them (they were closer to affiliation with the conservative or Cold Warrior branch of the Democratic Party). Kristol moved about, seeking a political belief system that served his longing for a robust political orthodoxy. When he finally embraced neoconservatism, that long search essentially ended, and he remained firmly planted on the right in the decades that followed. At last Kristol had discovered a political faith that satisfied his hunger for a fundamentalist-style perspective.

Irving Kristol's descriptions of the people and ideas that motivated him as a youth and young adult reveal an eagerness to find profound insights, a predisposition toward experiencing a life-changing intellectual discovery. Excitedly, he read Plato at City College in New York and agreed with many of the ideas in *The Republic*. Kristol found similar agreement when encountering the ideas of leftist radicals such as Vladimir Lenin, Leon Trotsky, and Rosa Luxemburg. Theologians such as Reinhold Niebuhr and Paul Tillich also excited him. Kristol recalled that he had been "sympathetic to all of them." Yet he reserves his most detailed and emphatic praise for the ideas and influence of two intellectual giants of his early years, Lionel Trilling and Leo Strauss. Trilling's perspectives "hit me with the force of revelation," he recalls.[12] Strauss (a favorite of many prominent neoconservatives) receives even higher praise. Kristol notes that the renowned scholar of political philosophy at the University of Chicago who revered the writings of the "ancients" was uniquely insightful. "Encountering Strauss' work produced the kind of intellectual shock that is a once-in-a-lifetime experience," Kristol reports. "[Strauss] turned one's intellectual universe upside down," says the adoring protégé. "Suddenly, one realized that one had been looking at the history of western political thought from the wrong end of the telescope."[13] By reading Strauss, evidently, Kristol discovered enduring truths that more effectively satisfied his intellectual needs than did the teachers who were the object of his enthusiasm in earlier years.

Interestingly, Anne Norton, author of an insightful study of Strauss and the Straussians, observes that followers of Straussian ideas have been described as a "cult" and a "priesthood" that is committed to "orthodoxy."[14] One of their "vices," she notes, is devotion to a "canon." Straussians act as if "all the knowledge of the universe can be found within a single text."[15] They think, also, in terms of prophets and followers, she observes. Students of Straussian ideas want a "master," and the "teacher wants disciples."[16] The language Norton employs sounds like a description of intellectuals in search of fundamentalist-style cerebral experiences.

Religious thought also attracted Kristol's interest during his years of ideological development. Though Jewish, Kristol found the King James

Bible inspiring when he read it in college. "What impressed me about the Christian theologians was their certainty, derived from the Bible, that the human condition placed inherent limitations on human possibility," he recalls. Certainty was a perspective he apparently treasured. Kristol reports that his parents observed Orthodox Jewish traditions but did not act like believers in God or the principles of Jewish theology. His mother kept a strictly kosher household, but his father went to the synagogue only once a year, for the high holy days. Kristol did not find their approach emotionally or intellectually satisfying. He studied at a yeshiva, and the spirit if not the details of Jewish orthodoxy attracted his interest. In later years Kristol demonstrated allegiance to the practices of traditional Orthodox Judaism and expressed suspicion of the modern "liberal" figures in Judaism that associated with the "Reform" movement.[17]

Michael Lind, a prolific commentator on political issues, maintains that Irving Kristol and other major Republican neoconservatives remained basically consistent over the years when they gave enthusiastic reception to ideologies of the left and then turned emphatically to ideologies of the right. Kristol was essentially antiliberal in mentality, Lind argues. He opposed liberalism as a communist and later opposed it as a neoconservative. Like several other prominent intellectual figures on the right, Irving Kristol had gone from standing as an illiberal radical of the left to standing as an illiberal radical of the right.[18]

## The Fundamentalist Experience

Political observers often employ religious metaphors when describing strongly partisan conservatives who seem to have had an epiphany at a key moment in their lives and changed their politics. Rather suddenly, these individuals discovered that conservatism represented Truth, and from that moment they committed themselves to the right's causes. Their reactions sound like conversion experiences. As in the case of many religious affirmations of devotion, often an inspiring individual excited their decision to make a life-changing political decision. This pattern is evident in the experiences of people who joined the conservative movement many years ago. In those times liberalism appeared to be the dominant intellectual perspective. Ideas of the far left had appeal, too (such as concepts related to Marxism, socialism, and the New Left), especially among young, intellectually curious Americans situated in large metropolitan regions. Several prominent rightists appeared to be in search of ways to reject current fashions dramatically. Recently, however, conservative ideas have become much more prevalent in American society and American homes. Many of the parents of today's younger conservatives already considered themselves strong advocates of right-wing politics when they raised their children and gave them a strongly ideological education at home. Their youngsters did not need a "conversion" experience. Consequently, political transformations tend to be more common among today's older figures on the right than among the younger partisans.

Authors who have written about youthful experiences of the older conservatives have noted the importance of these emotional events. In a book about the political fight over Robert Bork's nomination for the U.S. Supreme Court, Ethan Bronner reports on such an epiphany. Bork is the former judge and Yale Law School professor nominated to the Court by President Reagan. After a lengthy battle, the Senate chose not to confirm him. When Bork was a young man, Bonner writes, "he experienced what is frequently referred to as a conversion of religious proportions away from socialism toward conservatism."[19] The transformation came when Bork fell under the influence of a conservative professor at the University of Chicago. Similarly, journalist Nina J. Easton points out that Christian Coalition leader Ralph Reed found an inspiring prophet in the person of Grover Norquist, an intensely partisan political strategist of the right. Reed "glued himself to Grover's side with the religious zeal of a new convert, an evangelist in the Church of Holy Republicans," writes Easton.[20] For Ralph Reed, politics was not a sport but "a calling," and the political activist traded talk with other young conservatives about "political conversion experiences" as if "they were on some evangelical mission."[21] "Politics," concludes Easton, was his "faith."[22] Thomas Frank employs similar language when describing Sean Hannity's discovery of Truth on the right. Hannity, a right-wing radio and television commentator with a huge national audience, is often rude to guests he associates with the "left" and rude to individuals he considers "liberals" in crowds where he lectures. Frank observes that Hannity, like other conservatives, speaks of his "first bout of indignation as a sort of conversion experience, a quasi-religious revelation." In the course of listening to "dedicated patriot" Ollie North in the Iran-Contra hearings (and feeling anger over the treatment North was receiving),

Hannity found his "calling in life." This was, says Frank, "an epiphany, a revelation of the Christ-like nature of the right."[23]

Elements of a fundamentalist political faith are evident when conservatives speak in glowing terms about the way a particular publication made a tremendous impact in their lives. They often report on an intensely emotional experience during their youth, when they read a book that introduced them to conservative tenets. It is as if divine insight struck them. They describe an apocalyptic experience, a moment when drift and uncertainty ended and a confident understanding of the real meaning of life began. Not surprisingly, they view the authors of these respected tomes as prophets who opened their eyes to extraordinary wisdom.

When conservatives cite inspirational works that helped them to discover fundamental truths, they usually refer to commentaries that are broadly philosophical. Right-wing partisans favor writers who take the big view: thinkers who try to provide a broad framework for understanding the world's complexities. Many conservatives point to the tremendous influence in their lives of books by Richard Weaver (*Ideas Have Consequences,* 1948) and Russell Kirk (*The Conservative Mind,* 1953). In the 1950s those two publications were among the right's favorite intellectual tracts. Edwin Feulner, who served as president of the Heritage Foundation, read Kirk's book and Eric Kuehnelt-Leddihn's *Liberty or Equality* as a freshman in college. After that experience, reports Feulner, his mind was set, and it never wavered.[24] Kirk, in turn, found inspiration in the messages of a noted eighteenth-century English statesman. Edmund Burke had "prophetic powers," wrote Kirk. He provided "the true school" of conservative principles. Burke was the greatest of modern conservative thinkers, Kirk announced, and "the founder of our conservatism."[25] For others, Whittaker Chambers's *Witness* offered the greatest inspiration for their early political conversion. Chambers had been a member of a communist group in the 1930s but broke away and later denounced communism. Grover Glenn Norquist, the leader of the Republican antitax forces cited earlier, read *Witness* when he was in high school. That experience convinced him that the liberal media distorted reality (because many journalists had been critical of Chambers and sympathetic toward the man he named as a former communist, Alger Hiss).[26] Similarly, New Right political activist William Rusher reported that Whittaker Chambers's book had a "tremendous influence" on his thinking. The publication provided the "Alpha and Omega" for his understanding of the communist mind.[27]

As mentioned previously, some conservatives identify the University of Chicago's erudite political philosopher Leo Strauss as their principal source of inspiration. Strauss focused on the great works of the "Ancients," particularly Plato. An entry in the *Concise Conservative Encyclopedia* reports that Strauss was the only contemporary teacher of politics whose students are known as "disciples" (a term that fits the description identified earlier by Anne Norton).[28] Irving Kristol recalls that Strauss had great influence on his personal intellectual development and remembers that students who were enthusiastic about the revered professor became known as "Straussians."[29] Willmoore Kendall, who taught and inspired William F. Buckley and was an enthusiast of John Locke's ideas, suggested that two of Leo Strauss's books "should be not required reading but scripture for everyone who likes to think of himself as a conservative."[30]

Libertarian treatises also excite feelings of revelation. Partisans on the right sometimes describe these publications as treasured documents of the conservative canon. Edmund Optiz, a libertarian who emphasized Christian ethics, recalled reading *Our Enemy, the State* (1935), by Albert J. Nock, saying, "Nock has a way of becoming an event in a man's life." Optiz examined Nock's book while traveling by train across the United States. By the time he arrived at his destination, he had "chosen sides."[31] Others who became libertarians were persuaded by Ayn Rand's popular novels (*The Fountainhead* and *Atlas Shrugged*). Rand, an émigré from the Soviet Union, promoted a libertarian-style "objectivist" philosophy (not surprisingly, some libertarians who were contentious about principles objected to Rand's strong-minded views, atheistic inclinations, and dogmatic personal style). Mark Gerson, author and editor of books about neoconservatism, reports that Rand achieved a "cultist" following.[32] Barry Goldwater's 1960 publication, *The Conscience of a Conservative* (written with the assistance of William F. Buckley's brother-in-law, L. Brent Bozell), also pressed the libertarian case but avoided direct association with libertarian philosophy. Lee Edwards, a conservative activist and author of an important history of the American conservative movement, indicates his enthusiasm for the book by claiming that the 1960s "began with a book"—*The Conscience of a Conservative*.[33]

Many of the most prominent and influential conservative thinkers and activists who made their mark in the second half of the twentieth century adopted a hard-line perspective from the right after exhibiting an earlier enthusiasm for perspectives of the left. They were consistent in preferring a radical stance but switched to a different brand of radicalism. These individuals showed a proclivity for intensely partisan politics, and they consistently targeted the same enemy. Whether fighting from the left or the right, they were suspicious of people in the middle. Liberals, in both instances, represented their primary opponents. Like some religiously inclined individuals, they remained committed to a fundamentalist perspective. In the manner of Irving Kristol, these individuals substituted political fundamentalism of the left for political fundamentalism of the right. In both their earlier and later professional careers, they acted as True Believers in a political faith.

Several of the early leaders in the conservative intellectual movement started out on the left. Richard Weaver, the University of Chicago professor who wrote *Ideas Have Consequences,* joined Norman Thomas's Socialist Party of America as a young man, and he served for two years as the secretary of a local chapter. Weaver later switched to the Southern Agrarians' nostalgic brand of conservatism when he took up graduate studies at Vanderbilt University. Russell Kirk, author of the influential book *The Conservative Mind* and later a regular contributor to the *National Review,* voted for the Socialist Party's presidential candidate, Norman Thomas, in 1944, because Kirk took exception to Franklin D. Roosevelt's internationalist perspective when the United States entered World War II. Later Kirk served as one of the right's premier intellectual defenders of tradition.

Several major contributors to the *National Review* came out of leftist experiences. James Burnham, Frank Meyer, Whittaker Chambers, and William S. Schlamm were former communists. James Burnham was a Trotskyist in the 1930s and then broke from the left near the end of the decade. He became a passionate anticommunist and railed against "appeasement" in U.S. dealings with the Soviets.[34] Frank Meyer, an editor at the *National Review,* switched from advocating Marxism to championing extreme libertarian viewpoints.[35] Whittaker Chambers, of course, had known and worked with Alger Hiss during his communist days, but Chambers became a powerful voice on the right in the 1940s and 1950s. William S. Schlamm, a founder of the *National Review,* had been a communist in his teenage days in Austria. He defined himself as a "non-Marxist socialist" in the 1930s and then moved strongly to the right in later years.[36]

Many others who emerged as important spokesmen for the conservative cause in the later part of the twentieth century began on the left.

Joseph Epstein, a neoconservative literary commentator with *New Criterion* and editor of *American Scholar,* had been, in his own words, "a down-the-line, pull-the-lever man of the left."[37] Ronald Radosh, author of important scholarship on the espionage case of Ethel and Julius Rosenberg, identified himself as "an advocate of a socialist solution to America's domestic crisis" in a book published in 1975 but turned to the right in later years.[38] Robert Bork, the conservative jurist who wrote impassioned denunciations of liberalism after failing to win a seat on the Supreme Court, indicated that he read a Marxist analysis of capitalism when he was fifteen. "It hit me like a ton of bricks," Bork recalled. "It was very powerful stuff and I thought that was probably the truth."[39] In his later years Bork associated truth with ideas of the far right.[40] Richard John Neuhaus, a leading critic of secularized liberalism, was a strong-minded political activist on the left in the 1960s. He led angry protests against the supposedly racist and imperialistic "regime" in the United States, but turned radically to the right when he became disgusted with the moral and cultural relativism that seemed to permeate American life in the 1970s.[41] Neuhaus described his experiences in a book with a revealing subtitle: *Catholic Matters: Confusion, Controversy, and the Splendor of Truth* (2006).[42]

David Horowitz's journey from left to right is particularly interesting because he has written extensively about his personal transformation, and because he has applied religious metaphors to explain his experiences. His Jewish parents were enthusiastic Stalinists. During and after his studies at Columbia and Berkeley, Horowitz became prominent in leftist causes. He associated with the New Left, worked for Bertrand Russell's peace organization, and edited the radical publication *Ramparts.* Today he is one of the right's most active champions of its political causes. Interestingly, Horowitz sees religious implications in leftist thought but is less perceptive about the tendency of many on the right, including himself, to think in similar ways. Horowitz describes his father as a believer in orthodox ideas "that comprised the Stalinist faith," and he speaks of the outlook of American communists as a "totalitarian *faith.*"[43] Radical believers think "this idea is so beautiful it is like God himself," observes Horowitz. "It provides the meaning of a radical life."[44]

Horowitz reports that in the late 1960s and early 1970s he was still a partisan of the radical left, but once he recognized the faithlike quality of leftist ideas, he began to entertain doubts about that radical cause. David

Horowitz campaigned against the Vietnam War and later worked on a project with the Black Panthers that aimed to create a community learning center in an East Oakland ghetto. One of the events that especially drew him toward conservatism involved the brutal murder of a female member of the Sunnyside Young Progressives, an idealistic group on the left. The young woman had taken up residence in a poor neighborhood so that she could remain close to the people she wanted to help. She kept the door of her residence unlocked. One day a black youth whom she had been assisting entered, raped her, and then strangled her to death. Horowitz concluded that the woman "died a martyr to the political faith that made her blind."[45]

Shortly after this tragedy, Horowitz challenged his leftist friends to discuss the fundamentals of their political beliefs. He organized a seminar designed to confront leftist colleagues with a provocative question: "Is Socialism a Viable Idea?" When Horowitz realized his fellow radicals were not willing to engage the issue honestly, he became deeply disillusioned. David Horowitz describes the young socialists' attitudes in religious terms: "To ask whether the socialist idea was more than a fantasy was like asking believers about the existence of God."[46] Soon after, he became one of the right's most militant True Believers.

Some people who adopted militant conservatism tie their strong political beliefs to their strong religious sentiments. For instance, Michael Medved, a conservative radio figure and author, reports that he indulged in "messianic leftism" in his youth but eventually evolved in the direction of recognizing truths and rejecting "trendy notions of moral relativism." Medved announced confidently that his autobiography is not just about lessons from his personal experiences. Rather, the story about his discovery of conservative ideals represents an investigation into "the Truth, to the extent that I can comprehend and explain it." Medved's journey involved not only personal movement from the political left to the political right but also a growing commitment to Orthodox Judaism later in his life.[47]

Milton Friedman, a conservative economist and Nobel Prize winner, went from religious orthodoxy to a position of disbelief but confessed that he remained sympathetic to the spirit of orthodoxy through the rest of his life. In his early years he demonstrated fealty to Orthodox Judaism, but later Friedman transferred his penchant for strong beliefs into a commitment to orthodox libertarianism (which he called "classical liberalism").

Friedman recalls that he faced an intellectual crisis in his teenage years regarding religious beliefs. At first he had taken his faith seriously. Friedman says he was "fanatically religious, seeking to conform in every detail to the complex dietary and other requirements of Orthodox Judaism."[48] At about the age of twelve he decided there was no valid basis for the religious faith and rigid customs he followed. His parents' hypocritical religious practices played a role in this disillusionment. They kept kosher but exhibited no real observance of Jewish traditions and convictions. "If you believed in [Orthodox Judaism], you ought to do it right," Friedman concluded. "If you didn't, you ought not to pretend."[49] In later years Friedman did, in fact, "do it right" through a religionlike devotion to the ideal of laissez-faire. He projected an orthodox vision of libertarian philosophy.

## Undisturbed by Doubts

The radcons' interest in commitments to Truth rather than the uncertain, namby-pamby, relativist positions that the right associates with liberals often produces pressure for conformist thought. As the former conservative insider David Brock points out, a demand for certainty fosters a "stifling intellectual intolerance and the stamping out of dissent" on the right that is common to many political 'sects.'"[50] Brock recalls from his experiences as a prominent figure in the modern conservative movement that individuals on the right could be "excommunicated" if they were accused of tolerance for conflicting views and, particularly, if they compromised with liberals. Conservatives behave as people in cults do, says Brock. They denounce nonbelievers as heretics (as they did emphatically in his case, when he broke from the movement and later published sharply critical revelations about its activities).[51] Brock succinctly identified this mentality by citing a confession by a leading neoconservative, Bill Kristol (son of Irving Kristol): "There is a type of thinking on the right that if you don't agree with everything," said Kristol, "you're a traitor to the movement."[52]

Authors who have analyzed the ideas of major conservative leaders have often identified these characteristics. They point to an attitude of intolerance for dissenting opinions and note that leaders on the right frequently express a desire to purge the movement of individuals whose thinking appears to be compromised. Journalist Nina J. Easton notes, for instance, that Grover Norquist, the hard-core champion of tax reduction and limited government, scorns conservatives who compromise with liberals. He calls them "yellow-bellied conservatives" and "squishes" i.e., people who cave in to the enemy rather than standing up for their convictions.[53] Norquist has worked relentlessly (and often successfully) to replace "squishes" in Congress with committed radcons. David Alan Crawford describes similar attitudes in *Thunder on the Right: The 'New Right' and the Politics of Resentment* (1980). He says many conservative leaders treat people who make deals with the liberal enemy as scoundrels who have lost their integrity. Those who compromise are soft. "The good guys are those individuals who are untainted by liberalism or moderation," says Crawford. Right-wingers applaud heroic figures who oppose the left "to the last corral, shooting it out like some Wild West sheriff, holding off the outlaws of liberalism."[54]

## True Faith

Many of today's militant conservatives resemble religious fundamentalists in their zealotry for an ideological cause. Older ones often describe their political conversions from liberal or strongly leftist positions as apocalyptic experiences. Others who came into their political maturity well after Marxist and New Left causes had lost their intellectual clout grew up in strongly conservative households. They adopted right-wing, fundamentalist perspectives in the manner that children of religious fundamentalists often accept the religious outlook of their parents. Whatever their background, these partisans tend to be more enthusiastic about philosophical gurus than do liberals. They are also more committed to orthodox beliefs. Radical conservatives often proselytize the tenets of their faith in the manner of religious missionaries. Many of them treat those teachings as doctrine and dogma, and when they encounter people who do not share their uncompromising devotion to precepts of the right, they express profound distrust. Unsaved Americans are like heretics, followers of an alien creed—perhaps a competing errant religion. Political fundamentalists view their fellow conservatives, however, as the True Believers, the crusading soldiers of an esteemed political faith.

CHAPTER FOUR

# Stealth Libertarians

In 1995 the Republicans' feisty U.S. representative and House majority leader, Dick Armey, published a hard-hitting commentary that laid virtually all of the blame for the country's economic problems at the feet of liberal Democrats and identified conservative Republicans as saviors of the economy. Armey claimed the Democrats had been moving the nation on the road toward "statism" for many years. Since the days of the New Deal, he said, bureaucrats based in Washington, D.C., had been weighing down the nation's productive business people with hundreds of governmental regulations.[1] Armey considered Washington's bureaucratic interference grossly insulting to enterprising Americans who took economic risks and succeeded in building productive businesses. An army of little potentates on the Potomac had established costly obstacles to economic activity, he asserted.[2] Political "leftists" who supported this bureaucratic meddling did not understand that private enterprise worked much more effectively than government planning and regulation as the engine of growth. Armey found satisfaction in signs of a new political development that promised to remove these obstacles. Republicans had wrested control of the Congress in the 1990s after many years of liberal dominance. They ushered in a "Freedom Revolution" that promised to take the heavy hand of Washington bureaucrats off the backs of hard-working Americans.[3]

The champion of these ideas had been one of the principal leaders of the conservatives' surge to dominance in Congress in the 1990s. Armey, formerly an economics professor in Texas, had been a close ally of Newt Gingrich and one of the framers of Gingrich's "Contract with America," a plan to cut back many activities of the federal government. Dick Armey had been a strong voice for reducing taxes, privatizing Social Security, and phasing out farm subsidies. During the heyday of the Republicans' power in Congress after the 1994 elections, he served as the party's House majority leader.

Dick Armey's stunningly simplistic and partisan picture of recent U.S. economic history featured two characteristics that have become prominent in arguments of the radical right. First, Armey gave his fellow conservatives just about all of the credit for defending capitalism, and he cited liberals (sometimes identified as "the left" or Democrats) as the principal obstacles to advancement of the free enterprise system. Armey portrayed conservatives as promoters of an open-minded and expansive view of economic development and claimed that liberals were constantly undermining economic growth through their support of government intrusion in the affairs of business. Second, Armey supported an extreme version of laissez-faire when identifying a strategy for improving the nation's economic health. He did not temper his arguments about the negative consequences of governmental action with a consideration of government's usefulness. Dick Armey had virtually nothing positive to say about the state's potential for playing a useful role in fostering economic progress, ensuring fair business practices, or protecting the interests of consumers and workers. In grossly damning language, he described the federal government as a profoundly detrimental force in the economic life of the nation. The state was big, cumbersome, and costly, he insisted, and it usually brought more harm than help when it intervened in the economy.

Variations of these two themes have been central in the rhetoric of market radicals in recent decades. The paired ideas have served as a mantra for the political faithful. Just about every major writer and speaker of the radical right who discusses economic issues accentuates these two points. Partisans consistently identify laissez-faire as the appropriate philosophy for dealing with the U.S. economy, and they identify liberals as threats to free enterprise and economic progress.

This outlook is fundamentalist in its basic framework. Armey and others like him promote a highly simplistic and purist vision of economic problems and their remedies. In the familiar narrative virtually all of the difficulties can be laid at the feet of liberals (and the ideas that they advocate). Virtually all of the solutions to economic problems are associated with laissez-faire economic policies. Market fundamentalists persistently articulate an antigovernment narrative. State action in human and economic affairs is almost always bad. When these fundamentalists encounter facts that appear to contradict their conclusions, they often blithely dismiss the evidence as irrelevant or mistaken. Seemingly troublesome details fail to undermine their beliefs. Contrary interpretations do not weaken their convictions. Market fundamentalists invoke their cherished economic principles confidently, treating them almost as sacred concepts, as universal verities.

Libertarians are the best promoters of this fundamentalist-style economic vision. Of the many groups that have contributed to the thinking of leaders in the GOP regarding financial matters, libertarians have achieved distinction as the most principled and sophisticated articulators of the broad, philosophical rationale for unfettered markets. Many of today's Republicans and conservatives find their arguments enormously persuasive. They are attracted to a purist and Manichaean libertarian outlook that identifies private enterprise as inherently good and government intervention as fundamentally bad.

## The Libertarian Vision

Although many conservatives endorse an extreme version of market-oriented economic thought that resembles the concepts of economic libertarianism, they rarely acknowledge in public their association with this "ism." In fact, many of today's conservatives have heard libertarian principles articulated often in the national media and have not recognized that they were privy to a specifically libertarian philosophical outlook. These readers and listeners like what they see and hear and endorse the concepts without an appreciation of the source of these fundamentalist ideas about markets. Purveyors of libertarian ideals in the national media often conceal any association between their commentaries and their libertarian philosophy. They act by stealth, demonstrating sharp political sensitivity. To accept the libertarian label in public appears tantamount to confessing commitment to an extreme and radical view of economic issues, one not shared by most Americans.

Consequently, militant advocates of laissez-faire rarely mention the term in their political discourse.

Instead of identifying the basic framework that gives shape to their economic perspective, libertarians speak about details. These market radicals usually name governmental activities that they oppose, but they are loath to identify the ideological framework that best communicates their worldview. Like Richard Armey, market conservatives lambaste government as the primary source of the nation's economic problems. They urge Americans to reduce the role of the federal government and the states drastically, arguing that such action will improve economic conditions enormously. When addressing goals, they speak abstractly and vaguely about a fight for freedom from intrusive governmental controls. David Boaz, author of *Libertarianism: A Primer* (1997) and executive vice president of the libertarian Cato Institute, defines the outlook as a "view that each person has the right to live his life in any way he chooses so long as he respects the equal rights of others."[4] Boaz explains that libertarianism is "an advocacy of individual liberty, free markets and limited government rooted in a commitment to self-ownership, imprescriptible rights [fundamental ones that they cannot be denied] and the moral autonomy of the individual."[5] Libertarians especially celebrate the marketplace. Markets should operate freely, they insist, with little or no state interference. Libertarians call for limitations on state power, the privatizing of state enterprises, massive tax cuts, and strong protection for private property. Citing John Locke, they maintain that government should operate with the consent of the governed. Locke defended the right to life, liberty, and property, and libertarians emphasize the third element, property, as an essential foundation for enjoying life and liberty.

Libertarians express suspicion of government coercion. They often use the term "government" as if it is a naughty word. Libertarians want freedom from government intervention, including strong state involvement in taxation and regulation of business activities. As advocates of "free" markets, they generally oppose economic protectionism, tariffs, and labor laws that establish minimum wages or maximum hours. Many of them strongly oppose welfare programs, the social security program, and other forms of government assistance to individuals. While libertarians disagree among themselves about the limited responsibilities government ought to maintain, they are in general agreement that taxes collected by the state from people and businesses ought to be kept very low.

There is a utopian strain in much of libertarian thought. Like fundamentalist religionists who imagine possibilities for a marvelous society if only the serpent of liberal secularism can be removed from the garden, libertarians often speak as if Americans will realize extraordinary prosperity, freedom, and happiness if only they can get government off their backs.

The libertarian outlook applies to foreign policy, as well. Many, although not all libertarians, warn of the "warfare state." Military conflicts trouble them because wars can lead to high taxes, concentration of power in the hands of government leaders, and compulsory military service (the draft). Wars also disrupt business activities. Armed conflict can produce tremendous destruction of private property and the breakdown of national and international commerce.

Not surprisingly, partisans who value philosophical rigor fight about particulars. When trying to apply their ideas to the complex debates about politics in modern America, they often engage in lively internecine disputes. Some support open immigration because of their belief in freedom of movement; others think open borders lead to a form of legalized trespassing. Traditional libertarians are often suspicious of U.S. intervention in the affairs of other nations (including war), but some "neolibertarians" justify foreign entanglements, especially when those actions defend economic interests of the American people and the United States. Libertarian-minded partisans sometimes break off into factions so they can address specific goals more clearly. There are splinter groups of libertarians known as minarchists, anarchocapitalists, left-libertarians, and objectivists. Some libertarians side with liberals more than conservatives on specific issues, although libertarians generally tend to fall on the right in political and economic disputes. While fights among intellectuals in the movement remain intense, the thrust of libertarian thought in mainstream American politics remains rather clear and directed. Libertarian-minded radcons seek to diminish the role of the federal government drastically, to reduce taxes dramatically, and to accomplish a radical downsizing of the state's regulatory activities. Many of them advocate giant tax cuts, especially for the rich, so that they can "starve the beast" (the federal government). When the nation-state has to operate with drastically diminished revenues, they reason, politicians will have to eliminate many programs that had been initiated in the time of FDR's New Deal, Lyndon B. Johnson's Great Society, and subsequent Democratic administrations.

Libertarianism is not simply a bogeyman; its philosophy offers plenty of attractive features for people who are not among its partisans. The economic implications of libertarian thought sound reasonably appealing. Americans do not want government "on their backs." They wish to engage in private enterprise and take risks in making investments without state bureaucrats blocking their way. Americans generally love the concept of free markets. They wish to foster a business culture that welcomes entrepreneurship. A libertarian aversion to war is also generally appealing. Lots of Americans agree that warfare can produce terrible economic and human consequences.

Libertarianism looks problematic, however, upon a closer look at its proponents' attitudes, because enthusiasts of the cause tend to advocate extreme views. Many libertarians resist all kinds of state intervention in the public interest, such as pollution controls, government-initiated college loan programs, unemployment compensation, regulation of pharmaceutical products, monitoring toys for child safety, and providing housing and food stamps for the poor. Lots of libertarians are strongly critical of public education and advocate various forms of private education. They criticize efforts by representatives of the state to come to the aid of American citizens, as in welfare arrangements, Medicare and Medicaid programs, and the "government's retirement system" known as Social Security. Some libertarians wish to limit government's role to just a few services such as defending the nation from foreign attacks, fighting crime, and preventing fraud. Individual libertarians sometimes offer a degree of latitude in dealing with each of these matters, allowing a few small service activities, but generally they resist large-scale state actions, even when the importance of those activities to the public welfare seems apparent to many Americans.

Libertarians, like religious fundamentalists, tend to be sticklers for consistency. They are True Believers who promote a radical commitment to laissez-faire principles. Libertarians argue that government-led programs frequently produce unintended, negative consequences. Rather than take the chance of creating unexpected problems through state intervention, it is, they claim, best to place faith in actions of the marketplace. A system of free commerce will almost always deliver better economic solutions than intervention and regulation by fumbling and inefficient bureaucrats, libertarians argue. This hard-line philosophy offers almost no room for exceptions. It serves as a theology that gives believers answers for virtually all economic questions, and it provides convenient ways to dismiss evidence that conflicts with the group's teachings. Libertarianism promotes a more extreme stand against government action than most Americans favor.

There is also a social side to libertarianism that many Americans consider problematic. Libertarians are sticklers for consistency in their disdain for governmental restrictions, including curbs in social matters. Many of them insist that any activity involving consenting adults is OK as long as it does not harm innocent individuals or coerce them. Many (but not all) libertarians believe that Americans should have a complete right to gamble, indulge in drugs, consume alcohol, obtain or sell pornography, engage in prostitution, participate in gay marriage, choose euthanasia, or engage in many other affairs that do not, in their view, harm others. Of course, this social perspective is offensive to cultural conservatives who fear that libertarianism undermines societal norms and promotes nihilism. Consequently, libertarians generally avoid the label so they will not be associated with controversial issues that Culture Warriors treat as "moral" questions.

Libertarians exercise power and influence in the realm of conservative ideas that is greatly disproportionate to their actual numbers. A small Libertarian Party has been in operation since the early 1970s and has never attracted much support from the American electorate. The author Ayn Rand, with her "objectivist" school that resembles libertarianism in some important ways, drew supporters years ago, but many conservatives found her celebration of the "virtue of selfishness" anarchic, soul-less, and God-less (interestingly, the former Federal Reserve Chairman Alan Greenspan participated in these Rand-club activities in his younger days). Rand hated communism after her youthful experiences growing up in the Soviet Union. She became radically pro-capitalist and celebrated the heroic individual in two best-selling novels, *Atlas Shrugged* (1957) and *The Fountainhead* (1963). A libertarian think tank, the Cato Institute, created in 1977 by Edward Crane, directs most of its attention to the group's economic agenda. Crane had briefly chaired the Libertarian Party in the 1970s before leaving that organization in protest. He helped to establish the Cato Institute's agenda, which promoted deregulation, tax cuts, and free trade. Fellows at the institute are today among the nation's most vociferous champions of an unfettered market.

Libertarians speak and write often for the national media, but the communications industries usually feature these individuals as "conservatives." Despite the small size of the bona fide membership, libertarians make a substantial impact on the nation's discussions about business affairs. The *Wall Street Journal* and other business publications promote libertarian economic perspectives in their editorial commentaries. Leaders of the Republican Party frequently apply libertarian arguments in their analyses of the nation's economic problems and cite the comments of libertarian intellectuals to bolster their cases. Libertarians represent one of the nation's most forceful groups in advocating a greatly reduced role for the state in business affairs. When today's hard-line market-oriented conservatives endorse the laissez-faire perspective, they usually do not identify themselves specifically as libertarians (quite a few do not, in fact, know how to describe one). They think of themselves simply as conservatives. Yet these individuals address economic issues from the group's point of view. Most important, they subscribe to the radical laissez-faire outlook. Without recognizing the debt they owe to libertarians, right-wingers frequently approach economic questions by employing the language favored by followers of this small but prominent ideological "faith."

Libertarianism resembles the perspective of a fundamentalist secular religion. Its champions demonstrate enthusiasm for broad philosophical interpretations that appear to explain just about everything. Not surprisingly, then, libertarians are given to writing sweeping commentaries that apply their principles to diverse aspects of life. They do not simply limit judgments to economic affairs. Viewing their outlook as a valuable guide for understanding the world's complexities, they promote their philosophy as a useful template for considering moral, social, legal, and diplomatic questions as well. Like many other radicals, libertarians champion consistency. Buoyed by a sense of certainty about the truthfulness of their principles, they express discomfort with liberals' efforts to live with contradictions. Libertarians are often as intolerant of relativism as are religious fundamentalists. Once libertarians secure a strong view of supposedly fundamental truths, they are fiercely resistant to negotiating with people who, they think, accept falsehoods. For many of them, liberals and liberalism symbolize commitment to those fundamentally erroneous ideas. Libertarians tend to view the liberals' relativistic, flexible, and evolving perspective on economic issues as deeply mistaken. They apply much of their vitriol to this devil who is willing to employ a despised institution, the state, in efforts to improve conditions in the nation. In their eyes many of the country's most serious economic and social problems can be traced to activities of those advocates of state intrusion, the liberals.

## Four Libertarian Masters

A radical libertarian perspective is abundantly evident in the arguments of four prominent enthusiasts of the faith—Murray N. Rothbard, Milton Friedman, William E. Simon, and Charles A. Murray. The views of these individuals were not identical, yet each in specific ways contributed to the growing popularity of libertarian ideas in right-oriented circles. Rothbard, often considered the father of modern American libertarianism, catalogued his personal understanding of the group's ideas in a hard-hitting and controversial book, *For a New Liberty: A Libertarian Manifesto* (1973). Milton Friedman, a prominent economist associated with the University of Chicago (the training ground for many leading lights of the libertarian and conservative intelligentsia), provided an eloquent voice for the cause and, through his own prestige, gave it greater legitimacy. William E. Simon, with years of experience as a leader in business and government as well as prominence in conservative philanthropic activities, gave libertarianism a practical advantage. Simon usually identified himself as a conservative rather than a libertarian. Nevertheless, his applications of libertarian economic perspectives and sponsorship of libertarian activities through a well-endowed foundation made him one of the nation's most influential spokespeople for libertarian ideals. Charles A. Murray achieved fame as a conservatively oriented researcher in the social sciences. Well after he had published a number of provocative works of scholarship, Murray identified himself more clearly with the libertarian principles that inspired his investigations.

Each of these individuals took a religionlike, fundamentalist-style position on important societal issues. They established a clear vision of the True Faith in economic affairs. Once they identified its tenets, they defended their interpretation tenaciously. Like religious fundamentalists, their understanding of the faith was broadly philosophical. They promoted all-encompassing remedies for the good life. Like the people described by Thomas Frank, their libertarian framework ensured that "everything fits together, everything has its place." And like religious fundamentalists, these libertarians showed little inclination for compromise. They knew the correct answers; why negotiate with proponents of apparently mistaken ideas? The four libertarians under study here adhered to their principles because they were confident that those ideas were fundamentally true.

There are, of course, other figures that could be named as important contributors to the modern libertarian tradition. One of the conservatives' favorites from an earlier period of twentieth-century American history is Friedrich A. von Hayek. Many commentators on the right point respectfully to the influence of Hayek's writings, especially *Road to Serfdom,* published in 1944. Yet they overlook some of the arguments the Austrian-born scholar applied in that notable book. Hayek was not as much a market "fundamentalist" when he wrote *Road to Serfdom* as today's conservatives think. He was certainly not as vigorously libertarian then as he became in later years. In *Road to Serfdom* Hayek maintained that government had an important role to play in preventing fraud and deception and preventing the "exploitation of ignorance." Government needed, as well, to protect the populace from "acts of God," such as floods and earthquakes. The state could help, too, when human affairs led to calamities. Large-scale public works programs, for instance, could provide temporary jobs for the unemployed during an economic depression.[6] Furthermore, Hayek published *Road to Serfdom* as a means to criticize the strong socialist leanings of academics in England, where he had been teaching. Many of the claims he made in 1944 against collectivist planning and in support of free enterprise can be endorsed today by America's liberals as well as by conservatives.

### Murray N. Rothbard

Murray N. Rothbard's wide-ranging commentary, *For a New Liberty: A Libertarian Manifesto* (1973), suggests important foundations of the group's radical philosophical position. His book identifies principles that are close to the hearts of America's hard-core market conservatives. Rothbard (1926–1995) presents his case in extreme form, treating distrust of government as an article of faith. Libertarians today have learned to borrow essential elements of Rothbard's philosophy while toning down some of his sharply controversial proposals. Absent the rough edges,

Rothbard's interpretation of libertarianism outlines a number of the principal arguments espoused in recent years by market-oriented rad-cons in the United States.

Murray Rothbard seemed forever engaged in a search for causes to which he could devote the full measure of his enthusiasm, and this intensity led him in and out of numerous alliances and disputes during his years of public activity. Rothbard studied economics under the fiercely promarket and antisocialist Austrian professor Ludwig von Mises. For a while Rothbard was close to Ayn Rand, the strong-minded champion of a libertarian-style "objectivist" school, but later he got into disagreements with Rand and criticized her severely. When Rothbard became angry over the Vietnam War and disappointed about American conservatives' support for it, he briefly backed an alliance with the New Left. Later Rothbard became active in the Libertarian Party. He could not remain comfortable there, either, and eventually Rothbard expressed sharp disagreements with leaders in the organization. In 1992 he supported Pat Buchanan's candidacy for president of the United States but later became disillusioned with Buchanan as well. Rothbard remained fiercely independent. He was also a supremely restless and contentious individual.[7]

Rothbard's difficulty in maintaining alliances with people and movements can be traced not only to a feisty personality but also to his insistence on purity of beliefs—as he defined those beliefs. He was not tolerant of compromises in matters of interpreting the libertarian cause. Murray Rothbard developed a rather dogmatic, philosophical idea of extreme capitalism, and he did not appreciate criticisms from those who refused to accept his vision fully. Frank Sinatra's notable song *My Way* applies to Rothbard's outlook on ideology, and, not surprisingly, that hard-headed position led Rothbard into many quarrels.

In *For a New Liberty* Murray Rothbard firmly rejects the legitimacy and the efficacy of government's major place in the affairs of Americans. Whether the issue is taxation or welfare or warfare, Rothbard sticks to his principles. He outlines such a strongly partisan case for diminishing government's role in U.S. society that some critics have labeled him an anarchocapitalist. Rothbard expresses faith in extreme individualism and finds mostly trouble resulting when the state intervenes in economic matters. At first glance, his prescriptions for changing the country look like the wild-eyed recommendations of an idealistic radical who has little chance of achieving his goals. Yet Rothbard is not as far off the edge of mainstream social commentary as he appears to be when applying his radical principles to diverse aspects of American life. In *For a New Liberty* the father of modern American libertarianism outlines the basis for much of current right-wing thinking about government and the economy. Today's hard-core market conservatives avoid the controversial stands Rothbard presented, but they can trace a good deal of their economic thinking to concepts that were central to his philosophy. Indeed, many of Rothbard's points now sound familiar to Americans, for these principles have been developed into major elements of the right's political agenda. And, as is the case with the provocative points made by many other libertarians as well, radcons conveniently push aside the controversial aspects of Murray N. Rothbard's arguments.

Murray Rothbard presented a historical perspective when making his case. In *For a New Liberty* he claimed that American colonials assumed libertarian-style positions when they resisted the strangling economic regulations of British mercantilism. During the nineteenth century, Americans extended the protection of individual liberty by establishing guarantees against their own government's encroachments. By the late nineteenth century, principles of laissez-faire were everywhere in practice across the United States, and the federal government played a very limited role in American society. Unfortunately, said Rothbard, enthusiasts of state intervention in the economy stymied and reversed this progress when they gained a political advantage in the twentieth century. Progressives and New Dealers responded to the problems of the Industrial Age with plans for a welfare state and governmental regulation of business.[8] These mistaken individuals then appropriated the very term with which libertarian-minded Americans used to identify each other. Libertarians were the true liberals (in the classical sense), he insisted, yet politicians of the left, particularly the Democrats, called *themselves* "liberals" (in later years other libertarians imitated Rothbard, identifying themselves as "classical liberals"). Rothbard also expressed anger because enthusiasts of state action then proceeded to describe the advocates of laissez-faire as ignorant Neanderthals. They were wrong, Rothbard argued. Libertarians were not reactionaries. Rather, they were forward-looking champions of a dynamic economy and society and the bold defenders of individual liberty against encroachments by the state.[9]

Like many libertarians, Murray N. Rothbard employed sharply negative language when assessing the federal government's activities. He enjoyed making severe statements that expressed his opinions poignantly. Rothbard seemed to care little about antagonizing readers. In fact, he appeared to enjoy operating like a verbal provocateur, sensing that tough language helped to attract attention. Murray Rothbard called the state "parasitic" and described its leaders as "a band of robbers" and a "group of plunderers."[10] He compared the Internal Revenue Service to a mugger. Rothbard did not mince words, either, when speaking about federal programs to aid the needy. What can the state do for the poor, he asked? "The only correct answer is also the libertarian answer," he responded: "Get out of the way."[11] Welfare checks perpetuated cycles of poverty, he charged, and minimum wage laws failed to help the poor. In fact, regulations to guarantee wage minimums often destroyed the neediest people's jobs, he argued, since businesses tended to release workers whose wages proved too costly.[12]

Rothbard also exhibited little respect for public schools, since the government owned and operated these institutions. Schools were "cesspools" of crime, petty theft, and drug addiction, he claimed. Parents could better serve their children by training youngsters at home or outside of the public school environment.[13] The state had no right to require "compulsory" public schooling through attendance laws, and it should not require youngsters to remain in school until a certain age. Public schooling involved coercion of children, forcing them to spend many years in a "vast system of incarceration." In fact, the public educational system resembled involuntary servitude.[14] These observations provided a rationale for the modern idea of a school voucher system.

Murray Rothbard applied his laissez-faire principles to moral issues as well. His position on controversial topics associated with sex was consistent with his general attitude toward the state's intrusion in the lives of individuals. Not only did government need to give individuals liberty in economic affairs, Rothbard maintained, it should also leave them free to make their private choices as well—especially if those activities did not harm innocent third parties. The law should not attempt "to enforce anyone's conception of morality," he insisted.[15] Regulations applied to sexual relations were, for the most part, inappropriate. Associations between consenting adults deserved protection. Activities that did not injure innocent people were all right, including engagement in pornography and prostitution. Sexual relations were a "private aspect of life," he argued; they should not fall under the strong arm of the law.[16] Furthermore, Americans deserved a right to gamble, use narcotics and marijuana, and consume alcohol. Abortion was a private matter, too, as was gun ownership.[17]

Various conservatives parted company with Rothbard on specific issues. They found his libertarian ideas about reducing government's role in markets enticing but backed away from the hands-off philosophy with respect to social and moral questions. Religiously oriented radcons considered some of his libertarian views on sexual relations offensive, and other conservatives who were more secular in outlook understood the danger of upsetting their ideological colleagues, especially evangelical Christians, through attention to Rothbard's controversial positions.

Another broad issue addressed by this libertarian that lots of conservatives studiously avoided due to its controversial nature (and because many did not fully agree with it) was Rothbard's demand for a reduced governmental role in foreign affairs, including wars. Attempting to remain consistent in his commitment to laissez-faire, Rothbard called for a hands-off governmental approach to international relations. His agenda called for free trade, free migration, and free cultural exchanges.[18] Rothbard said government should refrain from interfering in the affairs of other countries. Nations should live in peaceful coexistence, "and this means total avoidance of war."[19] He qualified this remark, though: Libertarians did not advocate a completely pacifistic approach. The United States could employ violence to protect the home front from attack by enemies, but the government had no business conscripting young men and taxing citizens to support various military activities abroad.[20] The United States acted like an interventionist and imperial power when it sent its armed forces into trouble spots far away from the homeland, Rothbard argued. U.S. intervention in the Vietnam War was a prime example of an "imperial war."[21]

Murray Rothbard's enthusiasm for a reduced military presence in foreign affairs, his opposition to the U.S. engagement in the Vietnam conflict, and his tolerant position on "moral" issues led him and some of his libertarian colleagues into heated disputes with mainstream conservatives. Leaders on the right found the libertarians' advocacy of laissez-faire in economic matters attractive and often appropriated these ideas for their own cause, but they argued over the other controversial stands. Eventually, radcons learned to coexist with libertarians and profit from their intellectual contributions. They highlighted the arguments Rothbard and other market fundamentalists made about reducing the government's role in the economy while neglecting other ideas of the group that proved divisive. By cherry-picking the arguments, they were able to advance libertarian ideals without antagonizing large and powerful groups among the American electorate. Laissez-faire served as their principal ideal; compromises that limited its application were mistaken.

### Milton Friedman

No spokesman for a libertarian perspective on markets has done a better job winning mainstream respectability for that philosophical, fundamentalist-style "faith" than Milton Friedman (1912–). Whereas Murray Rothbard acted like a feisty rebel who was eager to provoke fights over doctrine and principles, Milton Friedman came across as a smiling and amiable scholar who simply wished to bring the fascinating discoveries of his research to the attention of the American people. Friedman made the libertarian perspective familiar to millions of Americans who did not even know that they were acquiring a taste for his philosophy. He is the quintessential Stealth Libertarian, flying comfortably under the radar screen, unrecognized as the spokesman for a fundamentalist faith. The University of Chicago economist does not even like to call himself a libertarian or a conservative. Demonstrating fussiness about labels, Friedman has insisted on identifying himself as a "classical liberal."

Libertarians, though, generally and correctly recognize Friedman as one of their fellow travelers. Conservatives adore him, too, although they describe Friedman as one of their own rather than as a libertarian. The petite scholar is a guru to many Americans on the right because of his brilliant and innovative articulation of a sweeping libertarian perspective that provides connected answers to diverse problems. In the manner that Thomas Frank described the right's religionlike devotion to markets, Friedman's theoretical schemes ensured that everything fits together and everything has its place.

Milton Friedman emerged quickly in the second half of the twentieth century as the nation's most prolific and ubiquitous champion of laissez-faire. He published several influential books, made numerous public-speaking appearances, wrote a regular column for *Newsweek*, appeared in his own television series on PBS, and won the Nobel Prize for Economics. Friedman also became a valued economic counselor to Republican presidential candidates. He assisted Barry Goldwater in 1964 and Richard M. Nixon in 1968 (Friedman parted with Nixon in 1971 when the president called himself a Keynesian and advocated wage-price controls). President Ronald Reagan hailed Friedman as one of the great prophets of market-based economics and proceeded to place advocates of Friedman's economic philosophy in prominent administrative positions.[22]

Milton Friedman rose from humble origins to a stellar position as one of the leading intellectual lights of American conservatism. His family of Jewish immigrants from Hungary lived in the New York City area. Friedman received an undergraduate degree from Rutgers University, an MA from the University of Chicago, and a PhD at Columbia. From 1946 to 1976 he taught at the University of Chicago, helping to make its economics department a prominent center for conservative thinkers. Later he became a fellow at the Hoover Institution at Stanford University.

Today's liberals find some of Milton Friedman's arguments for laissez-faire deeply troubling, but they cannot dismiss the economist as only a simplistic ideologue of the right. Friedman is an imaginative and innovative thinker. He made an extraordinary impact in the second half of the twentieth century and became a leading architect of the economic theory known as monetarism, which challenged Keynesian economics. He maintained that price levels are dependent on the monetary supply. Although many of his interpretations have provoked intense debates among economists, they certainly raised important new questions for consideration in the profession. Friedman was more persuasive than anyone in his time in arguing that errors by government leaders, including mistakes by officials at the Federal Reserve System, contributed significantly to the coming of the Great Depression. Politicians and economists who served in Washington, D.C., drew upon his wisdom regarding the value of free markets for stimulating growth. Advocates of Friedman's theories, known as the "Chicago Boys," applied his concepts to a reordering of Chile's economy in South America in the 1970s and succeeded in making growth in that country one of the most impressive examples of rapid economic progress in the developing world. Milton Friedman, who was sympathetic to many of the libertarian arguments made by Murray Rothbard, also devised ways to make Rothbard's criticisms of public schooling part of mainstream political discussions. Friedman became America's most prominent early advocate of a voucher program, an arrangement that proposed to give parents opportunities to use public money to choose schools for their children—even private schools.

A comparison of Milton Friedman's arguments in *Free to Choose* (1980) with Murray Rothbard's contentions in *For a New Liberty* reveals that the University of Chicago economist is much more adept than Rothbard in making the libertarian outlook persuasive to a broad readership. Friedman illustrates his ideas across a broad historical canvas and provides many more specific examples to show how his ideas could be put into practice. Friedman also has a stronger grounding in his profession's scholarship, a skill that has enabled him to back up concepts with specific evidence. Rothbard's book reads like a collection of abstract musings, a utopian dreamer's wish list for radical change. Friedman's book, by contrast, supports extreme arguments for laissez-faire with detailed information from national and global history.

In *Free to Choose,* Friedman and his wife, Rose, point to the historical development of ideas about free markets, as Rothbard does, but they provide intriguing examples that make their case compelling. When the Friedmans write about the failure of plans to give government extensive power over economic decision making, they offer an impressive comparison between the modern histories of India and Hong Kong. The Friedmans report that the Indians borrowed ideas from the British socialists, and the results were very disappointing. India's economic development languished. In contrast, the British opened markets for trade in Hong Kong and generally adopted a laissez-faire approach to that colony's development. Hong Kong's commercial success became legendary (interestingly, when Indians began applying free-market principles in the 1990s, their economy, too, began to surge).

No scholar in the economics profession mounted a more impressive challenge to the ideas of economist John Maynard Keynes (1883–1946), whose influence was huge through the middle years of the twentieth century. Keynes advocated a strong role for government, especially during times of slowdowns in business activity. The private sector sometimes failed to find equilibrium quickly, Keynes noted, leading to high unemployment and considerable social misery. Government could fine-tune the economy through the twin levers of fiscal and monetary policy. Milton Friedman—articulate, energetic, and prolific—relentlessly hammered at Keynes's prestige. He attempted to bring economists back to nineteenth-century concepts of classical liberalism and succeeded to a considerable degree in chipping away at Keynes's position of authority. By the end of the twentieth century, the ideas of Friedman and members of the "Chicago School" were influential in the economics and business departments of U.S. universities.

A critic's discomfort with Milton Friedman's arguments does not depend on blanket rejection of all of his contributions to economic thought. Critics, including liberals, can join Friedman in hailing the benefits of capitalism, cheering the progress of free enterprise in the United States, and recognizing the value of competitive markets. They can applaud Friedman's achievements in raising important questions about Keynesian economics and commend his efforts to establish new groundwork for a post-Keynesian perspective.

The primary objection to Friedman's outlook relates, instead, to his penchant for unbending, inflexible, and noncompromising adherence to laissez-faire principles. In the manner of Dick Armey and legions of other radcon critics of government's role in economic affairs, Milton Friedman presents the case against government regulation of business like a zealot from a fundamentalist religious faith. His proscriptions against state action sound like specific points in the Ten Commandments. Moses' code asked followers not to commit murder or adultery; Friedman's code warns them especially against turning to state action. Friedman views government essentially as a negative force in American economic life. He finds almost nothing of value in its regulatory activities and wishes for a return to classic nineteenth-century liberalism. In fact, Milton Friedman exhibits a somewhat romantic and nostalgic view of those supposedly good old days in America. He tells readers that in the nineteenth century, citizens enjoyed much more freedom from control by the state, and, under the circumstances, a spirit of charitable support for the needy was much more evident than today. The Gilded Age, which many historians view as a complex age of contrasts between glitter and misery, industrial boom and labor strife, looks glowingly attractive in Friedman's references.

Milton Friedman's libertarian commitment to the ideal of laissez-faire is so strong that he usually dismisses possibilities for any positive impact from state action. Friedman treats virtually all government regulation as mischievous and pernicious. He allows the state responsibility for protecting property, punishing criminals, and defending the country, but, like a purist-minded devotee of the libertarian ideal, Friedman wants to leave most other activities to the private sector.

Friedman's observations on issues concerning the federal government's role in the economy are often framed in contrasts of black and white. He promotes a Manichaean perspective, describing private activities in strongly positive light and public activities in the economy in dark tones. Friedman typically creates a mountain of ugly evidence about state meddling and provides hardly a molehill of information suggesting the value of government activity. In Milton and Rose Friedman's influential book *Capitalism and Freedom* (1962), the authors briefly acknowledge that "absolute freedom" is not feasible in a world of imperfect men but then cite example after example of ways that government intervention in the economy brings unintended problems.[23] This treatment of evidence makes their rejection of "absolute freedom" practically meaningless. When reviewing federal regulation of consumer products in *Free to Choose,* for example, the Friedmans briefly acknowledge that some governmental efforts to protect the public from unsafe or useless products is desirable, yet they devote their specific commentary to illustrations that show the folly of such regulation.[24] Even when dealing with the substantial problem of monopoly (a threat to the Friedmans' ideal of free, competitive markets), Friedman and Friedman refuse to relax their philosophical rigidity. Private monopolies, they state with confidence, are less evil than government regulation of them.[25] The Friedmans will not give an inch on the matter, because their faith in laissez-faire remains unshaken.

Just about any government-led action to protect the public receives their contemptuous scolding. The Friedmans assail the Food and Drug Administration (FDA) for doing "more harm by retarding progress in the production and distribution of valuable drugs than it has done good by preventing the distribution of harmful and ineffective drugs."[26] FDA officials display an "inevitable bias," they claim, that leads them to apply "unduly stringent standards" in the consideration of new remedies. Milton and Rose Friedman mock regulatory activities of the Consumer Products Safety Commission (CPSC), too. They think federal efforts to determine noise levels for cap guns used by children are silly. "The spectacle of trained, highly paid 'experts' with ear muffs shooting cap guns" to determine decibel levels "is hardly calculated to instill confidence in the taxpayer that his money is being used sensibly," they attest.[27] Similarly, Milton and Rose Friedman claim that regulations designed to reduce pollution are often imposed with inadequate weighing of costs against benefits.[28] The Friedmans characterize public discussion of environmental issues as driven by "emotion" more than "reason." Environmentalists demand the impossible. They propose choices between pollution and no pollution, and that "is clearly nonsense."[29]

Similarly, the Friedmans apply a condescending sense of humor (and exhibit a preference for extreme arguments) in their reports about regulations administered by the Occupational Safety and Health Administration (OSHA). "How many Americans does it take to screw in a light bulb?" they ask. "Five; one to screw in the bulb, four to fill out the environmental impact and OSHA reports."[30] OSHA, they argue, provides "a source of jobs for bureaucrats, while reducing the opportunities and income of ordinary workers." The federal agency has created a "bureaucratic nightmare" for manufacturers that adds greatly to the cost of doing business, they report.

Milton and Rose Friedman maintain that Washington officials intervene in the economy with a commendable intention to help the public, but usually their actions produce more problems than progress. In this fashion the Friedmans manage to acknowledge that regulation can promise Americans a degree of protection, yet they still conclude that the consequences of that security cause greater harm than good. They make a case against the federal minimum wage law, for example, by arguing that it forced northern manufacturers to close factories and shift their activities to the southern states, where wages were low and unions were weak.[31] Unintended consequences developed, too, say the Friedmans, when the federal government tried to take supposedly dangerous products off the market. For instance, Washington banned specific brands of aerosol spray adhesives. Federal bureaucrats took this action because some preliminary research indicated that the adhesives might be a source of birth defects. Several pregnant women reacted to this news by securing abortions. Later, more thorough research indicated that the initial reports about dangerous adhesives had been mistaken. Washington then removed the ban.[32]

What remedies do the Friedmans offer to American consumers who worry about unsafe products or unhealthy conditions in the workplace? Go to court or go shopping, they counsel, but do not seek help from Washington, D.C. Consumers can sue the makers of defective products. They can attempt to win sizable awards that will serve as impressive warnings to the makers of unsafe or defective products. Markets can also provide solutions for consumers. "If we buy an item that turns out to be defective, we are more likely to return it to the retailer from whom we bought it than to the manufacturer," they suggest. "The retailer is in a better position to judge quality than we are."[33] Americans should depend on the free enterprise system to look after their needs, the Friedmans advise. Sears, Roebuck or Montgomery Ward can serve as "effective consumer testing and certifying agencies as well as distributors."[34] Furthermore, the manufacturers can be expected to take actions that will protect their "good will" in the eyes of the public. Companies such as General Electric and General Motors will look after the quality and safety of their products because they do not want to lose customers.[35] If consumers find they have been sold defective goods, their remedy is to seek better goods at other stores. The sellers of bad products will lose customers and soon get the message. In fact, they will go bankrupt if they do not sell products that are acceptable to their customers.[36] Thus, the market, not the government, provides the best solutions to the needs of consumers.

Such is the Friedmans' radical, libertarian case against action by the federal government. It is an extreme argument for laissez-faire that would greatly displease many Americans if they fully sensed its broad implications. The sick, the elderly, the pregnant, parents, and many others who buy products would be alarmed if they were told to make their own judgments about the safety of new drugs, sprays, chemicals, or toys. Most of these citizens do not have the financial wherewithal to sue the makers of defective products in the courts (and they do not have the patience to wait years or decades for legal settlements in the event that they win their cases). Nor can they find satisfaction in the Friedmans' recommendation to deal with deceptive and unsafe marketing practices by directing their shopping to other vendors. They appreciate assistance from Washington, D.C., rather than bemoan it. Most of the nation's blue-collar workers who labor in the lower ranks of the pay scale would find the Friedman's contempt for minimum wage laws deeply troubling. Also, employees working in dangerous activities such as mining, steel-making, and bridge-building are unlikely to support the kind of contempt for OSHA's safety rules that the Friedmans express.

After hearing many such arguments by Milton Friedman against federal regulation of business, an interviewer tried to test the extent of the economist's commitment to laissez-faire. Friedman's libertarian perspective seemed to leave virtually no room for a governmental role in protecting the public. Was he truly outlining such an extraordinary position? The interviewer asked, "Do you think there's a constructive purpose to any government regulation of commerce?" Milton Friedman responded directly: "No, I don't." He acknowledged that various governmental regulations aimed to protect consumers and workers but claimed in the fashion of libertarians that "in fact, [these regulations] endanger the public interest."[37]

In 2002 George W. Bush honored Milton Friedman in Washington D.C., on the occasion of the economist's ninetieth birthday. The president recognized Friedman for providing an influential philosophical voice in defense of the deregulatory policies. These were the very policies Bush promoted while in office. The president called Friedman a "hero of freedom" who had used "a brilliant mind to advance a moral vision: the vision of a society where men and women are free, free to choose, but where government is not as free to override their decisions."[38] A more honest reporting on the economists' contribution might have noted that he sometimes advanced the freedom of manufacturers to operate machinery and sell products that were unhealthy and unsafe for human consumption. A more truthful acknowledgement of Friedman's contribution to recent American life would have identified him as one of the nation's most influential promoters of libertarian ideas and as a leading oracle of the kind of market fundamentalism that Bush and many of his appointees adored.

Whereas the Friedmans bemoan the United States Food and Drug Administration's interference in the market, claiming that the FDA prevents the development and distribution of products needed by the public, Americans can easily recognize the many valuable public services provided by the FDA. That agency's interference in the market has required labels that inform vulnerable citizens about trans-fat and allergens in food products. Many individuals with heart or other health problems appreciate this information about fat content, and consumers who react badly to gluten, peanuts, or other allergens in food products are likewise thankful for the FDA's labeling requirements.[39] Americans receiving medical treatment appreciate the FDA's watchdog activities and its clearinghouse efforts that involve reporting on defective instruments. For instance, the FDA noted in 2005 that a urinary catheterization device required a recall because of uncertainties about its sterility, and another report dealt with the recall of syringe products used to inject fluids during angiographic procedures for fluoroscopic imaging. This equipment appeared to have the potential for air aspiration or fluid leakage from a faulty syringe tip.[40]

In one of the most notable problems with a medical product in the early twenty-first century, many Americans wished that the FDA had been *more* aggressive in looking after their interests. Research evidence indicated troubles with Cox–2 inhibitors, which were widely used to reduced pain from arthritis. Tests showed that one of the most popular inhibitors, Vioxx, could double the risk of a heart attack or a stroke after eighteen or more months of use. Merck & Company, the manufacturer of Vioxx, recalled the drug in 2004.[41]

The Friedmans want the federal government to maintain a largely noninterventionist stand in dealing with the environment, but many Americans prefer vigorous federal action in situations where their health is at risk. One of the most stunning examples of public frustration with weak regulatory action on the part of the Environmental Protection Agency (EPA) during the time of President George W. Bush's leadership related to the emission of dangerous pollutants by coal-fired power plants. The Bush-influenced EPA took such a relaxed stand in dealing with the issue that officials from twelve states announced that they would pursue court action to invalidate the agency's loose standards for mercury regulation. Recent reports of mercury contamination in fish consumed by the American public, including canned tuna, had excited considerable alarm. Mercury ingestion can cause reproductive, behavioral, neurological, and physiological problems. Late in the Clinton administration the EPA set up strict regulation of mercury under the terms of the Clean Air Act. Bush officials, instead, put deregulation into action. They advocated a much slower approach to reducing mercury levels. Interestingly, their approach drew fire from ten GOP House members, led by the chair of the Science Committee, who sent a letter to the EPA administrator expressing "deep disappointment" with the ruling.[42]

The Bush administration also put the Friedmans' economic philosophy into practice when dealing with power plants in the Midwest and Northeast, a policy that led to significant health concerns for people in those regions. EPA officials appointed by George W. Bush rewrote the rules in ways that restricted the EPA's ability to require pollution-control devices on newly built facilities. Scientists found an unusual opportunity to test the extent of the pollution problem in 2003, when a massive power blackout shut down power plants over much of the Midwest and the

Northeast. Significant changes in air quality appeared quickly. Researchers flew over central Pennsylvania and collected air samples. They found a 90 percent drop in levels of sulfur dioxide and a 50 percent reduction in ozone. Visibility increased by more than twenty-five miles. The report by the head of the researchers noted that "the improvement in air quality was so great that you could not only measure it, but could actually see it as a much clearer, less hazy sky." When the power plants were up and running again, American citizens were once again at risk. According to a study by Abt Associates, a technical consulting firm, the loss to public health from this air pollution might be catastrophic. Polluted air can result in thousands of premature deaths every year. Chronic lung disease and cardiovascular diseases that could have been prevented under the old rules would likely trouble people living downwind from the power plants. This report indicated that Americans living near Cincinnati, Ohio; Pittsburgh, Pennsylvania; and Charleston, West Virginia—cities close to the power plants—were particularly vulnerable.[43]

With mockery and disdain, the Friedmans reported that members of the Consumer Products Safety Commission test-fired cap guns for children. In the Friedmans' libertarian interpretation of this activity, the CPSC was meddling in ways that were likely to produce more harm than good for the public and create unnecessary bureaucratic hurdles for American businesspeople. Yet if that commission did not monitor the safety of products used by children, who would? Linda Ginzel, a professor at the University of Chicago's Graduate School of Business, called for vigorous monitoring of unsafe products in day-care facilities after her son was strangled in a crib at a licensed facility. The crib had been recalled in 1993, she discovered, but information had not come to the attention of day-care administrators in many locations. Two other youngsters had also died in that model of crib following the recall.[44] More aggressive intervention by the CPSC might have saved the lives of those children. Frequently the CPSC does perform a valuable service by monitoring the safety of children's toys that are distributed with meals at fast-food restaurants. The agency recalled 3.8 million model planets distributed by Chick-Fil-A because of a choking hazard from suction cups. Other recalls involved 234,000 Scooter Bugs available at McDonald's because broken antennas could cause choking, 400,000 Riverboat toys featured at Burger King (due to a choking hazard), 25 million Pokemon balls at the same restaurant because of the suffocation of two children, and 425,000 Tangled Treeples available at KFC after packaging got stuck over a child's face.[45]

Of course, the CPSC looks after the health and safety of adults, too. Recently it required warning labels for cookware using a nonstick coating, including a warning related to the popular Teflon brand. Studies revealed that the compound used to make the coating can break down into toxic particles and gases when heated at normal cooking temperatures.[46] Another initiative of the CPSC informed the public that some power lawnmowers (among the most familiar household tools) could pose significant dangers to operators or bystanders. The commission had been pushing for stronger safety standards for walk-behind and riding mowers since the 1980s, and it estimated that by the year 2000 approximately 80,000 injuries nationwide had occurred in connection with the mowers. Many of these injuries were preventable, especially to operators younger than fourteen years of age.[47]

Americans, especially parents, could appreciate these efforts by the Consumer Products Safety Commission to monitor the safety of equipment. To the Friedmans, though, such activities could be considered disturbing examples of bureaucratic meddling. In the libertarian perspective on market affairs, governmental regulatory activity was fundamentally suspect.

Milton Friedman is an innovative thinker who has contributed significantly to modern economic thought. Yet he is also a market fundamentalist who addresses questions about government action in the economic sphere with the conviction of a religious enthusiast. Friedman acts like he has discovered the true faith, a belief system that presents correct answers to virtually all of life's economic challenges. In his scheme government almost always has a negative impact on people, and private activity is almost always beneficial. There is little room for compromise in his dualistic worldview. Like many other market zealots who adore libertarian-style outlooks, Friedman comfortably disregards evidence that does not jive with his philosophical scheme. He approaches complex economic problems with the firm confidence of a person of faith, an elated individual who thinks he has discovered the key to basic universal truths.

## William E. Simon

Whereas Rothbard and Friedman provided important intellectual foundations for libertarian thought, William E. Simon (1927–2000) helped to put libertarian ideas into practice in the highest offices in Washington, D.C. He espoused those ideals while serving in important administrative posts and after leaving Washington. Simon promoted the careers of many young advocates of laissez-faire by funding their activities during the time that he was president of the conservatively oriented John M. Olin Foundation. With the exception of Ronald Reagan, Simon was possibly the most influential market conservative to maneuver libertarians into the halls of government leadership. Through stealth—speaking frequently about "markets" and "competition" while tending to avoid direct public association with the libertarian-style philosophy that guided his outlook—Simon opened the way for a mass migration of the antigovernment zealots into the nation's top policy-making positions. In later years many conservatives followed the paths he helped to clear. By the time of George W. Bush's administration in the early twenty-first century, a virtual takeover had been achieved. Libertarians who did not openly acknowledge their philosophical faith were sitting in the nation's most important administrative positions in government agencies and in the Congress. From those powerful vantage points, they steered the country on a course toward the implementation of radical laissez-faire policies.

William E. Simon was the epitome of an Establishment insider. He was a wealthy businessman, a top administrator in Washington, and president of a conservative foundation. With an athletic figure and in possession of a booming voice that suggested he enjoyed operating from a commanding position, Simon cast a large shadow during his years of work in government and business. He was a senior partner at Solomon Brothers investment firm when he received an appointment from Richard M. Nixon to serve as the nation's energy czar. Later he worked as secretary of the treasury under presidents Nixon and Ford and as chairman of the Economic Policy Board under Ford. After leaving the federal government, Simon became president of the conservatively oriented Olin Foundation. He continued to enhance his economic status by working on mergers and acquisitions and by creating new financial services organizations. Simon served on the boards of the Heritage Foundation and the Hoover Institution, and he was president of the U.S. Olympic Committee.

William E. Simon's indebtedness to Milton Friedman (the libertarian who called himself a "classical liberal") was particularly evident in Simon's 1978 book, *A Time for Truth*. Friedman wrote the foreword. Like many faith-driven enthusiasts of laissez-faire, Milton Friedman employed strident language when criticizing people who advocated an important role for government in American society. In contrast, he praised William E. Simon for offering a profound analysis of this "suicidal course."[48] Friedman argued that Simon's book came at a precious moment, because the time had arrived to rescue American society. An important change in direction could be achieved by supporting a philosophy of "individualism" (Friedman would not acknowledge the idea as libertarianism).

William E. Simon then gave Friedman's general call to ideological arms support with specific recommendations. In *A Time for Truth,* ghost-written by Edith Efron, and in his 1980 book, *A Time for Action,* Simon portrayed private enterprise as the source of virtually all of the American economy's attractive developments, and he lambasted the federal government, considering it responsible for virtually all of the economic problems.[49] Simon had often stressed this theme when speaking as the U.S. energy czar and testifying before congressional committees. Repeatedly he stated that the government in general and the Congress in particular were responsible for the major economic difficulty of the time, the energy crisis. Simon berated Democrats for displaying an inability to comprehend the mischief they had wrought through state intervention in economic and petroleum matters.[50] Oil exploration had been "strangled" by environmentalists, Simon argued. He offered a simple solution for energy problems: leave businesspeople free of the state's intervention and regulation, and huge improvements would result.[51] Through a greater commitment to laissez-faire, the United States could obtain "energy independence."[52]

Simon's diagnosis of the energy crisis was, of course, grossly simplistic. While competition could and did help to alleviate the crisis in later years, it is clear that the actions of the Organization of the Petroleum Exporting Countries (OPEC) were the primary cause of energy problems faced by Americans in the 1970s. The major oil-producing nations, not the U.S. government, had created the international economic crisis by limiting production and substantially raising the price of petroleum. Furthermore, as the U.S. and other economies grew in later years, the world's appetite for petroleum expanded enormously. Demand expanded faster than supply, and the price per barrel of oil shot upward. Simon failed to recognize these larger causes of the energy crisis because, like a deeply committed libertarian, he was obsessed with criticizing actions of the government.

Like Milton Friedman, Simon showed a strong distaste for federal regulations designed to protect the public. He complained loudly about the FDA's watchdog activities, assuming that the organization's interference in the market hurt citizens far more than it helped them. Simon mocked the activities of officials at the Food and Drug Administration in the manner of libertarians, claiming that "it is doubtful that if penicillin were introduced today—or aspirin—either would survive the obstacle course erected by the FDA."[53] Too often, he said, representatives of the news media tell the public about a life saved through the FDA's intervention, but Americans do not hear about the deaths of tens of thousands of people who may have expired because the FDA did not permit the manufacture of beneficial medicines.[54] In these remarks Simon appeared oblivious to the dangers of profit-hungry pharmaceutical companies promoting drugs that failed to deliver promised cures or created dangerous side-effects. His easy dismissal of the FDA's value would find little appreciation from citizens and health-care professions who have received useful information from the FDA about flu protection, counterfeit drugs, toxicology, radiation safety, and dangerous medical devices. The FDA's warnings and labeling requirements helped to alert citizens to the dangers of particular pharmaceutical products. OxyContin was one of them, a drug for pain relief that had strong narcotic characteristics (as was noted in Chapter 1, Rush Limbaugh had become dependent on it when he used the medicine to relieve pain).[55]

Like other libertarians, William E. Simon berated the bureaucrats at government agencies. He claimed they acted like "Big Brother," wastefully intervening in the lives of the American people.[56] The Environmental Protection Agency was staffed with antibusiness partisans, environmentalist extremists, and youthful "Naderites" (allies of Ralph Nader), he charged. Through regulations, federal lawmakers and bureaucrats sucked the lifeblood out of states and local communities.[57] OSHA officials earned his wrath, too. Simon said they worked with an original statute of just thirty pages, but over the years the list of OSHA rules grew to over 800 pages of regulations.[58] He expressed contempt, as well, for regulatory officials who worked with the Federal Trade Commission and the Consumer Products Safety Commission.[59] In case after case, Simon expressed a libertarian's contempt for regulatory activities designed to protect the public. A consideration of specific regulations did not appear to call for open-minded and objective investigation of possible benefits to the public. Instead, it provided an opportunity to deliver a sermon on the libertarian faith.

An unbending commitment to laissez-faire principles is evident throughout Simon's two book-length commentaries on America's economic challenges. When confronting issue after issue, Simon offers abundant praise for economic actions taken by businesses while, in contrast, communicating broad-based hostility and contempt for measures undertaken by the federal government. Simon displays almost no sympathy for the state's efforts to ensure that the rule of law applies to business activities or to protect the public from business corruption and unsafe or unhealthy products. Journalist Sidney Blumenthal described Simon succinctly and perceptively when he identified him as a leading spokesman for "fundamentalist free-market views."[60]

### Charles A. Murray

Charles A. Murray (1943–), one of the most notable libertarians of the late twentieth century, achieved prominence as a social scientist who addressed controversial public issues in a scholarly manner. In provocative publications bulging with statistical evidence Murray challenged conventional wisdom concerning poverty, welfare, and related subjects. His interpretations received considerable attention in the national media. Some who reviewed his books were initially dazzled by Murray's skill in mustering diverse economic and social information to support his interpretations. They assumed that Murray had carried out this seemingly impressive research in the manner of a sophisticated social scientist, drawing conclusions through an open-minded analysis of complex data. Eventually, details about Charles A. Murray's handling of evidence came to light that cast doubt on his interpretations. Critics reported that his scholarship had been richly funded by agenda-driven right-wingers. Murray's highly selective use of statistics came under question by investigators who found his research techniques were disturbingly biased. Critics also noted that many of the sources Murray employed in his publications were strongly suspect. After these revelations, Murray's work looked more like lamentable exercises in political propaganda than ground-breaking discoveries in social science.

While much of this scholarly debate about Murray's work concentrated on concerns about the agenda of his sponsors, his use of statistics, and his choice of sources, critics generally missed opportunities to view

Murray's approach to controversial issues as a reflection of his strong philosophical commitment. The absence of attention to Murray's ideological underpinnings is not surprising, since he did not broadly identify the outlook that influenced his interpretations until long after he had made noisy entrances into policy debates. Charles Murray had been a libertarian, but that interest was not well publicized until a 1997 book appeared in which he proudly associated with the perspective. In *What It Means to Be a Libertarian: A Personal Interpretation* Murray tried to put his philosophical imagination and sophistication on display, yet this work also revealed the thinking of a firmly committed ideologue. Murray exhibited a fundamentalist-style libertarian faith. He approached complex social and economic problems with the simplistic self-assurance of a True Believer.[61]

Sugar Daddies who were eager to support conservative causes gave Charles Murray a huge career boost over several years. These promoters of a "counterintelligentsia" (who aimed, specifically, to counter the influence of liberalism among the intellectual elite) chose Murray as a promising candidate to promote libertarian antigovernment scholarship. They funded his professional development lavishly, supporting him with one million dollars for research and writing. Murray, a graduate of Harvard with a PhD from the Massachusetts Institute of Technology in political science, looked like an ideal figure to give the right intellectual gravitas. He not only held degrees from prestigious institutions but also had experience outside of academia that was likely to impress liberal scholars: he had spent five years working with the Peace Corps in rural Thailand. Most important, in early publications Murray had demonstrated a strong interest in challenging the effectiveness of the federal government's welfare programs.

Benefactors offered valuable assistance to this potentially influential right-oriented researcher. William Hammett, president of the conservative Manhattan Institute, provided financial support that gave Murray two years of free time to work on *Losing Ground,* his 1984 book that sharply criticized the welfare system. Hammett also contributed $15,000 that facilitated the sending of 700 copies of *Losing Ground* to leading figures in universities, think tanks, politics, and the media. Additionally, Hammett hired a publicist who helped to turn Murray into a celebrity intellectual. As Charles Lane and Michael Lind have pointed out, the Manhattan Institute also provided generous honoraria to well-known journalists and politicians who participated in seminars that focused on Murray's ideas. Eventually, the Manhattan Institute broke off its support of Murray when its leaders discovered that the author was working on a book with Richard Herrnstein that would make a strong case for genetic differences between races, but other organizations filled the void and provided continued sponsorship beginning in 1990. The Lynde and Harry Bradley Foundation offered hundreds of thousands of dollars in support of Murray's writing projects, and another right-oriented institution, the John M. Olin Foundation, delivered additional funding. Later Murray worked at the conservative American Enterprise Institute (AEI) as a Bradley Fellow. The benefactor in that case was the family of William H. Bradley, a generous supporter of the *National Review* and the Heritage Foundation. Grants from the Bradley organization had assisted the work of various figures on the right, including Lynne Cheney, a prominent commentator on academic issues in Republican circles and wife of Dick Cheney, who later served as George W. Bush's vice president.

*Losing Ground* challenged what Murray called the "elite wisdom" of his time. Charles Murray questioned the view that welfare programs, especially those created or expanded through Lyndon B. Johnson's Great Society initiatives, helped the poor. Garnering a vast array of statistics, Murray claimed that scholars who believed welfare programs had been successful in assisting the needy were dead wrong. Rather than help the poor, federal programs often hurt them by removing incentives for industrious behavior. The state's initiatives often produced unintended consequences. Welfare payments established incentives for impoverished, often unemployed unmarried women to produce babies, Murray concluded. Reformers had hoped to reduce poverty through federal intervention in the lives of the needy, but instead their efforts created many new problems. Murray claimed that economic dependency, unemployment, poor education, crime, and breakdowns in the nuclear family could be traced in large part to expanded entitlements for the poor.

Charles Murray strongly emphasized the empirical basis of his case. Throughout the book he draws attention to a supposedly rich treasure of data that supports his interpretation. *Losing Ground* starts with "A Note on Presentation," which informs readers that the analysis grew out of a "varied technical body of social science data," and Murray points to additional sources of evidence. *Losing Ground,* he proclaims, offers numerous graphs and lengthy footnotes that read like small essays as well as an elaborate appendix featuring numerical tables. Much of this information came from standard, valuable sources, he announces—from the U.S. Census Bureau and information in the Library of Congress.[62] The text, too, provides readers an "accurate understanding of argument and evidence," he reports. When Murray reaches the end of his study and summarizes the meaning of this plethora of evidence, he concludes that the lives of the poor could be radically changed for the better through the elimination of federal programs. This thesis, he announces, is supported by "powerful, collaborative" evidence featured in the book.[63]

While Murray collected some positive reviews by writers who were impressed with his use of quantitative data, other scholars who were skilled at number crunching challenged him regarding his supposed strength—the use of statistics. They found that Murray tended to privilege details that supported his thesis and overlook evidence that undermined it. One of the most impressive challenges came from Christopher Jencks, author, with others, of a book on a related topic, *Inequality: A Reassessment of the Effect of Family and Schooling in America*.[64] In a lengthy analysis published in the *New York Review of Books,* Jencks criticized Murray for using data selectively. Christopher Jencks showed that the official federal poverty statistics did not take account of changes in "need," since federal programs providing food stamps, Medicaid, subsidized housing, and other benefits had, in fact, made the life of the poor in America much more comfortable than Murray suggests. Government statistics from the mid-1970s revealed that the number of Americans in poverty had dropped dramatically by that time (shortly after implementation of Johnson's "War on Poverty"). Furthermore, Jencks noted that Murray failed to take adequate account of changes in general economic conditions. Charles Murray drew attention to gains for the poor in the 1950 to 1965 period—the years before dramatic expansion of welfare benefits—and then wrote critically about hardships for the poor from 1965 to 1980, years when the welfare expansion went into effect. The first period was a time of unprecedented economic growth, noted Jencks. In the years between 1965 and 1980, however, the overall economy became deeply troubled by recession, unemployment, and inflation. In these and other examples, Jencks showed that Murray built his case on a very shaky and debatable statistical foundation.[65]

Similar criticisms hounded another book that Murray co-wrote, this time with Harvard psychologist Richard Herrnstein, *The Bell Curve: Intelligence and Class Structure in American Life* (1994). In it, Murray and Herrnstein maintain that intelligence quotient (IQ) is more predictive than any other factor in affecting people's success in life or their condition of poverty and general failure. Some sections of the book draw attention to the disproportionate representation of African Americans in poverty and suggest that blacks' economic problems are due essentially to low mental ability. Nicholas Lemann summarized the discoveries of several scholars who examined the authors' use of statistical evidence in the three years subsequent to the book's publication. Those investigations revealed that the book is "full of mistakes ranging from sloppy reasoning to mis-citations of sources to outright mathematical errors. Unsurprisingly, all of the mistakes are in the direction of supporting the authors' thesis."[66]

Problems with sources drew considerable attention, too, especially after Christopher Lane published an article in the *New York Review of Books* carrying a poignant title, "The Tainted Sources of 'The Bell Curve.'" Lane noted that Murray and Herrnstein had not completed new research on intelligence but were, essentially, interpreting the conclusions of various other investigators (as well as information released by the U.S. Census Bureau). Thus, the validity of the Murray/Herrnstein conclusion depended in large part on the quality of their sources. Lane found many of those citations highly questionable. *The Bell Curve* cites a number of research papers published in *Mankind Quarterly,* Lane noted. Ten of those citations relate to the work of people who were present or former editors of the journal. *Mankind Quarterly* had been founded by men who believed in the genetic superiority of the white race. Robert Gayle, the publication's editor in chief until the late 1970s, had been a champion of apartheid in South Africa and belonged to an ultra right-wing group associated with the idea of white rule in Rhodesia. Another founder of the journal had been a pamphleteer for the White Citizens' Council in the American South. The journal also published research undertaken by Ottmar von Verschuer, an individual interested in "race science" in Hitler's Germany and a mentor to Josef Mengele. Additionally, Lane found that Herrnstein and Murray cited thirteen researchers who benefited from grants provided by the Pioneer Fund. That organization, according to its charter, was devoted to "race betterment," with special reference to the people of the United States. A 1989 statement from the Pioneer Fund proposed the abandonment of integration in the United States on the grounds that "raising the intelligence of the blacks or others still remains beyond our capabilities." Lane provided other examples, too, that questioned sources employed in the Herrnstein/Murray interpretation.[67]

Critics who have been troubled by Charles Murray's influence in debates over welfare, race, and other issues have concentrated their arguments on the ways in which he used statistical data or relied on scholarship written by questionable figures, but they have given relatively little attention to the impact of Murray's philosophical leanings on his interpretations. Charles Murray was an enthusiast of the libertarian faith, although he did not identify this interest clearly in public forums until well after he published his provocative books on social issues. In the fashion of many libertarians, Murray showed an inclination to privilege evidence that supported his preconceptions and screen out information that contradicted it. His treatment of evidence in *The Bell Curve* demonstrated a libertarian bias, for the book's conclusions about the power of genetically based mental differences suggested that government-generated affirmative action programs were unlikely to succeed. Murray's revealing statements in *What It Means to Be a Libertarian: A Personal Interpretation* (1997) identify the foundations of this outlook.

Charles A. Murray did not present *Losing Ground* as a treatise inspired by libertarianism (the term does not even appear in the book's index, nor does the index include references to Hayek or Rothbard), but Murray offers libertarian messages indirectly in his concluding remarks. There he suggests that the nation needs to scrap the entire welfare and income support structure, including Aid to Families with Dependent Children, Medicaid, food stamps, workers' compensation, subsidized housing, and disability insurance. Murray also argues the case against public schools by advocating school vouchers.[68] Much later, in *What It Means to Be a Libertarian: A Personal Interpretation* (1997), Murray associates his sympathies openly with libertarian ideals. He presents a wish list for change that resembles the goals of other advocates of a sharp turn toward laissez-faire, such as Murray Rothbard and Milton Friedman.

As in *Losing Ground*, Murray presents these ideas as a "thought experiment," hinting that he understands that it would be difficult to realize the libertarian goals he outlines in view of the political environment of the United States in the late 1990s. Still, he leaves no doubt that he is serious in presenting a lengthy exposition on the need for broad changes. Murray argues emphatically that intervention by the state has been leading the nation down a path of trouble for years. It was time to reverse course—radically. His remarks in *What It Means to Be a Libertarian* give a fuller picture of the negative perspective on action by the federal government that characterizes his commentary throughout and, especially, at the end of *Losing Ground*. As his 1997 publication reveals, Murray had not just discovered a specific problem with governmental planning for welfare; he shared the libertarian distrust of almost all forms of federal involvement in the economic and social life of Americans.

Like other libertarian True Believers, Charles Murray shows particular contempt for government regulations. He argues, for example, that there should be no laws regulating employment, including hours or wages, and no regulations regarding conditions of the workplace. Murray suggests that Americans "throw out all regulation of business" except in the extraordinary cases of natural monopolies and serious pollution. Congress could provide for the enforcement of laws against fraud and deceptive practices, but it should not otherwise get in the way of Americans seeking to provide services or manufacture or sell products.[69] Far too often, writes Murray, government regulations interfere with efforts by individuals to go about their business of making a living, and these rules prevent society from developing new products. Regulatory interference is so offensive that one could "rightly call it oppression."[70] Americans should ensure that bureaucrats "will not have the right to run other people's lives for them."[71]

Murray believes many of the federal government's regulatory programs are unnecessary, because progress has already been made in the United States toward solving problems. Often "the government displaces the civil response that would have continued to evolve and expand if the government had done nothing," he writes.[72] Furthermore, OSHA "has inflicted great harm on the freedom of people to pursue their vocations," and many jobs have disappeared because of the organization's annoying interference with business affairs. Murray also maintains that on-the-job deaths had been declining before the formation of OSHA, so it is difficult to claim that OSHA has made much difference in saving lives.[73] His lecture on this subject, no doubt, would be of great interest to the families that lost fifteen loved ones in a fire at a Texas City oil refinery. The company that ran the facility agreed to pay OSHA a fine of $21.3 million after the discovery of 300 separate alleged violations of OSHA safety regulations at the work site.[74]

Like many libertarians, Murray offers an alternative to Americans who seek protection through their government. He urges them to find solutions in the courts instead of the legislature. Good tort law—suits for injury, for instance—can provide opportunities to deal with problems in the workplace currently handled by OSHA.[75] If employers provide faulty equipment that harms workers, the employer is liable.[76] If manufacturers produce unsafe products or service professionals provide faulty assistance to their customers, they should be subject to suits in the courts for the harm they cause.[77] In this instance, too, Murray's lecture on individual initiative rather than support for citizens through governmental action would be of dubious value to the family of a man whose feet and one arm had to be amputated after a mishap at a Sunrise, Florida, job site. According to an OSHA report, an exposed screw head on a boom brought the lineman into contact with energized lines, causing an electrical current to run through him. OSHA fined the company $35,000 for allowing employees to work too close to power lines, especially since the company had previously been cited for a similar violation of OSHA standards. Charles Murray's libertarian perspective (as well as that of Milton Friedman) suggests that the aggrieved family members should have turned to lengthy action in court against the company and that OSHA should never have engaged in its intrusive rule making. Yet in this case, careful attention to OSHA's standards might have prevented the tragedy in the first place.[78]

On virtually every other matter of liberal reform, Murray claims that progress had already been well under way before the government attempted regulation. The state deserves little or no credit for protecting the public over modern American history, and, again, the state's intervention often produces unintended negative consequences, he asserts. Murray claims that health care had been improving substantially in the decades before the creation of Medicare and Medicaid in the 1960s (his lecture on this matter to a group of elderly and poor recipients of assistance from Medicare and Medicaid would likely draw an angry response from individuals who greatly appreciated the help). Murray surmises in Losing Ground that the record of economic and social gains made in the United States before the introduction of new federal programs suggests that greater progress can be realized if the national government does nothing at all. From this perspective, Murray argues that many programs could be disbanded.[79] The solution for health care (and educational needs, as well) is to "let people shop for what they want and pay for what they get."[80]

Similarly, Murray argues that minorities had been making gains toward civil rights before passage of the civil rights laws of the 1960s.[81] In dealing with future needs of minorities, he suggests a constitutional amendment: government should not be able to pass any law that requires discrimination on the basis of ethnicity, race, religion, or creed, nor should government pass any law limiting the freedom of association for private individuals and associations.[82] Murray's amendment, sounding fair in principle, would be distinctly unfair in practice. It could give legitimacy to practices of exclusion that had been very much in evidence across American society before passage of the civil rights laws.

Murray's ideal society would wipe out most of the federal government's major social and economic functions. His "thought experiment" calls for abolition of the U.S. Post Office and the Federal Communications Commission (which regulates the stock market). It would terminate welfare programs, of course, including food stamps, public housing, social services, and supplemental security income.[83] The environmentalist movement is "dominated by people who tend to be hostile to free markets, technology, and economic growth," he claims.[84] Environmental problems should be handled in the justice system rather than through regulations. If fumes were covering an individual's property, the courts could deal with complaints "promptly and inexpensively."[85] (In practice these legal challenges often take years or decades and cost a great deal in legal fees, but such evidence is not troublesome to Murray, who blithely suggests solutions.) Here, again, is a remedy based on faith rather than a realistic sense of the problematic implications of putting libertarian ideas into practice.

On issues that conservative Republicans often associate with morality, Murray takes the familiar libertarian stand, claiming that vices thrive when the public attempts to ban or regulate them.[86] Prostitution deserves protection as long as it does not involve solicitation on street corners. Government should not intervene when a man and a woman wish to set a price for sex. Some restrictions on pornography could apply to media accessed by minors, and laws could be enforced to prevent force or fraud. "That is as far as government can legitimately go," Murray concludes.[87]

Federal and state laws regarding alcohol, drugs, and gambling should be repealed except for matters involving minors.[88] Even crack cocaine is OK if the people consuming it do not abuse their spouse or children, show up sober for work, and pay their taxes.

Much of Murray's interpretation of data in *Losing Ground* and *The Bell Curve* involves exercises in propaganda rather than impressive research in the field of social science. Fortified with charts and tables, Murray presents his investigations as models of scholarship, yet his publications show a closer resemblance to ideological campaigning presented under the guise of scientific inquiry. The Manhattan Institute and AEI "scholar" and "research scientist" has not approached his subjects in a manner that suggests readiness to accept evidence that proves favorable to governmental programs designed to aid the poor—in the event that some or much of the data point in that direction. Nor has his technique evinced much openness to the possibility that environmental factors are often as important as, and sometimes more important than, IQ in explaining individuals' economic successes.

It is entirely understandable that Murray concludes his work with research results that bring considerable satisfaction to leaders in the ideologically oriented institutions that so generously sponsor his labors and publications. Murray's financial benefactors, who think governmental programs to help the poor are almost always counterproductive, find confirmation of their beliefs in his work. So do sponsors who disapprove of governmental actions on behalf of minorities. Many of them despise affirmative action programs and claim they are worthless. Murray and Herrnstein confirmed their ideas by arguing that state intervention is likely to prove disappointing because recipients lack the intelligence to benefit substantially from it. Charles Murray had performed marvelously for the institutions and individuals who had thrown cash at him throughout the decades. He delivered well-publicized books that looked like social science research. His libertarian-inspired interpretations suggest that government intervention in human affairs is often worthless and frequently downright detrimental to progress.

## Libertarian Policy Making in the
## Years of George W. Bush's Presidency

Economic advisers who were inspired by libertarian perspectives turned up at the White House in significant numbers during the time of Ronald Reagan's leadership in Washington, D.C., but those market fundamentalists made a much more impressive appearance in Washington when George W. Bush entered the Oval Office. Bush gave libertarian-style thinkers unprecedented power and influence thanks to appointments made by members of Bush's executive team. President George W. Bush did not publicly and eagerly associate himself with the libertarian philosophy (he is too savvy a politician to do that), but the approach he and his aides took in dealing with economic issues betrayed a libertarian bias. Since Bush and others in his administration usually operated by stealth when promoting their outlook in practice (except on occasions when they praised the work of fellows at the Cato Institute), their application of libertarian principles generally went unnoticed by the national media. Newspaper and magazine journalists and the television and radio-based pundits focused attention on the details of these policies rather than on the broad ideals that inspired them. A brief examination of two policy applications suggests that libertarian convictions—commitments to market fundamentalism—had much to do with the way Republican leaders adopted economic stands. Stealth Libertarianism can be seen in the way Bush administration officials promoted Social Security "reform" and blithely accepted budget deficits (despite the traditional conservative abhorrence for red ink in governmental affairs).

### The Libertarian Assault on Social Security

President Bush provided a good example of this kind of cherry-picking from the libertarian orchard by promoting radical reorganization of the nation's Social Security program. When Bush fought for these changes in 2005, millions of Americans who viewed Social Security as one of the most successful programs ever created by the U.S. government found the president's talk about the system's supposed failures puzzling. They recognized that the system of Social Security was extraordinarily popular and understood that some adjustments to its financing could sustain it long past the middle of the twenty-first century, the time when shortfalls would likely develop because of an aging population. Yet President Bush continued to make frightening predictions about the system's coming "bankruptcy" and "collapse." Furthermore, his proposal to shift funds to private accounts would add about $2.5 trillion to the already huge national debt, since cash would have to come from somewhere to pay current benefits after the change to private accounts.

Why would the president put the nation's finances and the well-being of future retirees at great risk, many asked? Was there more to his opposition to Social Security than met the eye?

There was. A key to the Bush administration's hostility to Social Security could be found in ideology. The president and many of his top advisers viewed the issue in the manner of libertarians. They projected a fundamentalist-style approach to the related issues. Faith in the libertarian ideal of a severely limited role for the federal government inspired their actions. When championing their goals in public, however, they preferred not to frighten the American people. Avoiding the L-word was essential. Stealth Libertarianism worked best.

George W. Bush did not suddenly discover a need to change the Social Security program radically because of the appearance of disturbing new statistical evidence about the system's future difficulties. He expressed libertarian-style contempt for the system decades earlier, when he first ran for public office in Texas. Bush's readiness to scrap Social Security sprang especially from his philosophical outlook, not from his discovery of new data. The president viewed economic issues in the manner of a libertarian and took advice on economic policy from many people who promoted libertarian viewpoints, but he remained careful not to identify himself openly with their ideology.

Quite a few libertarian-minded Americans, including President Bush, select some libertarian themes and turn away from others. Bush gave particular attention to libertarian ideas about the economy and often expressed enthusiasm for free markets and small government. He did not, however, publicly promote libertarian social themes, including the idea that citizens have the right to live in any way they choose as long as they respect the rights of others. And, of course, the president showed little public interest in the traditional libertarian advocacy of peace over war.

When President Bush and other hard-line, market-oriented conservatives presented their case for limited government, they usually called for specific measures to deal with specific problems, concealing their larger ideological interests. They offered proposals in ways that made the recommended changes seem like needed solutions to save the nation from a crisis. These market fundamentalists did not attribute their actions to a commitment to libertarian philosophical perspectives. Cleverly, they avoided mention of their quasi-religious enthusiasm for this outlook. Furthermore, it is likely that Bush, a born-again Christian who expressed strong evangelical interests, did not find the libertarian position on social issues such as drugs and pornography personally appealing. Like many other modern libertarian-minded conservatives, he only accentuated the libertarian themes that worked for him.

Washington-based libertarians (such as those associated with the Cato Institute) have frequently provided the news media with data suggesting that government programs are failing, then offer radical measures to remedy the problem. Libertarians talk about failing "government" schools and then propose vouchers to support private school education. They describe Medicare programs as unsustainable and then recommend private insurance programs to replace them. And, of course, they talk about a Social Security crisis in the manner of President Bush and then point to privatization as a remedy (although they chose other terms to describe their program for Social Security after polls showed that many Americans reacted negatively to the word "privatization").

When discussing the debates over Social Security, the media and the public failed to look beyond familiar disagreements over interpreting demographic data. They focused on discussions about the merits of long-term investments in stocks and treasury bonds rather than the merits of the antigovernment philosophy inspired by opponents of this popular program. The clash over Social Security involved more than just disputes about crunching numbers. It was also about ideology. The libertarian-minded assault on Social Security represented one battle in a full-scale war that aimed to defeat many of the principal reforms of the twentieth century that gave the state a vital role in the lives of the American people.

### Budget Deficits: Beliefs Trump Facts

By the 1980s and 1990s, America's radical conservatives were expressing libertarian ideas frequently in their comments on the economic issues of the day. Of course, many of these speakers and writers did not identify themselves specifically as libertarians (stealth remained the practice), and they disagreed with some of the libertarian positions on social, moral, diplomatic, and military issues. They did, however, find the libertarian position on business affairs highly persuasive. Some of these commentators sounded like Richard Armey and William E. Simon, whose simple language parroted favorite shibboleths of the faithful. Others offered more philosophical support for their positions in the manner of Rothbard, Friedman, and Murray. All drew upon the familiar libertarian-style appeal to make their case. Consistently they argued that laissez-faire was the proper solution to America's economic problems, and they claimed that liberals were the principal obstacles to putting that ideal into practice. Grover G. Norquist, head of Americans for Tax Reform, communicated this message frequently when he campaigned vigorously for gigantic tax cuts that would reduce the potential of federal administrators to regulate the nation's economic life.[89] Norquist became a powerful designer of political strategy for Republican efforts to reduce the size of the federal government. At one point Norquist said that he wanted to reduce the size of government to the point where he could drag it into the bathroom and drown it. He also compared the estate tax to the Holocaust. The power of this modern libertarian-style belief in laissez-faire has been abundantly evident in recent years in the manner that many conservatives dropped their historic support for balanced budgets. This shift in attitudes dramatically reveals the power of faith over facts. Market conservatives have become so committed to their libertarian creed that they are willing to give short shrift to a sensible and responsible economic idea when it appears to conflict with the tenets of their faith. The right's recent disregard for balanced budgets indicates that libertarian ideas do, indeed, have consequences.

Until the days of Ronald Reagan's leadership, conservatives had ranked among the nation's leading advocates of fiscal responsibility. Frequently they warned Americans about the dangers of excessive government spending. Washington needed to keep the nation's books balanced, said these traditional conservatives. Deficit spending spurred by the creation of new federal programs represented a disturbing development. Yet conservatives began to relegate this fear to a minor consideration in the age of rising political faith. They subscribed so strongly to the libertarian view of limited government that they learned to treat the looming budget deficits as only minor nuisances.

Republicans of the mid-twentieth century made balanced budgets central to their economic appeal. Robert Taft, an Ohio senator who led his party's conservative forces in the 1940s and early 1950s, tried to win the Republican nomination for the presidency through demands for fiscal responsibility. He blamed the social programs of Franklin D. Roosevelt and Harry Truman for the nation's deficit problems. Then Dwight D. Eisenhower, the hero of the American victory in Europe during World War II, defeated Taft in a 1952 struggle for the Republican nomination, but Eisenhower did not dispute the importance of Taft's attention to budgets. As president, Eisenhower promised to balance the federal books during his administration and expressed regret that he was unable to accomplish the goal during his first years in office (expenses associated with the Korean War and the Cold War complicated his efforts). Eventually, in 1956 Ike was able to boast that his administration had achieved the traditional conservative goal of fiscal discipline: a balanced budget.

From the 1950s to the 1980s, many conservatives endorsed the idea of fiscal responsibility in their public statements. Barry Goldwater pressed the case for cuts in federal spending during the years when the Eisenhower administration failed to achieve a balanced budget. Deficit spending, he charged, was inconsistent with Republican principles and represented a betrayal of public trust.[90] The Arizona senator also made the issue of balanced budgets an important facet of his presidential appeal in 1964. Later, North Carolina's hard-line conservative senator, Jesse Helms, complained that the huge federal deficit of the mid-1970s was larger than the federal expenditure for an entire year when he had arrived in Washington as a Senate aide in 1956. Deficit spending, Helms warned, could lead America down the path of "penury and stagnation," as it had in postwar Britain.[91] In the Reagan years, too, a number of conservatives voiced strong opposition to the build-up of federal deficits. Richard Viguerie, the Populist-style leader of the New Right, warned that a massive debt complicated the federal government's efforts to battle inflation since it necessitated hikes in interest rates. Deficits were delaying the nation's economic recovery, Viguerie charged.[92] Similarly, William E. Simon argued in the 1980s that the ever-increasing national debt was "devouring the funds needed for capital investment in our productive system."[93] James G. Watt, who served as secretary of the interior in the Reagan administration, also saw serious economic troubles associated with deficits. He observed that Washington needed to commit a huge portion of its revenues to pay interest on the nation's debt. Federal borrowing seemed to increase each year.[94] Liberals had made a terrible mistake advocating the strategies of economist John Maynard Keynes, Watt argued. Political leaders acted irresponsibly when justifying deficit spending, thereby placing the nation's future at risk.[95]

Ronald Reagan, too, complained about the deficit when he campaigned for the presidency against Jimmy Carter and promised not to spend more than the government took in once he moved into the White House. Nevertheless, Reagan accepted the smoke and mirrors promises of supply-side advocates once he took office. The concept of supply-side economics had not emerged at the time as a respected scholarly interpretation of the economics profession, but it got a boost from some strategically placed radcon authors and received lots of favorable attention in the *Wall Street Journal*. Reagan initially found the concept intriguing and thought it workable. Supply-siders said the best way to stimulate and grow the economy was to cut the taxes, especially those of wealthy Americans. This would free money for business leaders to invest in their enterprises and to expand them. In the long run, said the supply-siders, the economy would grow back into prosperity and the tax cuts would essentially pay for themselves. During booming economic times, the government would bring in plenty of revenue, even with the reduced tax rates.

When federal deficits climbed dramatically in the 1980s, in large part from Reagan's massive tax cuts, some Republicans resisted the new conservative mentality and heeded the old conservative call for fiscal responsibility. They complained about the disturbing trend and urged leaders in Congress and the White House to take the painful actions necessary to balance the government's books. Senator Bob Dole, who claimed that the supply-side argument did not make much sense, joked about it. "The good news," said Dole, "is a busload of supply-siders went over the cliff. The bad news is there were three empty seats." As a leader of Republicans in the Senate, Dole tried to raise taxes in the 1980s to help close the gap.[96] After Reagan left the White House and George H. W. Bush took over the presidency, Richard Darman (Bush's director of the Office of Management and Budget) and others in the Republican Party joined Democrats in supporting increased taxes.[97] Republicans and Democrats came up with the Gramm-Rudman-Hollings Act, which aimed to move the government forcefully in the direction of a balanced budget. Then, in a stunning reversal of opinion, the president turned away from his firmly stated presidential campaign pledge of the 1988 campaign ("Read my lips: no new taxes"). He boldly supported tax increases in order to secure a more stable and healthy economy. George H. W. Bush deserved applause for his controversial but fiscally responsible action, but angry Republicans, particularly hard-line conservatives, drowned out the praise with boos. They insisted that Bush give no ground in his opposition to taxes. By the early 1990s, their libertarian-style contempt for federal taxation had emerged as a far more important element of the conservative faith than the earlier commitment to balanced budgets.

This posture of forceful resistance also made sense for True Believers of supply-side mythology. These hard-line conservatives were not going to compromise on essentials of a faith they had come to adore in the period when libertarian economic ideas found an increasingly prominent place in mainstream Republican thought. Government was bad, they firmly concluded, and the best way to starve and weaken it was to stand firmly against taxes. Compromise was out of the question. Enthusiasts of a religionlike economic belief should not surrender on fundamentals.[98]

By the time George W. Bush ascended to the White House in 2001, faith in the libertarian view of economic issues had become so firm that the president could send federal budget deficits soaring to unprecedented levels and still earn mostly fawning praise from the right for his economic leadership. Bush inherited record budget *surpluses* from the Clinton administration in 2001 but squandered that advantage by slashing taxes dramatically and requesting huge spending allowances for a war in Iraq. Many enthusiasts of supply-side economics applauded his actions. The curse of the Reagan years—massive deficits—returned, but the Republican faithful had little to say at first about this growing difficulty. They approached the subject as if it represented the Democratic Party's partisan issue. Acknowledging the deficit problem seemed tantamount to accepting the legitimacy of the Democrats' complaints. The Republican Party's maverick senator, John McCain, showed courage in warning that the Bush administration was spending money like a "drunken sailor." Few Republicans joined him in sounding an alarm at the time. Eventually, a number of conservative Republicans—the so-called fiscal hawks—began to speak out in protest of the expanding deficit. Their courage was on display much too late.

By early 2004, a presidential and congressional election year, some conservatives began to give more public attention to the problem of deficits, but they were reluctant to sway from the libertarian elements of their economic faith when proposing remedies. In January 2004, for example, Brian M. Riedl of the Heritage Foundation called for "smaller government and less spending" and Edward H. Crane of the libertarian Cato Institute challenged politicians to show the political courage needed to make spending cuts. Noticeably absent from these proposals was a demand for major tax increases to deal with the government's increasingly serious problem with red ink. Nor was there a strong demand for President Bush to abandon his tax cuts for the rich or step back from his expensive engagements in Iraq in order to bring relief to the federal budget.[99] Riedl, Crane, and others stuck to the libertarian message of demanding reductions in social spending as the catch-all solution to budgetary difficulties.

Of course, some libertarians do not fear budget deficits, because they suspect that a sense of crisis will convince the American people of the need to accept severe declines in domestic spending. Libertarians tend to be less troubled by gargantuan deficits than moderate conservatives and liberals since those imbalances can force changes that they promote. They love the tax cuts that contributed to deficits, and they know that the public's fears about a growing fiscal crisis will justify finance-chopping actions against entitlement programs that are popular with liberals. These libertarians aim to "starve the beast" (government) by fostering budget crises and then denying social and regulatory programs the nourishment of federal funding.

During the years of George W. Bush's presidency, when the budget deficit grew to enormous proportions, many of the nation's political leaders as well as their conservative constituents were wearing blinders—libertarian blinders. They had become True Believers of a radical faith that projected dramatic visions of heaven and hell. Paradise was associated with the almost stateless nirvana achieved in a society dedicated to the principles of laissez-faire. Purgatory was confinement in a society where the long arm of the federal government reached out to grasp independent people by the shoulders while they were in motion, reducing their energy and stifling their enterprise. For the philosophically inclined, the devil was in the details of "planning" and regulatory action, as Rothbard, Friedman, and Murray had argued. For the rhetorically inclined, such as William E. Simon and Dick Armey, a more specific image of Satan served better to rally the forces of opposition to government. References to the "liberal" worked best to identify libertarians' principal enemy.

George W. Bush's economic leadership was libertarian in spirit, but the American people did not hear reference to this philosophy emanating from his lips or from the many other enthusiasts of radical laissez-faire who served in top positions in his administration. The real nature of their faith remained under the covers, concealed from public view. These leaders were not partisans of a radical "ism," they suggested in their speeches, just advocates of free enterprise, free markets, and free people. This strategy served wonderfully to ease libertarians through the doors of government in Washington without much notice. Once inside, libertarians went about their business of dismantling the supposedly evil creations of an earlier generation of liberal legislators. Like religious fundamentalists who succeeded in cleansing the churches of moderate religionists, these Stealth Libertarians looked like elated victors who, at last, had restored the True Faith to Washington, D.C.

## CHAPTER FIVE

# Culture Warriors

Militant conservatives have shown impressive resilience. Communism, the Great Beast that excited their impassioned rhetoric during four decades of the Cold War, transformed into a mere mouse in 1989–1991 when the Soviet Union and its empire collapsed, yet they continued to gain momentum in the following years. These radicals achieved notable political gains in the 1994 congressional elections and managed to place a politician in the White House in 2000 who spoke energetically for their cause. Strongly partisan commentators on radio and television gained larger audiences after the end of the Cold War, and hard-core conservative columnists in newspapers and magazines found a broader readership in the 1990s. Despite the virtual disappearance of communism as the major enemy that had brought together diverse right-wing interests against a common foe, militant conservatives continued their march toward influence and power. How did they hold and even enlarge their base in the absence of a traditional communist threat?

The decline and near-disappearance of the communist enemy in the late 1980s and early 1990s did little to diminish the intensity of right-wing passion, because by that time ultraconservatives were well on the way toward identifying a different threat to the American way of life. Liberalism, an internal enemy, had become a useful reference for deviltry. Ugly references to liberals had been evident in right-wing rhetoric for decades, especially since the days of the New Deal, but in the late twentieth century partisans gave even stronger attention to these negative points of reference. Commentators of the radical right identified liberalism as a particularly broad-based and multifaceted menace. They suggested that it could be blamed for just about everything. Was the economy in trouble? Wrong-headed liberals had created a mess. Was immorality plaguing U.S. society? Liberal attitudes must be the source of the problem. Were enemies abroad giving the United States trouble? No doubt liberal naïveté, weakness, and appeasement were to blame. This Manichaean symbolism that identified liberalism with all that was despised served nicely in the emerging political environment. By the 1990s, right-wingers had discovered that nothing worked as effectively to replace communism as a bugaboo than fear of liberalism's advancement in the culture wars. Comments about supposed struggles against liberal evil were accentuated in the right's parlance during the 1980s, and, especially, in the 1990s.

Reference to culture wars suggested clashes between worldviews, reports James Davison Hunter, a professor of sociology and religious studies at the University of Virginia and the author of an influential book on the phenomenon published in 1991 titled *Culture Wars: The Struggle to Define America*.[1] Hunter observes that Americans were deeply divided over a variety of symbolic issues that had little to do with traditional political disputes about the economy or foreign policy. Americans engaged, for instance, in arguments about funding for the arts, prayer in public schools, and multicultural education. These debates were not easily resolved, Hunter stresses, because the disagreements concerned fundamental assumptions and beliefs. Each side appeared to claim a monopoly on truth.[2] Conservatives and liberals were fighting over basic questions about how people should live and the kind of society they wished to build. The clashes involved religion as well, Hunter acknowledges, but he emphasizes that they were not entirely about religion. Some partisans on the right were generally secular in outlook, he notes, yet they also stressed "moral" issues and showed an impulse toward orthodoxy.[3]

Hunter attempts to treat liberals and conservatives in a balanced manner when interpreting the culture wars, claiming that people on both sides of the social divide exaggerated their claims and described opponents in sensationally negative language. He writes that partisans of the right and left typically inflated the nature, size, and political power of their adversaries.[4] They exhibited "symmetry in antipathy," mirroring each other's hatred.[5] Hunter favors a social scientist's neutrality when studying this subject. He announces in the book that he does not wish to determine who was right or wrong in these cultural disputes. As a sociologist aiming to provide objectivity, Hunter's principal goal is to understand the language and symbols each group employed to identify and discredit its opponents.[6]

Although Hunter provides many useful insights, his exaggerated effort to balance judgments suggests that both sides in the debates were equally responsible for picking fights and employing strident language. Liberals, he should have noted, did not typically initiate these "wars." They did not seek fights over sex education in the schools or call for battles over school prayer. Liberals were not the principal instigators of protests against the art of Robert Mapplethorpe and Snoop Doggy Dogg. They did not lead the charge against *Murphy Brown,* the character in a television sitcom who decided to have a child out of wedlock, and they did not initiate protests against Ellen's decision in another TV sitcom to come out of the closet as a lesbian. Nor did liberals provoke many other controversies that appeared on the battlegrounds of the culture wars.

Culture Warriors of the right fired the initial shots in these "wars" because they were suspicious of modernity.[7] The complex, pluralistic, and fast-paced conditions of contemporary life disturbed them, much as they did some fundamentalists of Tennessee in 1925 who struggled against modern ideas and lifestyles through a symbolic fight over the teaching of evolution in the public schools. In recent years Culture Warriors have found a bevy of new symbolic issues around which they can rally the frightened faithful (and a few Culture Warriors have actually returned to the old battles over evolution). In each case the radicals act as if they are fighting to save the soul of American civilization. They attempt to protect the nation's morality by impeaching Bill Clinton or try to defend traditional marriage between men and women by supporting a constitutional amendment to ban gay marriage. In each instance the political campaign is symbolic of their broad effort to counter the supposedly wicked influences of modernity. Like religious fundamentalists, the Culture Warriors of American politics act like they are engaged in a cosmic struggle to save the civilization from nefarious liberal forces.

The ultras' critique of American society, though varied and often complex, exhibits some common features. Major themes emerge in much of the partisan literature. The right's cultural narrative generally reads like this:

There has been a serious decline in the quality of American life in recent years. A prime cause of this deterioration is the public's growing disrespect for values. Liberal Americans no longer look to the Bible for moral standards, and the public now shows inadequate interest in the great teachings of literature and philosophy passed down over the centuries under the rubric of Western civilization. Liberals have lost their moral and intellectual compass. They adopt almost any fashion of their age because they have no fixed principles on which to base their ideas and actions. Liberals lack the direction that tradition provides. Wallowing in "relativism," they are often enamored of radical and mischievous forms of modernity. Some flirt with nihilism. Liberal intellectuals are very much to blame for the society's indulgences in relativism. Influential professors and writers, operating in prestigious universities, foundations, think tanks, and media organizations, foster disrespect for traditions. Their attitudes promote irreverence, narcissism, and rebellion. They have contributed to the development of rootless, anarchic culture in modern America that is dramatically and sadly different from the generally conservative culture based on traditional values that prevailed in the United States before the 1960s.

At first glance this argument sounds like the exclusive jeremiad of religious fundamentalists, but upon closer examination of conservative activities it is clear that the outlook appeals as well to many staunch conservatives who do not associate with evangelical and Pentecostal movements or other church-based organizations. Secular-minded rightists in institutions of higher learning are also in the crusade for values, standards, morals, and traditions. The right's social agenda—ironic in that it makes radical claims for tradition—has received energetic support as well from intellectuals operating outside of the universities. Quite a few representatives of this conservative intelligentsia are situated in the nation's large metropolitan areas. They include federal judges, pundits of the mass media, and "social scientists" holding fellowships at leading conservative think tanks. A number of neoconservative intellectuals cherish these traditions as well. Of course, all of these rightists understand that the language of cultural warfare has practical value to the conservative cause. They recognize that the appeal against "liberal" thought and fashions helps to attract millions to GOP candidates during election campaigns. In short, America's "enthusiastic religionists" contribute powerful political support for the culture radcons' perspective, but they do not monopolize communication of this viewpoint. Secularly oriented rightists have made important contributions, too.

## The Closing of the American Mind

A publication that was arguably the most significant early verbal assault in the modern American culture wars came from the mind of a sophisticated, erudite, and generally secular-minded intellectual who worked at one of the nation's most prestigious institutions. The University of Chicago's political philosopher Allan Bloom achieved distinction as a leading light of the Culture Warriors with his publication of a wide-ranging commentary on social change called *The Closing of the American Mind: How Higher Education Failed Democracy and Impoverished the Souls of Today's Students*. Bloom's 1987 book pulled together diverse arguments that had been generating for years among conservatives and tied them together in an impressive scholarly package. While many other protesters against liberalism had sounded like shrill reactionaries, Bloom gave this litany of complaints the appearance of sophisticated criticism. Embellishing his critique of American society with references to many of the West's leading philosophical and political thinkers, Bloom provided gravitas and legitimacy to cultural conservatism.

Allan Bloom (1930–1992), a scholarly type who seemed more at home in the life of the mind on a university campus than in the hurly-burly of American politics, rather suddenly became a hero to American conservatives with the publication of his book in 1987. The only son of parents who had been social workers, Bloom was greatly influenced by the political philosopher Leo Strauss at the University of Chicago. Bloom, one of Strauss's "disciples," also attracted a loyal following of students at Chicago. Before the release of *The Closing of the American Mind,* Bloom was best known as the translator and interpreter of an impressive scholarly work, *The Republic of Plato* (1968). He gained academic fame, too, for encouraging students to read "the Great Books" (noted works in Western intellectual thought). Bloom was horrified by the examples of student rebellion on college campuses in the late 1960s and compared that tumult to troubles in the Weimar Republic in Germany during the pre-Hitler years. He thought some student radicals in the United States were acting like the Nazi ruffians who wrecked German society's democratic hopes.

The publishing success of *The Closing of the American Mind* made Allan Bloom an academic superstar. His book soared to the top of the nonfiction best-seller list. Howard Cosell, William F. Buckley, and David Brinkley interviewed Bloom on their television programs, and his picture adorned the covers of the nation's major newsmagazines. Soon many other writers on the right were trying to imitate Bloom's success. They published books of their own that accentuated specific themes addressed in *The Closing of the American Mind,* and, like Bloom, supported their ideas with scholarly references and numerous commentaries about activities in the nation's universities. The right's criticisms of higher education had been growing for years, but no one did a better job than Allan Bloom in bringing intellectual respectability to cultural conservatism. Through an impressive display of erudition, Bloom left the impression that the liberals' social ideas could be confronted effectively in the highest levels of discourse.

Bloom's assault was decorated so impressively with the panoply of scholarship that some book reviewers initially greeted his publication as a balanced and objective exploration of cultural issues that carried no specific ideological bias. Will Morrisey, writing in *Interpretation: A Journal of Political Philosophy,* concluded that Bloom's book could appeal to both liberals and conservatives, and Michael W. Hirschorn praised Bloom in *The Chronicle of Higher Education* for eschewing a narrow political agenda.[8] These and other commentators on *The Closing of the American Mind* did not recognize the publication's value as an important catalyst for the right's emerging crusade against a supposedly powerful liberal elite.

Most reviewers, however, revealed their political sympathies when they lined up to hail or rail against Bloom's arguments. Radcons such as Roger Kimball and John Podhoretz commended the University of Chicago professor for his wisdom in identifying societal flaws, and William Kristol gushed in the *Wall Street Journal* that "no other recent book so brilliantly knits together such astute perceptions of the contemporary scene with such depth of scholarship and philosophical learning."[9] Commentators on the right quickly recognized the power of Bloom's wide-ranging assault. They believed *The Closing of the American Mind* represented a devastating denouncement of liberalism even though the author did not employ that word frequently in his discourse. Others struck at Bloom for displaying contempt for the progressive elements of modern education. Attacking from the left, Robert Pattison (in *The Nation*), Richard Rorty (in the *New Republic*), and Louis Menand (also in the *New Republic*) criticized Bloom's right-oriented interpretations sharply and suggested the author's own mind was not as open as it ought to be.[10]

The reviewers who politicized their analyses of *The Closing of the American Mind* were on the right track. Bloom's book packed ideological punch. His interpretations highlighted most of the key points that social conservatives mustered in subsequent years when they marched into battle in the culture wars. *The Closing of the American Mind* serves as a useful template for identifying essential elements of militant conservatism's cultural persuasion. The book's comprehensive critique of U.S. higher education specifically and American society generally employs many ideas that became central in the arguments of America's Culture Warriors.

### Bloom's Appeal

Allan Bloom's timing was superb because by 1987 two of modern conservatism's principal critiques were losing political clout. Complaints about liberal economic policies and communism excited less public interest in the late 1980s than they had in earlier years. By 1987 the nation had pulled out of the long recession that had troubled the country since the early 1970s. Ronald Reagan's control of the White House and Republican gains in Congress took some of the edge off of the right's claims, familiar in the late 1970s, that liberalism was to blame for the nation's economic crises. Also, by 1987 the Cold War had begun to look less threatening, as a younger and friendlier premier of the Soviet Union, Mikhail Gorbachev, appeared ready to support improved relationships between the two superpowers. Fear of communism was losing much of its potential to anger and energize conservatives. The moment was right for a shift toward cultural issues, and *The Closing of the American Mind* demonstrated how this transference could be achieved through a multifaceted diatribe against current societal conditions.

Bloom directs his attack in *The Closing of the American Mind* against conditions in the universities, but his principal arguments resemble Culture Warriors' criticism of American society in general. A central feature of this claim is a charge that privileged and powerful intellectuals who harbor dangerously mistaken beliefs enjoy extraordinary influence in

American society. Bloom's villains are liberal-minded professors and administrators in higher education. Many other radicals have since repeated this accusation. They have also expanded Bloom's attack on
"elites" to figures outside academia, including editors and journalists,
television news anchors, Hollywood executives and actors, directors of
prestigious foundations, liberal-minded religious leaders, and others who
operate from prominent positions in American society. The villains in
these radcon indictments vary, but their ideological character is rather
similar. From the Culture Warriors' perspective, the powerful elites are,
essentially, liberals. They are the supposed source of numerous modern-
day social, cultural, and educational problems in America.

Bloom's *The Closing of the American Mind* represents a splendid display of erudition, but it also reflects the thinking of a fundamentalist-
minded Culture Warrior who grossly and rather simplistically attributes
the nation's social and intellectual shortcomings to a common internal
enemy. Like many other Culture Warriors, Bloom loosely conflates liberals and radical-leftists, making the two groups look similar or, at least,
like partners in a common enterprise that deeply undermines precious
traditional values. At its base, Bloom's vision is Manichaean. He identifies the forces of right and wrong in dramatic, emotion-laden terms, and
that is the key to his book's enormous appeal among conservatives who
were deeply suspicious of liberals.

Allan Bloom's critique of society and education is worth a close, detailed viewing, because it recites so many of the fundamental premises
of culture-minded radical conservatives. Bloom's popular book offers a
framework of social criticism from the right that attracted numerous imitators in later years. His hard-hitting treatise contains the essential elements of the modern Culture Warriors' rejection of liberalism. The following discussion offers a summary of Bloom's main arguments, an
indication of the way various other Culture Warriors have employed
seven essential principles in Bloom's book, and a reflection on the ways
moderate conservatives and liberals often disagree strongly with these
key points in the Culture Warriors perspective.

### Bloom's Case

Bloom offers a disturbing, almost prophetic vision in *The Closing of
the American Mind*. He discerns, as his title suggests, a severe intellectual crisis. The American mind is "closing." Higher education has failed

democracy and "impoverished the souls" of the nation's students. The difficulty, then, is a matter of deep importance. Tomorrow's leaders will be intellectually crippled if the current failures expand through higher education in the United States. Allan Bloom focuses on the world he knows best—the university—and claims that undergraduates are woefully lacking in the knowledge and interests expressed by earlier generations of college students. Today's undergraduates, he says, have little appreciation of the great works of literature or the ideas of the great philosophers. They are steeped, instead, in the culture of movies and rock music. Students live for the moment and have little use for traditions that represent the foundations of the culture and values of the West. Their awareness of the Great Books diminished greatly during the radical 1960s, when campus revolutionaries forced drastic changes in the university curricula. Courses about race and ethnic relations, feminism, and other trendy topics replaced study of the classics. Student appreciation of fine music also dropped significantly in the 1960s, Bloom argues. Gone was the enthusiasm for Wagner, Beethoven, Chopin, and Brahms expressed by previous generations of music lovers. Instead, students demonstrated a passion for "orgasmic rhythms" that took the campuses by storm. Rock and roll, attests Bloom, offered the young little more than a prepackaged "masturbational fantasy."[11]

Students, he writes, are suffering from "great spiritual bleeding" and a "spiritual entropy or an evaporation of the soul's boiling blood." The consequences of this slippage are disturbing. Citing Friedrich Nietzsche's concerns, Bloom claims that a decay of culture can lead to a "decay of man." He observes that "today's select students know so much less, are so much more cut off from tradition, are so much slacker intellectually that they make their predecessors look like prodigies of culture."[12] In these and other remarks Bloom communicates the dire conclusion that America's educational and cultural crisis is not an inconsequential matter. It is a monumental problem.

What is the source of this crisis? For Bloom, much of the difficulty can be traced to the perspective of "relativism" that has become fashionable among many of the teachers and scholars at U.S. universities. These professors maintain that there are no fixed ideals with inherent value. "Liberal thought" contributed to this indiscriminate outlook, Bloom claims. Academicians said "there are no absolutes"; only "freedom is absolute."[13] Bloom cites some specific examples of cultural relativism to illustrate the

problem. He notes, for instance, that college students who had been exposed to relativist teachings said they had no right to claim that one culture is better than another. Bloom responded in the classroom with the
implied suggestion that in some matters Western traditions *are* truly
superior to those of non-Western societies (i.e., true standards of decency
and morality can be ascertained). Bloom asked the students: "If you had
been a British administrator in India, would you have let the natives
under your governance burn the widow at the funeral of a man who had
died?"[14] There *are* higher standards of human decency.

Relativism has extinguished the real motive of education, Bloom says,
which is "the search for the good life."[15] Students cannot recognize truths
because their beliefs are nonjudgmental and often politicized. They have
been trained, for instance, to denigrate crimes of the right but have learned
to excuse crimes of the left. When asked to identify evil, students frequently mention Hitler but rarely mention Stalin.[16] Bloom also cites the
example of one of Ronald Reagan's most memorable statements, criticizing
liberal reactions to it in a way that many conservatives often repeated in
later years. He recalls that when President Reagan denounced the Soviet
Union as "an evil empire," campus relativists denounced him for using provocative rhetoric and indulging in simplistic notions of good and evil.[17]
Bloom maintains that Reagan made an important and necessary moral
judgment when he described the communist empire in blunt fashion. Academics and students steeped in "values relativism" were ill-equipped to
understand, let alone express, a moral conviction so forthrightly.

The proper response to relativism, Bloom suggests, is greater attention to fixed points of light and guidance. Thousands of years of Western
thought have produced great ideas worthy of study and reflection.
Bloom, the translator of Plato's *Republic*, finds much wisdom in the writings of notable philosophers of ancient Greece. He also praises the Great
Books of Western civilization and draws on the insights of major European thinkers over the ages.[18] A good deal of Bloom's interpretation de-
rives from the teachings of his academic mentor, the University of
Chicago's Leo Strauss, who was also a critic of relativism. Bloom men-
tions Strauss only briefly in *The Closing of the American Mind,* yet he
draws much insight from the political philosopher who emphasized the
wisdom of the great thinkers of antiquity.[19]

Bloom turns to the Bible, too, as a valuable fixed point of light. The author accentuates the importance of religious study in his book, observing

that through much of history, moral teaching was essentially religious teaching.[20] The Bible long served as a key to the common Western culture, Bloom notes, and it inspired many great works of art and literature. Ironically, some Culture Warriors criticized Bloom for failing to base his ideas on religious precepts. They should have read his work more closely. The professor made brief but nevertheless serious appeals in favor of religious teachings.

Allan Bloom sounds nostalgic when commenting on the lack of adequate attention to the classics in American universities. He looks back, describing the 1950s and early 1960s as a sort of Golden Age of university life in the United States.[21] In those earlier times American colleges were the most envied in the world, he informs readers. Students pursued their studies in the 1950s and early 1960s with a greater degree of seriousness, and America's campuses were not disrupted by political activities.

Then the terrible 1960s rocked the campuses and permanently changed university life. Under pressure from protesting students, the colleges abolished fundamental course requirements that exposed students to the great ideas of Western culture. Fashionable new courses on "relevant" subjects replaced the classics in the core curriculum. Many professors gave favored attention to the ideas of Marx and Freud, and they asked students to read trendy books by Norman O. Brown, Charles Reich, and other authors. Those publications faded quickly into insignificance as the 1960s passed from view.[22] Professors and administrators were responsible for the sorry conditions in the universities, Bloom charges. In the 1960s leaders in American universities made mistakes similar to those of leaders in German universities in the 1930s. Academicians tolerated the dismantling of rational inquiry and left "the university prey to whatever intense passion moved the masses."[23]

Liberal faculty members are the targets of much of Allan Bloom's invective in *The Closing of the American Mind,* but the author only rarely identifies them as such. At one point in the book he states bluntly that "liberalism is what prepared us for cultural relativism," and in another discussion he recalls that all of the university professors who trained him when he was an undergraduate student were Marxists or New Deal liberals. Scholars of the left dominated the classrooms in the post–World War II era, he says, and promoted ideas that contributed to the spread of "value relativism."[24] Many of them went on "to become very famous," and from influential positions they preached the flawed view that bold new ideas from the social sciences could produce social and political progress. These scholars were in positions of great intellectual power, Bloom observes, but they did not fully understand the potential for mischief laden in their devotion to their "values relativism." Allan Bloom knows better. "There is no doubt," he says, "that values relativism, if it is true and it is believed in, takes one into very dark regions of the soul and very dangerous political experiments."[25]

Bloom lays a good deal of the blame for university troubles in the 1960s at the feet of students and professors who campaigned on the campuses for identity politics, particularly feminists and blacks. Both groups, he says, called attention to their distinctive needs and attempted to force changes in the curriculum to reflect their groups' interests. Universities responded to the feminists' demands with courses in Women's Studies and Gender Studies and reacted to the African Americans' pressures by scheduling Black Studies and Black English. The resulting courses, he argues, were superficial and inappropriate for a respectable curriculum in higher education. Even more disturbing, their placement in the core programs often led to the deletion of courses dealing with the classics.

The author blames feminists not only for pushing the study of gender onto the curriculum but also for helping to precipitate a breakdown in sexual mores. Men, he argues, are not as responsible as many think for this breakdown, because, by their very nature, they are *always* eager to achieve immediate carnal gratification. Traditionally, it has been the responsibility of women to resist pressures for sexual engagement. Feminism undermined this tradition of female "modesty," Bloom claims, and promised to liberate women from "nature." The result, seen in 1960s college life, was cohabitation without demands of marriage. The feminist quest for equality and justice led eventually to the neglect of children. When both wives and husbands are in hot pursuit of their professional careers, who was to care for the children?[26] Not surprisingly, says Bloom, a spike in divorce rates accompanied the feminist revolution.[27]

Blacks also receive a firm scolding in *The Closing of the American Mind*. Bloom writes that African Americans sought separation rather than integration, power rather than rights, identity rather than opportunity. He notes that the Black Power movement took control of the civil rights movement in the late 1960s and brought aggressive, bullying tactics to the campuses. Once black militants gained a foothold in the universities, they pressed for social distance from white students and demanded that universities fund their separatist organizations.

Allan Bloom saves his sharpest criticism for the university administrators and faculty members who caved in when radical students and their supporters among the faculty made irresponsible statements and pressed for drastic changes. Bloom was teaching at Cornell University in the late 1960s, and he cites examples from his experiences there, arguing that weak-willed leaders at Cornell demonstrated cowardice when dealing with militant black students who threatened violence if they did not get their way. Frightened administrators and instructors agreed to jettison the traditional core curriculum to satisfy the angry protesters.[28] Scholars without backbone proceeded to describe the changes as progress and hail campus radicalism as a contribution to the cause of civil rights. In reality, says Bloom, physical intimidation succeeded in reducing academic freedom and setting back higher education.

Allan Bloom cites a specific example from the student confrontations of the 1960s to make his point about the harmful consequences of intimidation. He relates the story of a group of black activists on campus who disrupted the class of an economics teacher. The blacks claimed that the economics instructor was a racist because he used a Western standard for judging the efficiency of African economic performance. These militant students marched to the department chairman's office and held him and his secretary hostage for thirteen hours. Some professors at the university praised the radical students for calling attention to a problem, Bloom recalls with disgust, and the teacher "disappeared miraculously from campus, never to be seen again."[29]

These excesses are symptomatic of a grave crisis that struck higher education in the late 1960s, says Bloom, and the radical outlook began to make a profound impact on university teaching. "Every conceivable radical view concerning domestic or foreign policy demanded support from the social sciences," he argues. Radicals asked historians to rewrite the history of the world to show that leaders in Europe generally and the United States in particular had been involved in conspiratorial plans for domination and exploitation. Partisans of the left also pestered psychologists to prove that economic inequality and the existence of nuclear weapons created psychological damage and that Americans were paranoid in their view of the Soviet Union. Radicals insisted, too, that political scientists describe the North Vietnamese as nationalists and remove the stigma of totalitarianism when speaking or writing about the Soviet Union. Political correctness on the campus called for professors to denounce racism, sexism, elitism, and imperialism. If they resisted, they could face ostracism from their peers. The academic mind had truly closed.[30]

Bloom is quite blunt and severe when criticizing American society and the universities in particular, yet for all of the directness of his tirades, they are also characterized by considerable vagueness. The author is nebulous when considering solutions to the problems he identifies. He argues clearly for a return to the traditional core curriculum, but that proposal can hardly provide a remedy for all of the cultural ailments he reviews in his lengthy diatribe. Bloom displays much more assurance when assailing modern life than in prescribing ways to deal with its challenges. He leaves important questions unanswered: Must *all* changes be stonewalled? Is *some* degree of curriculum reform useful? Are *some* goals of blacks and feminists worthy of an appreciative reception? Did modern music deserve *a degree* of respect, especially in view of its vast popularity? Do *all* professional courses in the universities (as opposed to general liberal arts courses) threaten the foundations of liberal learning? Does *all* critical scholarship from the social sciences deserve reproach?

Bloom's ambiguity in addressing the implications of his sharp critique provoked criticism from those who assessed *The Closing of the American Mind*. Some reviewers thought that he displayed a tendency to dance around important controversies by concealing his opinions in esoteric verbiage. Quite a few said they detected a subtle contempt for democracy, modernism, and liberalism in the pages of *The Closing of the American Mind*, a contempt that was not directly articulated but strongly implied. Christopher Lehmann-Haupt, writing in the *New York Times*, was generally enthusiastic about Bloom's lively intellectual foray, but Lehmann-Haupt recognized that the vague complaints leveled in the book left the author vulnerable to charges of "elitism, antiquarianism, exaggerated subjectivity and skewed generalization from the particular." Bloom could be judged as "reactionary and cranky" as well as passionate and witty, Lehmann-Haupt concluded in a mixed reaction.[31]

This dichotomy, evident in Bloom's book—sharp complaints about American society followed by only vague suggestions about remedies—found expression in many publications of the Culture Warriors that preceded and followed release of *The Closing of the American Mind*. Militants

often presented scathing critiques of the social order and the universities, and they left no doubt about identifying culprits who were responsible for the supposed cultural decline. "Values relativists," academics,
curriculum reformers, militant feminists, black radicals, and others of
the "left" were to blame. When presenting a vision of actions that could
lead to a better world, though, Culture Warriors often slipped into hazy
commentaries that in effect concealed their thoughts about remedies for
the problems that troubled them.

## Seven Themes of Cultural Warfare

Seven fundamental elements of the Culture Warriors' persuasion are salient in Allan Bloom's presentation. These arguments were evident in
disparate writings of the conservative ultras before 1987, and they appeared more prominently as the culture wars grew in intensity during
the 1990s and into the twenty-first century. Of course, individual crusaders gave emphasis to specific themes and neglected others. Yet all seven
elements are essential to the genre. These ideas appear frequently in the
major speeches and publications of most militant conservatives who address cultural issues. In fact, the list of seven principal themes serves as
a useful check-sheet for partisans of the right who wish to participate in
this verbal warfare. Employment of some of these major points in their
attacks (or, ideally, invocation of all seven) can almost guarantee an appreciative audience of angry right-wing partisans.

### Theme One: Blame Liberals for Creating a Social Crisis

Allan Bloom's book warns about "the closing of the American mind"
and also informs readers that "higher education has failed democracy
and impoverished the souls of today's students." These statements con-
vey a sense of crisis: grave problems are at hand; dangerous forces
threaten American life; the situation calls for drastic action.

Bloom's admonition resembles the language and spirit of many warnings delivered by radcons in the culture wars. Partisans frequently claim
that the stakes are high in current clashes. They offer a prophetic vision
of serious problems straining American society. In this Manichaean vision the fate of mankind is hanging in the balance. If drastic action is not
taken quickly by people of good will, much will be lost. Culture Warriors

insist that tinkering will not correct the ills. Radical change is necessary. Huge problems require huge responses (like religious fundamentalists, they believe that strong beliefs are necessary to combat the supposedly strong ideas of their enemies). Reacting to a sense of profound crisis, the commentators show enthusiasm for sweeping philosophical and religious proposals. They prefer broad answers to modern life's diverse challenges, not small adjustments.

Paul Weyrich, an important figure in the New Right's culture wars, provided a representative example of this notion of crisis when he responded to Bill Clinton's success in holding on to the presidency in the face of tremendous Republican pressures for impeachment. Weyrich, one of the principal founders of the Heritage Foundation, had championed the causes of both laissez-faire economics and religious-based social protest in many years of influential activity with conservative organizations. When Clinton's problems with the Monica Lewinsky affair became front-page news in the late 1990s, Weyrich expressed disgust with the reluctance of many Americans to demand the president's resignation. American culture had become "an ever-wider sewer" that "has decayed into something approaching barbarism," Weyrich complained.[32] "In truth," he said, "I think we are caught up in a cultural collapse of historic proportions, a collapse so great that it simply overwhelms politics."[33] Weyrich traced the nation's troubles in large part to the influence of advocates of "political correctness." Cultural Marxism threatened "to control literally every aspect of our lives," he argued.[34]

This kind of harsh language supported by frightening references to an impending decline of values in U.S. society is a familiar element in radcon rhetoric. Culture Warriors often frame their criticisms in terms that suggest Western civilization's progress is in serious jeopardy.

The right's political literature is replete with commentary on threats posed to society by liberal ideas. Radcons view liberalism not just as a competing perspective coming out of the political mainstream. It is, instead, an extremist outlook that has already created considerable social upheaval in the United States. Liberalism, in the language of the culture-conscious right, serves as a catch-all phrase for identifying the troubling forces of modernity that undermine American traditions. The "liberal," in turn, represents an individual who is responsible for many of the disturbing social problems that have accompanied modernity. These characterizations of liberals are, of course, grossly simplistic and emotion-laden.

They identify liberals as radical straw men, extremists who bare little resemblance to actual liberal-minded individuals in modern American society. Yet these images of the liberal Devil serve the conservative movement well, for they excite the contempt, anger, and hatred of the faithful.
Political mobilization is easy when the supposed enemy appears to represent significant threats to fundamental values.

Arguments in the culture wars often sound apocalyptic. Commentators define the struggle between right and left as a fundamental clash
between good and evil. Two hard-line cultural conservatives, James G.
Watt and Pat Buchanan, have communicated this perspective forcefully.
Watt, a born-again Christian who served as Ronald Reagan's secretary of
the interior, characterized disagreements in the culture wars as a "moral"
battle. "It is a contest over who is right and who is wrong," Watt declared.
The former government official acknowledged that many liberal observers thought his talk about a moral clash "smacks too much of religion."
But "this is the truth," Watt insisted.[35] The conflict really is about differences between people who respect or abandon religious values. It is a
fight between a correct and an incorrect vision of America's choices. Pat
Buchanan characterized the disagreements in similar terms. The Republican speechwriter, presidential candidate, and paleoconservative pundit
offered his most memorable description of the moral clash in a provocative speech at the 1992 Republican national convention. In strident language Buchanan described the conflict with liberals as a "religious war
for the soul of America" that is "as critical to the kind of nation we will
one day be as the Cold War itself."[36] Journalists and historians often mention Buchanan's speech as a striking example of the kind of rhetorical ex-
cess that harmed President George H. W. Bush's campaign for reelection
in 1992. Yet Buchanan was not acting as an eccentric and unusually shrill
demagogue of the right when he made the controversial statements at
the 1992 convention. His dramatic description of the clash was representative of the Culture Warriors' rhetorical mainstream. Many other figures
on the right have employed similar language in attempts to characterize
their differences with liberals.

When radical rightists use this metaphor of a battle for the country's
soul, they usually blame liberals for a broad range of ills plaguing American society. Conservatives claim divorce, venereal disease, and teen sui-
cides are the consequences of liberal teachings. Such "scourges" are "the
direct result of the liberal social agenda, spearheaded by the judicial fiats

handed down by an activist Supreme Court," claims Gregory Wolfe.[37] In a similar fashion, Senator Jesse Helms blamed liberalism for precipitating a social breakdown. Helms, a controversial former senator from North Carolina, made clashes over political ideas sound like fights between the forces of religion and atheism. The essential problem, Helms declared, is that liberals believe in a "Superstate" rather than God. Their secular outlook undermines respect for the moral teachings of the Bible. Liberalism has contributed significantly to the growing incidence of crime, divorce, drugs, abortion, and pornography in the United States, says Helms.[38]

Some Culture Warriors charge that the left's warped sense of "freedom" is a primary cause of America's social problems. Liberals, they say, express an exaggerated notion of freedom because they lack standards. They do not identify boundaries that mark off acceptable and unacceptable comportment. The acerbic and humorous radio host Rush Limbaugh illustrated the point by noting that youngsters in the urban ghettos were shooting each other over a pair of sneakers. He traced these outrageous activities to a decline in public behavioral standards fostered by liberals. Limbaugh declared that liberals are hedonists. They do not want to impose any standards on personal behavior. "That's what freedom means to them: no responsibility, no consequences for anything. It's whatever feels good." Liberals "excuse bad behavior," said Limbaugh. They rationalize it and give it "political legitimacy and credence." The breakdown of standards in the United States, Limbaugh judged, "is the liberals' forte."[39]

Journalists who find Rush Limbaugh's pungent remarks highly irritating often dismiss his observations as extreme, over-the-top versions of right-wing thought. Limbaugh's style and language are, indeed, more abrasive and provocative than that of most Warriors, and fact-checkers who have examined his many statements on the air have demonstrated that he often distorts his evidence or reports it incorrectly. Yet Limbaugh's fundamental message remains very appealing to conservatives, and it is similar to the one delivered by many other militants on the right. Fans of the media-based Culture Warriors *expect* to encounter frequent denunciations of liberal deviltry. As David Brock observes, a conservative spokesperson who wishes to become popular with the modern right's membership must denounce liberals frequently and in strong language. Those who do not participate in this political ritual are quickly pushed aside.[40] Brock, who formerly worked as a leading right-wing ultraconservative before defecting, recalls that Newt Gingrich was a master of this technique. The former leader of the Republicans in the House of Representatives who masterminded his party's takeover of Congress in 1994 by promoting a "Contract with America" understood that conservative audiences love to hear shrill denunciations of the domestic enemy. After leaving Congress in the late 1990s, Gingrich became a fellow at the American Enterprise Institute and commented frequently on the Fox News Channel. Gingrich could electrify listeners with descriptions of titanic battles between the forces of right and wrong.[41] He often warned that the challenge of dealing with such a sinister enemy called for more than just fierce political competition. The opposition has to be destroyed, Gingrich insisted. "This war has to be fought on a scale and a duration and savagery that is only true of civil wars."[42]

How long had this "war" against the liberals been in the making? Pat Robertson, the conservative religious leader and contestant for the GOP's presidential ticket in 1988, claimed the fighting had been under way since Biblical times. Robertson, the televangelist who founded the Christian Broadcasting Network, stated that throughout history, liberals, leftists, and nihilists had "tried to reduce humanity with the slime and ooze of the earth, rather than identifying humanity as children of the living God and fellow heirs of the kingdom of heaven."[43] The left is guided by an Orwellian vision of social equality, Robertson declared, that aims to level the entire culture.[44] Senator Helms saw religious implications as well, but he found most of the deviltry originating in modern times. "Atheism and socialism—or liberalism, which tends in the same direction—are inseparable entities," Helms said. When men no longer believe in God, they replace Him with an "all-provident Government."[45] America had become especially demoralized since the 1940s, Helms maintained. Since that time, liberals had been "dynamiting the foundations of our liberties on the pretext of accomplishing some overriding social good." America was in crisis because of the "incompatibility of liberalism with political freedom and biblical morality," he said.[46]

The Culture Warriors' outlook does not suggest that political groups disagree over small matters of interpretation. The chasm between conservatives and liberals appears huge. On one cliff stand heroic crusaders for light and decency. On the other are America's sinister champions of dark ideas that can tear society apart. From this perspective, Patrick Buchanan was correct. The clash of viewpoints represents "a religious war for the soul of America." Whether the battle involves social practices, religious ideas, or the fundamental nature of the university, as Allan Bloom framed the debate, stakes in the culture wars appear high, and the right's crusade appears noble. The battles look very much like a struggle to save the soul of American civilization. These descriptions of titanic struggles against evil forces resemble the outlook of fundamentalist religionists.

The prevalence of this apocalyptic rhetoric in radcon commentaries since the 1990s suggests that James Davison Hunter spread the blame for cultural warfare much too widely when he published his influential book, *Culture Wars: The Struggle to Define America* (1991). Hunter attempted to offer an even-handed evaluation of the problem, laying responsibility for the clashes at the feet of both conservatives and liberals. The record of abundant right-wing hammering at cultural themes in years subsequent to publication of Hunter's book reveals that radcons, not liberals or even moderate Republicans, were the principal promoters of these clashes. Many Americans who were not enthusiasts of the radical right found the strident writing and oratory of Culture Warriors embarrassing and disturbing. They did not characterize major social changes in American society as evidence of the deterioration of the people's morality or evidence of a significant decline in American civilization. They understood that the angry rhetoric of the right was deeply dividing the American people.

Culture Warriors continually stoke the fires of conflict even though a good deal of social science research suggests that most Americans do not wish to be forced to choose sides. Alan Wolfe, the prolific sociologist at Boston College, provides evidence of generally moderate and tolerant attitudes in eight suburban areas around the country in his 1998 book, *One Nation, After All*. He writes that the two sides supposedly fighting the culture war did not so much represent a divide between one group of Americans and another as a divide between sets of values important to most Americans. Unlike the Culture Warriors of the right who seem eager for battle, the Americans Wolfe and his research team interviewed were reluctant to pass judgment about their fellow Americans.[47] Also, Morris P. Fiorina, Samuel J. Adams, and Jeremy Pope reported in *Culture War? The Myth of a Polarized America* (2004) that Americans are much less split on social issues than news stories about a Red State/Blue State divide appear to suggest. Nonpartisan public opinion polls show that most Americans are moderate and centrist. They are not more polarized today than they were decades ago, say Fiorina, Abrams, and Pope. Americans agree remarkably on most important social questions, even though they live in different regions and hold different religious beliefs.[48]

### Theme Two: Criticize Relativism and Demand "Truth"

Allan Bloom makes a critique of "relativism" central to his thesis, as do many who participate in the culture wars. Often these critics lament the passing of traditions, morals, and values. They claim their political opponents lack standards. Liberals, they argue, are excessively fearful about making judgments regarding superiority and inferiority, morality and immorality. Liberals resist taking strong positions because they have been trained to be nonjudgmental when dealing with peoples, cultures, and ideas. This relativist outlook is dangerous, Culture Warriors warn, because it promotes the acceptance of mediocrity and tolerance of evil.

Culture-minded conservatives try to combat the relativist mindset by promoting notions about higher values, moral absolutes, and traditional points of light. Some seek guiding principles from secular learning; others turn to religious precepts. They insist that firm, conservative ideas can lead humankind out of the relativistic morass. Direction to the good life can be found. Truths can be ascertained. Canons can be consulted for wisdom. Firm responses are available to questions that liberal relativists treat as unanswerable.

The godfather of this outlook was an obscure university professor at the University of Chicago with rather eccentric views. Richard M. Weaver abandoned his earlier ideal of socialism for a highly traditional perspective that he associated with the ways of the Old South. While studying English at Vanderbilt University, Weaver came under the influence of intellectuals known as the Southern Agrarians (champions of a rural ethos, conservative Christian values, Jeffersonian principles of local and limited government, and southern civility). Doctoral work followed at Louisiana State University, where Weaver produced a dissertation called "The Confederate South, 1865–1910: A Study in the Survival of a Mind and Culture." Eventually he settled at the University of Chicago, teaching composition and rhetoric there and writing in praise of traditional ideas and lifestyles. Weaver became an influential conservative voice in opposition to modernism.

*Eccentric* is an appropriate word for characterizing Weaver's ideas, since many political observers operating outside the right-wing network of True Believers have expressed surprise that a nostalgic and cranky commentator on the affairs of humankind such as Weaver could appeal to many right-wingers in modern times. Yet Weaver holds that influential position in the minds of many culture-minded conservatives. When they identify books that helped to shape their fundamental outlook, many of them cite Weaver's most notable work, *Ideas Have Consequences* (1948), as a particularly important source for their thinking. Emmett Tyrrell Jr., editor of *American Spectator,* recalls that *Ideas Have Consequences* "became a revered text for generals of the movement conservatives." George H. Nash, author of one of the most respected intellectual histories of the American right, called Weaver's tome the "source of origin" for America's contemporary conservative movement.[49]

If *Ideas Have Consequences* reveals much about the nature of conservative thought, it is a strange ideology, indeed, since Weaver sounds like he wishes that modern life had never intruded in humankind's Garden of Eden. Weaver anticipates the argument of numerous values-oriented conservatives when he identifies *relativism* as a profound problem in modern life. He attributes the West's mistaken shift toward relativist ideas to the contributions of a fourteenth-century figure, William of Occam. That individual, Weaver claims, pushed Europeans in the direction of a "fateful doctrine" of "nominalism." William of Occam denied that "universals" had real existence or represented sources of "higher truth," he reports.[50] Occam rejected God, spiritual belief, and moral absolutes. Then, writes Weaver in this historical treatment of the breakdown of moral standards in the West, new support for relativist ideas came into fashion in the Enlightenment through the teachings of Thomas Hobbes and John Locke. In that era religion became much less important in the life of man. In fact, Weaver writes, man began serving as his own "priest" and as his own "professor of ethics." Individuals created their own values rather than draw insight from the "universals." They substituted facts for "truth" and "empiricism" for "belief."[51] Europeans, and Americans who followed them, turned away from moral absolutes and religious faith.[52] A secular, materialist, relativist society was at hand. Some called this "progress," but Weaver offers a different perspective. He sees a profound spiritual void, a decline in the character of Western civilization.

In the 1950s William F. Buckley Jr., a more sophisticated and worldly conservative, rose to prominence on the right, and Buckley, too, eschewed relativism and called for greater respect for standards, canons, and traditional principles. A bright and diversely talented individual, Buckley became a noted columnist, novelist, political philosopher, magazine editor, talk show host, and businessman. He demonstrated skill as a harpsichordist, a yachtsman, and a fluent speaker of Spanish. Born to privilege thanks to his father's successful oil ventures, William F. Buckley Jr. found comfort with traditionalist, conservative perspectives from the time of his youth. He became an orthodox-minded Catholic and sharpened his rightist political ideas after meeting the far-right thinker Albert J. Nock, a friend of Buckley's father. Following Buckley's graduation from Yale, he quickly emerged as an eloquent champion of conservative causes. Interestingly, his first major book attacked liberalism at Yale, and his second major publication, coauthored with his college roommate, L. Brent Bozell, defended Senator Joseph McCarthy.

In *God and Man at Yale* (1951) Buckley turns on many of his former university professors not only for being insufficiently critical of communism and the welfare state but also for promoting secularist and relativist values. In an influential later book, *Up from Liberalism* (1959), Buckley accentuates these themes. Again he lambastes university professors for treating good and evil in relativistic terms.[53] In addition, he writes that college students in the 1950s sound like a "silent generation" because they do not passionately defend their convictions. "We don't feel deeply because there are no fixed, acknowledged norms," he asserts. Americans recognize some norms, Buckley acknowledges, but these seem "merely conventional." He laments that these ideas "are not rooted in the natural order."[54] Liberals were to blame for much of the problem, while conservatives were capable of identifying the much-needed points of light. Spokespeople for the right held that "great truths" had already been discovered through humankind's searches and teachings over hundreds of years. "Certain problems have been disposed of," Buckley insists in his defense of traditions. "Certain questions are closed." Whatever comes in the future, he guesses, "cannot outweigh the importance to man of what has gone before."[55]

In later decades religious-minded Culture Warriors often employed an emotion-laden catchword to identify the supposedly dangerous liberal attitudes that fostered relativism. Liberals who believed that humans, not God, were the source of truth practiced "secular humanism," they charged. As James Davison Hunter has observed, secular humanism quickly became "the bogeyman of the religious right." This reference served as a convenient label for beliefs that right-wing ultras associated with a variety of ills.[56] A society that acknowledges no higher standards of truth based on religious principles is a society without commonly recognized values, the Warriors claimed. Such a community, cut off from its moral moorings, could drift toward nihilism. Quite a few conservatives have pointed to the threat of secular humanist influences in the nation's public schools. If American youngsters were taught humanist values rather than religious ones, they warn, the traditional teachings of parents and church leaders might be greatly undermined.[57] Radical conservatives fear that educational programs not influenced by religion are, essentially, controlled by the state's ideological doctrines.

Some religious-minded conservatives have described secular humanists as people who practice a counterreligion. This image of a competing creed has served wonderfully to alarm the faithful. Church-oriented conservatives are frightened by the prospect of facing challenges from another kind of religion—an alien one whose followers supposedly seek to win over the hearts and minds of the American people (and possibly to convert fellow traditionalists and religionists). Senator Jesse Helms played on this fear when he declared that secular humanism is a state religion that made a "god of government." It is really a "counterfeit religion." Helms explained that secular humanism is comprised of a hodgepodge of ideas from Karl Marx, Sigmund Freud, John Maynard Keynes, John Dewey, and other intellectual gurus who were congenial to the liberal mind. The North Carolina senator claimed secular humanists want to replace Christian religion with their own alien beliefs.[58]

Paul Weyrich and James Watt have offered similar views of secular humanism. Both Weyrich and Watt consider the "ism" a serious threat to religious values. Weyrich, like Helms, describes the concept as a "religion" and, in the manner of Helms, argues that it is human-centered rather than God-centered. Secular humanists follow a dogma, Weyrich asserts. They believe you can change man if you can change his environment. That outlook produces a whole set of pernicious social values and ethical notions that clash with Christian views drawn from the Gospels.[59] In a related manner Watt worries that secular humanists believe man can attain fulfillment and ethical conduct without resort to supernatural religion.[60] Rather than characterize this "ism" as a counterreligion in the style of Helms and Weyrich, however, Watt calls it a form of "militant atheism." He writes that secular humanism mixes concepts from Marx and Freud and communicates the ideas of liberals who were not sympathetic to religious traditions.[61] Most liberals do not identify themselves as secular humanists, Watt acknowledges, but he believes their attitudes clearly reflect troublesome humanist concepts.[62]

Neoconservatives also have contributed to this assault on relativism and called for greater attention to standards, morals, and religious values. Irving Kristol, the Jewish former Trotskyist who became one of the key early leaders of neoconservatism (see Chapter 3), sometimes employed the term "secular humanism" in his publications, maintaining that the idea did, indeed, represent a sort of counterreligion. Kristol said that "clergymen" in the "church" of this ideology believed that "man makes himself."[63] Secular humanists believe humankind has the power to control, manipulate, and improve its condition without any consideration of man's special place in a "transcendent universe." Secular humanism is bound to fail, Kristol concluded, because it leaves its followers believing life is meaningless in a meaningless world.[64] Among the neoconservatives who made contributions to the campaign against relativism is James Q. Wilson, a prominent criminologist with an affinity for philosophical discourse, who called for greater attention to humankind's "moral sense." Values are important, he insisted. The country needs greater expression of moral judgments rather than indulgence in cultural "relativism."[65] Richard John Neuhaus joined the cause by drawing attention to a supposed decline in religious commitments among the American people. Neuhaus, founder of the right-oriented journal *First Things,* was an ordained Lutheran minister before he converted to Catholicism in 1990 and became an ordained priest. He argues that religion needs to be honored and accorded a stronger presence in America's public square.

Quite a few neoconservatives are agnostics in terms of their personal religious views yet express strong respect for religious values in their public statements, believing that support for spiritual teachings has helped greatly to promote social cohesion and moral behavior. Many Straussians among the neoconservatives have viewed religion in this manner. Some of these intellectuals, disciples of University of Chicago philosopher Leo Strauss, have not personally accepted organized religion's deistic and theocratic teachings, but they sense that people who believe in religion are likely to behave as virtuous citizens. Religious piety does not appear necessary for their individual perspective on life, these neocons conclude, but it provides a useful service to the masses. Religion offers a "noble myth."

Commentators from the right, whether religiously or secularly oriented, have been communicating this theme about alien values for decades, and in recent years their comments have taken on a particularly strident tone. The Culture Warriors' familiar descriptions of struggles between believers and nonbelievers make political conflicts look like epic battles for the salvation of the American people. This perspective appears notably in the writings of Dinesh D'Souza, a facile wordsmith of the right who favors stinging indictments of liberalism. D'Souza served as a John M. Olin Fellow at the American Enterprise Institute before joining the Hoover Institution. He cut his teeth on conservative campaigning as a student at Dartmouth, where he waged a form of guerrilla warfare against the supposedly liberal administration and faculty (his writing in the *Dartmouth Review* also insulted blacks, women, and gays). Evidently leaders at the Heritage Foundation were impressed with this display of aggressive commentary, for they soon made him managing editor of their publication, *Policy Review*. Later D'Souza took a post as a policy adviser in the Reagan administration. In recent years he has published several provocative books that promote strongly right-wing perspectives on race, affirmative action, multiculturalism, feminism, and related issues.

In *Letters to a Young Conservative* (2002) D'Souza argues that immorality has spread across the United States because liberal scholars reject the Greek view of a moral order in the universe. D'Souza suggests these liberals think there is no moral truth, since each culture treats questions about morality differently. When confronted with serious problems of public immorality, liberals have no answer. In fact, they welcome the breakdown of traditions and moral standards in the name of freedom. In an especially provocative statement, D'Souza hints of connections between liberal ideas and the rise of totalitarianism. Relativistic liberalism, he writes, helped to spawn Nazism and communism, and related difficulties have appeared in more recent times. "The liberal commune, based on shared possessions and free love, is one such experiment," D'Souza explains in a provocative innuendo. "The Nazis and the Communists also tried to create new men and new values, with less benign results."[66] Conservatives challenge this relativist attitude, reports D'Souza. They understand that the absence of public belief in a moral order can create a new "crisis of the West."[67]

Michael Barone, another prolific conservative author, also communicated the strident, hard-core assault on relativism recently when he characterized issues in the 2000 presidential election in apocalyptic terms. Barone, a senior writer for *U.S. News and World Report,* is a frequent speaker for right-wing perspectives on the Fox News Channel and NBC's *The McLaughlin Group* and is principal author of the *Almanac of American Politics.* Barone interprets political differences between Republicans and Democrats as a clash between two dramatically different worldviews. One political group (the Republicans) is clearly "observant, tradition-minded, [and] moralistic," he observes. The other appears "unobservant, liberation-minded, [and] relativistic."[68] Like many on the right, Barone believes conservatism offers a route for escape from the aimlessness and confusion of liberalism and its supposed rejection of any notion of a transcendent moral order.

Through the publications of D'Souza, Barone, and many other Culture Warriors of modern times, Richard Weaver's troubled ruminations about the fatal turn toward "nominalism" has found abundant expression. Like religious fundamentalists, the Culture Warriors seek fixed points of wisdom. Denouncing relativism, they counsel greater attention to the canons of Western culture and to the values of Judeo-Christian traditions. Their strident and simplistic diatribes make liberalism appear to be a nihilistic, directionless attitude that is, evidently, the primary source of many of the problems in modern American society.

These frightening descriptions of liberalism have almost no relationship to reality. Liberals are hardly the rudderless relativists described so negatively in the rhetoric of Culture Warriors. American liberals gather under a large political tent, bringing together diverse interests and beliefs. There are certainly more secular-minded individuals among liberals than among conservatives, but the presence of many seculars does not suggest the absence of moral concerns, disrespect for traditions, or contempt for "family values," which the radical right frequently associates with liberals. Nor do other Americans who stand outside the right's fold endorse the kind of moral relativism that rightists often associate with people outside of their movement. Moderate Republicans and independents cannot be characterized as individuals who have lost their moral moorings simply because they reject the self-righteous and contemptuous views of the Culture Warriors.

Democrats have found the assault on "liberal" values particularly troubling, because the charges appear to have sticking power in the minds of many voters at election time. Many constituents cast their votes for Republicans because they hear repeated characterizations of Democrats as individuals who reject family and religious values. Presidential candidate Al Gore embraced and kissed his wife at length before giving his acceptance speech at the 2000 Democratic national convention, hoping to send a strong message about family commitment. While on the campaign trail, Gore also spoke frequently about the importance of family ties and the need to help working families. Candidate John Kerry tried also to demonstrate his love for his wife and children when addressing the 2004 Democratic convention, and he identified himself proudly as a practicing Catholic during his campaign appearances. These and other efforts by Democratic candidates generally failed to combat the effect of right-wing image-making. Lots of voters viewed Republicans as the principal champions of family values and religious commitment. The impact of the Culture Warriors' politicized definitions of standards, principles, and values remains substantial.

Many Democrats were shocked after George W. Bush won his reelection fight in 2004 and Republicans won impressive victories in Senate and House races. There were many reasons for the Republicans' successes, but the one that received accentuated attention from Democrats in the months after November 2004 related to values. Democrats sensed that the Culture Warriors had defined them as antireligious and antifamily, and that many voters accepted this bogus description. Anger over the examples of irresponsible labeling led Democrats to accentuate their concern for values. Some sought help from an insightful linguistics professor, George Lakoff, who advised Democrats to work more effectively in framing the language of political discussions. Republican strategists understood how to make language work for their benefit, said Lakoff. They succeeded in making voters think the GOP represented their values. Democrats needed lessons in political linguistics.[69] The Reverend Jim Wallis served as another appreciated adviser in "progressive" circles because he promoted the idea that liberals and centrists should not allow conservatives to use Christianity as a political tool. The right's religiously oriented campaigns against abortion and gay rights represented "bad theology," Wallis asserted. He urged voters of the left and the center to mobilize their forces behind more tolerant and compassionate forms of political involvement. Religious values *could* have a major place in the political campaigns of progressive figures, Wallis argued. Efforts to alleviate poverty and challenge racism represented attractive examples of political support for religious ideals. Not surprisingly, Wallis's book, *God's Politics: Why the Right Gets It Wrong and the Left Doesn't Get It* (2005), became a best-seller and the object of much discussion among Democrats who were eager to show that they, too, care about values.[70]

Other Americans who consider themselves moderate conservatives, centrists, independents, and religiously oriented Democrats have joined the efforts to challenge the simple-minded characterizations of the Culture Warriors. Some come from evangelical backgrounds yet were disturbed by the radical right's apparent eagerness to mix religion and politics. These evangelicals do not want specific religious groups in America to force their own faith upon others.[71] In 2005 a mixed gathering of Jews, Christians, Muslims, and Hindus as well as some theologically inclined liberals and evangelicals affirmed their interests in traditions, family, and religious values, and expressed disgust that members of the radical right are attempting to monopolize an association with these ideals.[72] These and other efforts reveal a belated but nevertheless serious effort to challenge the theme that Allan Bloom had articulated in *The Closing of the American Mind* and that many other Culture Warriors stressed in subsequent years.

### Theme Three: Point to the 1960s as the Source of Modern Social Problems

Allan Bloom viewed the late 1960s as a troublesome era. It was a time, he said, when universities dropped curricular standards and American culture turned crass. Classical music lost favor while the crude sounds of rock and roll turned popular. The rules of civility in romantic affairs gave way to sexual explicitness and cohabitation. In these realms and many others, Americans of the 1960s quickly lost direction, and society never recovered from those shock effects. A decent and sophisticated culture that Bloom appreciated as a young professor in the 1950s and early 1960s appeared to pass from view, sadly gone, but with hope, not forever.

This anxious view of societal decline is a familiar theme in the rhetoric of the right. Culture Warriors often treat the 1960s as a significant turning point in recent U.S. history because this interpretation nicely supports their thesis about dangerous liberals dominating modern American society. The 1960s radicals have grown up, these conservatives point out, and they now hold prominent positions in the universities, the media, and other institutions. From centers of social power, liberals can now make an extraordinary impact on the American people's values. This influence is most unfortunate, Culture Warriors conclude. Important elements of social breakdown in modern America, they charge, can be traced to ideas and attitudes that liberals introduced in the 1960s.

The effort to blame virtually all of the nation's modern-day social problems on liberalism's influence in the 1960s and early 1970s ought to provoke amused disbelief from any reasonable observer, but it does not strike many writers from the right in that fashion. Consider the argument of R. Emmett Tyrrell Jr., the prominent conservative editor and author who has associated liberalism with just about every controversial social development that appeared in the culture revolutions of the 1960s. Tyrrell, a caustic critic of liberalism (and of some fellow conservatives), is founder of the right-wing journal *American Spectator,* an adjunct fellow at the Hudson Institute, and the author of a stinging political attack book called *Boy Clinton: The Political Biography* (1997). In *The Liberal Crack-Up* (1984) Tyrrell declares that liberals created "a riot of enthusiasms, usually contradictory, always extremist," in the late 1960s and early 1970s.[73] Virtually everything that seemed out of the mainstream and kooky could be identified with liberalism. Wacky fashions such as consciousness-raising, self-realization, and group therapy had their origins in the liberal perspective, Tyrrell asserts. Responsibility for black separatism, extremist opposition to the Vietnam War, and the drug culture could be placed at the feet of liberals. Tyrrell also claims that liberals used government's power to experiment with social engineering. Bureaucratic liberals were spreading the "chloroform of egalitarianism" because they "heaved overboard" the earlier American values of self-reliance, personal liberty, and competence.[74] Others, the "prophets of catastrophe," introduced fanatical environmentalism in the 1960s and 1970s. Tyrrell reserves his greatest sarcasm for feminism, which he considers an extension of liberalism. The feminist movement in the United States, he writes, "evolved into a lunatic jihad against femininity and manliness, a neurotic flight from biology, reproduction, and history itself."[75] Feminist "storm troopers" were rebelling "against the heterosexual paradise."[76] Liberalism was, in sum, "responsible for modern American life," particularly its crazy, extremist elements.[77]

A dozen years later Robert Bork published one of the most influential examples of the right's nostalgia for pre-1960s sobriety and civility in *Slouching toward Gomorrah: Modern Liberalism and American Decline* (1996). Before his controversial nomination to serve on the Supreme Court, Bork was best known as the solicitor general who had carried out President Richard M. Nixon's order to fire Watergate special prosecutor Archibald Cox after Cox had requested tape recordings of conversations in the Oval Office. Others had refused to participate in several firings that became known as the Saturday Night Massacre. Bork, a federal judge, spent many years as a law professor at Yale, where he established a strong reputation as the champion of the judicial philosophy known as "originalism." Bork argued that the Constitution needed to be understood in terms of the framers' original understanding of the document's terms. He looked critically upon supposedly loose interpretations of the Constitution that took into consideration the modern needs of society. Such exercises represented attempts to "legislate from the bench," said the originalists. When Ronald Reagan nominated Bork for the position of justice of the U.S. Supreme Court, many groups that were concerned about the rights of racial minorities and women lobbied against his nomination. Bork would not fully recognize a "right to privacy" in those hearings, a position that suggested he might vote to reverse *Roe v. Wade,* the Court's decision that established constitutional grounds for the right of a woman to have an abortion.

In *Slouching toward Gomorrah,* which contains numerous critical remarks on the cultural changes of the 1960s, Robert Bork approvingly recalls the calm ways of university life when he began his teaching career. Then everything seemed to come unraveled. America started a long period of "decline" beginning in the late 1960s, and the slippage has not been reversed, Bork concludes. In fact, the "rot is spreading."[78] University faculty members are to blame for much of the misery that entered American life in those years, he reports. They preached the principles of a "bankrupt philosophy" (liberalism) to their students.[79] Modern liberalism is a "corrosive agent" that expresses hostility to bourgeois society and culture, Bork maintains.[80] It is hostile to American values and the American nation. During the 1960s, many liberals argued that America was deeply immoral, racist, sexist, authoritarian, and imperialist. In turn, students were influenced by their professors' contempt for the society and expressed "rage against their own country."[81] They called U.S.

attempts to contain communism immoral and indulged in the rhetoric of Marxist revolution.

Liberalism in the 1960s also spawned social radicalism, Bork declares. It led to the removal of religion from the public arena, to the legitimizing of abortion, the sanctioning of sodomy as a private right, and the promotion of a radical form of feminism that viewed "the family as oppressive to individuals."[82] Bork, like Allan Bloom, associates liberalism with a breakdown in standards of musical appreciation. Americans no longer favored sophisticated musical entertainment after liberalism made its impact in the 1960s, he observes. They changed quickly from a fondness for the classics to a penchant for rap music, with its frequent references to dead policemen and mutilated women. In short, every branch of American culture was worse than it was before because values promoted by the liberals came into fashion in the 1960s.[83]

These lamentations about lost innocence in the 1960s have become a staple of the Culture Warriors' appeal. Over the years, critics on the right, such as Russell Kirk, Robert Nisbet, and David Horowitz, have expressed disgust with the way liberal teachings spawned revolutionary thinking and radical behavior on university campuses. Sixties liberalism ushered in these attitudes, they argue, and a 1960s-style outlook remains strong today.[84]

The modern-day relevance of the problem, according to these Culture Warriors, is the presence of 1960s radicals in prominent positions of power. As an editor for the *New Criterion* reports, the radical movement of the 1960s "is nowadays in the hands of the offspring of the counterculture."[85] Rush Limbaugh identifies this view in his usual hyperbolic language, claiming that "we're still reaping a bitter harvest from the seeds that were planted by the sixties kids. And now they're running things."[86] Limbaugh claims that many leaders in the Clinton administration were originally the flower children of the 1960s.[87]

Some Culture Warriors seem unable to get over the social disruptions of the 1960s. Elliott Abrams, a neoconservative hard-liner, is among the 1960s-obsessed ultras. Abrams, son-in-law of the noted neoconservative hawk Norman Podhoretz, served in high-ranking State Department and national security posts in the Reagan administration as well as in the administrations of President George H. W. Bush and his son George W. Bush. During the Reagan years Abrams faced accusations of covering up atrocities of right-wing regimes in Central America that had been supported by the

Reagan White House. Abrams was indicted for giving false testimony about illicit money raised in association with the Iran-Contra Affair. His guilty plea on two minor violations allowed him to return to political prominence in later years. Usually a hawk on foreign policy matters, Abrams appeared among the names of prominent conservative thinkers who signed a document in the late 1990s calling for regime change in Iraq.

Elliott Abrams appeared to be deeply moved by events on college campuses in the 1960s. A friend said Abrams acted as if he thought about half of the modern Democratic Party is made up of former radical members of the Students for a Democratic Society who had been taking over the universities during the tumultuous decade. "Elliott's still living in the world of the 1960s, where Harvard is about to be destroyed by revolutionaries who happen to be his fellow students," the friend noted. He called Abrams' perspective "a fixation in the past."[88]

The persistently negative images of the 1960s promoted by Allan Bloom and many others who fight the culture wars tend to astonish many scholars who stand outside the conservative movement. They are amused to see militant conservatives reading so much significance into this brief but tumultuous period. These observers recognize that a substantial number of young people in the late 1960s and early 1970s engaged in confrontational politics, radicalism, and "countercultural" activities (often identified in shorthand as sex, drugs, and rock 'n' roll). They understand, however, that much of that extraordinary behavior was ephemeral. Political radicalism passed quickly when the United States military pulled out of Vietnam and racial tensions diminished. Sex, drugs, and the new music remained, but later generations of youths did not worship at the Dionysian altar as naïvely as young Americans in the late 1960s did. In fact, many of the 1960s radicals later became fathers and mothers in suburbia, and, yes, some became stockbrokers. The Culture Warriors' efforts to treat 1960s-style cultural radicalism as if it is still in fashion and represents a key to understanding modern societal problems strikes many scholars as an exercise in exaggeration, simple-mindedness, and historical amnesia. Furthermore, that radicalism of the 1960s was not quintessentially liberal. Many liberals in the universities and the media complained during the 1960s about cultural radicalism. Observers note, too, that the legacy of the 1960s recalled by Americans in recent years is not particularly political or radical. When the U.S. Postal Service asked Americans to vote in 1998 on the subjects that best commemorated the 1960s, the winning topics related to cultural favorites, not political interests. The favorite themes for commemorative stamps were the Beatles, Woodstock, and *Star Trek*.[89]

Modern historical research suggests that American society and politics in the 1960s were not nearly as radical or liberal as the Culture Warriors often suggest. In their broad analysis of developments in the decade published in 2000 (*America Divided: The Civil War of the 1960s*), Maurice Isserman and Michael Kazin report that liberals did not perform very well in elections during the decade, and they usually constituted only a minority in Congress. For a brief time President Lyndon Johnson led a liberal resurgence with his Great Society programs, but his governmental efforts were poorly funded, and the war in Vietnam quickly eclipsed his War on Poverty. Toward the end of the decade, evidence of a newly vibrant conservative movement was already taking shape. It was noticeable in the growing ranks of evangelical Protestants, in the activities of business people, and among working-class Americans who demanded "law and order" in response to crime and riots.[90]

Other authors, too, find conservatism played a significant role in the 1960s, particularly radical forms of conservatism. David Farber and Jeff Roche provide more focused discussion of these conservative trends in an edited book appropriately titled *The Conservative Sixties* (2003). Contributors to the volume point to diverse signs of a growing conservative coalition in the 1960s that later made a tremendous impact on American culture and politics. The authors discuss themes such as "Cowboy Conservatism" in the Southwest, Ronald Reagan's political emergence in California, the importance of Phyllis Schlafly in promoting grassroots conservatism, the efforts of Protestant evangelicals to mobilize resistance to abortion, and the popularity of "law and order" appeals.[91] In other books scholars have thrown light on the importance of diverse conservative activities in the decade that Culture Warriors typically associate with leftist rebellion. Mary Brennan and Rick Perlstein have shown that Barry Goldwater's 1964 campaign set the stage for later conservative politics (Goldwater's fight was not, as is often assumed, the last gasp of the ultra-right).[92] Important studies of grassroots politics also reveal the emergence of strong local campaigns on the right. Particularly intriguing is Lisa McGirr's study *Suburban Warriors* (2001), which examines the ideas and campaign strategies of local conservatives in southern California. These works of scholarship reveal other sides of the 1960s that are not particularly liberal and certainly not radical leftist.[93] The investigations do not support simplistic characterizations of the period such as those employed by Culture Warriors.

### Theme Four: Identify the Enemy with Positions of Power and Influence in the Universities

Allan Bloom characterizes himself as a lonely crusader in *The Closing of the American Mind*. Throughout the book he suggests that U.S. universities are largely in the hands of liberals (although, for the most part, he uses other terms, including "relativists," to describe the dominant groups). Bloom suggests that someone like himself who wishes to challenge the ideas of influential liberal groups feels persecuted in the stifling campus environment of political correctness. His criticisms of professors and university administrators imply that he has been engaged in a noble but difficult fight against powerful forces. Advocates of the mistaken vision are corrupting the minds of the nation's students. They control the campuses and have managed to promote their outlook as the only authentic and legitimate perspective. Since academicians of the left hold positions of substantial influence, defying their authority takes great courage.

Bloom's characterization of political correctness is a familiar theme in the rhetoric of Culture Warriors. Militant right-wingers often describe liberals as possessors of enormous influence over ideas in American society. They claim that liberals dominate Hollywood, the news media, the government bureaucracies, and the nation's think tanks. Right-wing combatants in the culture wars give particular attention to the universities for two reasons. First, a critique of professors serves nicely to arouse class resentments. It suggests that privileged elitists working in ivory towers have little knowledge of the needs of average Americans, yet these haughty intellectuals are in the habit of pontificating about what is good for America's nonacademic citizens. Second, attention to the professors' writing and teaching suggests that these influential college instructors preach liberal propaganda to their impressionable students. Culture Warriors imply that liberals in the academy use their positions of prestige and power to ensure that their viewpoints remain ascendant and to censor conservative ideas in the campus environment. Also disturbing, say the Warriors, is the way liberal academics block access to membership in the university faculty. Liberals practice favoritism, they say, by placing only their compatriots in prominent teaching and administrative positions. In this manner, the intellectual left is engaged in a sort of conspiracy to insure that only one viewpoint—its own—prevails.

This criticism of universities resembles the fundamentalists' criticism of religious institutions. Like some evangelical Protestants and Orthodox Jews who have expressed disgust with modernist and secular-minded teachings in mainstream churches and synagogues, political fundamentalists often hurl their rhetorical axes at liberal education. In the manner of evangelical and Pentecostal spiritual leaders who were determined to challenge the prevalence of liberal theologians in religious seminaries, Culture Warriors seek to challenge the supposed dominance of liberals in America's institutions of higher learning.

Roger Kimball, author of the provocatively titled book *Tenured Radicals: How Politics Has Corrupted Our Higher Education* (1990), outlines some of the main points in this semiconspiratorial view of the liberal academics' supposed success in taking over the nation's universities. Kimball, an American art critic and copublisher of the *New Criterion,* has attacked political correctness in the world of art. He has contributed numerous articles to mainstream conservative publications, such as the *National Review,* the *Weekly Standard,* the *National Interest,* and the *Public Interest.* Kimball speaks alarmingly about the fate of U.S. higher education. He argues that conservatives need to take back the campuses and rescue students from the propaganda of liberal and radical professors. The left is working with a "blueprint for a radical social transformation," the author charges. It aims to "revolutionize every aspect of social and political life, from the independent place we grant high culture within society to the way we relate to one another as men and women."[94]

One important way to achieve that radicalization is through reorganizing the university curricula, Kimball proffers. Academic leftists are pushing traditional courses out of the list of core programs of study required of all students, he warns. Classes on the writings of Shakespeare and Milton are disappearing from the basic curriculum. The works of white European males are no longer required reading. Leftist professors substitute, instead, books and plays written by ethnic Americans, African Americans, Latinos, gays, and feminists, he declares.[95] Instructors are also offering courses that deal with popular culture, such as Hollywood movies, rock music, and comic strips. Some instructors, he notes, pander to students by teaching courses on the songs of Bruce Springsteen or the stories of television's *Star Trek* episodes. Other leftists, the deconstructionists, eagerly promote fashionable theories, including postmodernism and the new historicism.[96]

Like many radcon critics of academia in the late 1980s and early 1990s, Kimball draws attention to curricular changes that had occurred at Stanford University. He worries about the influence of the prestigious California institution that abandoned its traditional undergraduate core curriculum. Stanford's earlier program had concentrated on the great writers of Western civilization, but then it shifted to incorporate writers from the newly fashionable subjects. Kimball disdainfully reports that when Stanford's faculty debated issues concerning the core curriculum, Jesse Jackson and about 500 students marched on the campus, chanting, "Hey, hey, ho, ho, Western culture's got to go."[97]

William J. Bennett, who served Republican administrations as head of the National Endowment for the Humanities, secretary of education, and national drug czar, attacks liberal influence in the universities in a similar manner in *The De-Valuing of America: The Fight for Our Culture and Our Children* (1995). After leaving government positions, Bennett became a prolific author of conservatively oriented books, host of a radio program, *Morning in America,* and a Distinguished Fellow at the Heritage Foundation. Bennett fancies himself a lonely crusader against dangerous intellectuals in the universities. He writes in the fashion of a bold Cassandra who warns excitedly that radicals are taking control of America's institutions of higher learning while hardly anyone is prepared to accept the painful truth. Bennett claims that representatives of the academic left are indoctrinating students in the classrooms. Modern universities resemble medieval churches, he suggests. Leftist academicians are pontificating like the monks of yesteryear. Convinced of their own "purity," they believe they can make pronouncements on virtually anything with an air of "moral authority."[98] Bennett warns that Americans must reclaim their educational institutions in order to take back their culture. The battle against leftist bias in education is becoming "*the* central political debate" of modern times.[99]

Whereas Kimball and Bennett effectively display the radcons' case against political correctness in academic life, another conservative writer, the ever-combative Dinesh D'Souza, demonstrates skill in casting suspicion on virtually all professors who are not on the conservative bandwagon. D'Souza loosely conflates liberalism with radicalism, leaving the impression that there is little difference between the various academic intellectuals that stand outside the conservative realm. In *Letters to a Young Conservative* D'Souza tosses barbs at liberalism and radicalism continuously, making virtually no distinction between them. From paragraph to paragraph, he mixes, often indiscriminately, information about the academic left with comments about academic liberals. Frequently he offers an anecdote about a particular abuse by a radical figure in the university environment and then proceeds to make a general statement about liberals' ideas. Through much of the book, D'Souza practices guilt by association. He characterizes virtually all debates as two-part clashes. On one side are conservatives, defenders of sobriety, moderation, virtue, and wisdom. D'Souza places just about everyone else on the other side, identifying them, essentially, as extremists.

Dinesh D'Souza suggests that liberals harbor deep, hostile attitudes toward capitalism. He claims that deans and professors are "overwhelmingly" from the generation of the 1960s, implying not only that they had been students in that period but also that they have embraced the radical politics of the era. In those days, D'Souza explains, radical students believed that capitalism would disintegrate from its inner contradictions. They also expected Marxist guerrilla revolutions to break out all over the globe.[100] Eventually these former students became university professors and administrators. Their expectations have been dashed in modern times, the author notes. In recent years these leftist teachers and university officials have been "distressed" because the world is moving in a conservative direction. They cannot reverse the trend, he notes, but, at least, they can assert power in the one place where they have a chance to take control: the English Department, where leftists can dominate "their fetid little ponds."[101]

The charge made by D'Souza, Bloom, and others that liberals have enjoyed inordinate influence over ideas in the United States represents a gross exaggeration of a small reality. The circumstances are far more complex and the evidence of leftist bias much less impressive than Culture Warriors suggest in their heated rhetoric against political correctness on the campuses. In the 1970s and 1980s, especially, some leftists had gained a notable presence in specific sectors of American universities, although their prominence and power were never as hegemonic as critics from the militant right proclaimed. The academic left included professors who thought of themselves as socialists, Marxists, or neo-Marxists. Others were not sympathetic to communism or socialism but expressed much more enthusiasm for the welfare state and federal action than the American public. Some were cultural radicals. Several fancied themselves postmodernists or radical multiculturalists.

These academics never saw their influence spread broadly across the campuses and the nation; rather, the impact of their work was concentrated in particular university departments and in particular geographic areas. The academic left's clout was more evident in universities near the Atlantic and Pacific coasts of the Northeast and California than in the South, Southwest, Midwest, or the Rocky Mountain region. It was also more prominent in elite institutions. Complaints about university radicals were more applicable to the fields of literary and cultural studies, American studies, Latin American studies, and film studies than to other fields. Not many academic leftists (in the truly radical sense) held teaching positions in schools of education, business, the sciences, or engineering. Some academic leftists gained a footing in traditional fields of study such as history, philosophy, English, and sociology, but militant rightists exaggerate grossly when they charge that tenured radicals took over higher education.

Hard-core right-wing critics of academia never give much attention to the temporal nature of this condition. The influence of the political and cultural left, limited as it was, had its greatest effect in university departments during the 1970s and 1980s. Political disenchantment associated with the Vietnam War helped to make sharply critical perspectives on American society and history fashionable in some areas of university-based scholarship. In the 1970s and 1980s a new generation of scholars sometimes called Revisionists or the New Left offered damning indictments of American society and history. Their discontent over U.S. warmaking in Southeast Asia and conservative politics at home inspired sharply negative views of the United States and its legacy. By the late 1990s, however, the radical perspective had lost considerable support. In that period many more academics were challenging political correctness in higher education. Liberal historians themselves attacked the New Left's "revisionist" interpretations, including some of its sweeping critiques of American capitalism and foreign policy. Academic liberals also led the charge against postmodern excesses in literary studies and against radical multiculturalism. They were prominent leaders in campus efforts to restore elements of the core curriculum.

A variety of factors contributed to the decline of the academic left. The fall of the Soviet Union, the tragedy at Tiananmen Square, and other unflattering news about developments in communist states deeply weakened the left's case for intellectual legitimacy. Furthermore, during the 1990s, U.S. foreign policy was not as much an object of scorn as it had been in the tense years during and immediately after the Vietnam War. Also, during the 1990s leftist faculty members discovered that they had a substantial investment in the capitalist system. Successful marketing of their academic books, advancement to higher salaries associated with senior professorships, and mounting retirement funds amplified by a surge in the value of securities marketed on Wall Street took the edge off some of their discontent. Many of them had obtained a substantial stake in the "capitalist system" they had scorned in previous years.

Culture Warriors never tired of blaming liberals for the leftward tilt of some departments in some universities, but they rarely acknowledged the limited scope of the radicals' influence, and they paid little attention to changes in society and the universities that were reducing rather than augmenting the academic left's impact. Instead, Culture Warriors expanded their warnings. They spoke and wrote as if the specific conditions applied to all of the humanities and social sciences, and they acted as if trends in interpretation that had gained some favor in academia during the 1970s and 1980s had never fallen out of fashion. Their simplistic outlook, which cast suspicion on virtually all academicians who stood outside their conservative faith, left them blind to the liberals' struggle. They demonstrated almost no appreciation for the liberals' discomfort with the academic left and resistance to it.

In fact, it was the liberal faculty members who were most vociferous in challenging radical thought in scholarship and teaching. Conservative faculty members in the humanities and social sciences were less prominent in these academic battles during the 1980s and 1990s (and less numerous in these academic departments in the liberal arts and social sciences). Campus struggles for intellectual and scholarly influence in the 1980s and 1990s were essentially contests between liberal and leftist professors. Furthermore, liberals had been under attack in the 1960s and after not only from student radicals on the campuses but from scholars of the New Left who challenged their ideas about American history and politics. As John P. Diggins points out in his study of these divisions in academic settings, scholars representing the New Left pummeled liberals, saying they were too sympathetic to bourgeoisie, middle-class values and insufficiently critical of American capitalism and values. Liberalism did not adequately explain the nation's historical development, these leftists charged. Real insights required the mentality and tools of analysis employed by more radically inclined scholars. The New Left's representatives in the academy lost their influence in debates about history and politics, but some leftists in academia continued to exercise clout in intellectual exchanges by promoting esoteric European theories identified with "postmodernism."[102]

As in many other claims about liberal mischief, Culture Warriors blurred distinctions between liberals and radicals when commenting on university affairs. They bunched liberals and leftist ultras together and spoke anxiously about the ascendancy of the "left" in the nation's institutions of higher learning. In their interpretive scheme, anybody in academia who was not conservative was on the left and suspect. Employing generalizations with frequency, they treated moderates and radicals as one. By concealing the liberal academic's own discomfort with radical perspectives, radcons appropriated all credit for confronting political correctness in the universities. In their heroic narrative, they, alone, courageously took up the challenge against leftist excesses in the academy.

Distinctions are important in any discussion of the role of "liberalism" in the academy, and they are particularly important in discussions about the political proclivities of university professors. Radcons are eager to point out that inquiries made during the time of the 2004 presidential elections indicated that a substantial majority of university faculty members considered themselves Democrats and supported Senator John Kerry for president. Conservative pundit David Brooks was particularly eager to draw broad conclusions from this evidence about the political leanings of academics. He made an invidious comparison, suggesting that Americans who worked primarily with language, such as college professors, leaned heavily toward the Democrats, but people who dealt with numbers, such as accountants and business executives, preferred Republican candidates. The numerically oriented voters, Brooks hinted, had their feet on the ground and knew how to meet a payroll.

This kind of criticism, found in various forms of conservative rhetoric, obscures rather than clarifies the nature of political views in academia. The preference of university personnel for Democrats and Kerry in 2004 certainly does not indicate support for the radical left or rejection of hard-nosed, realistic concerns about economic conditions. Academia's greater comfort with Kerry and other Democratic candidates revealed a strong preference for centrist liberalism and conservatism and a clear rejection of the politics that George W. Bush's administration had been advancing energetically through four years of ultra-right leadership. If David Brooks believes professors should have embraced the Republicans' wreckage of the nation's budget surpluses, gigantic tax breaks for the rich, the undermining of work by agencies such as the Food and Drug Administration and the Environmental Protection Agency, a disastrous march into a quagmire in Iraq, and the campaign for an amendment on gay marriage, he is living in a dream world. Academics were turned off by the Republicans' wooing of Americans who oppose the teaching of evolution in public schools. They were appalled by George W. Bush's suggestion that *both* evolution and Intelligent Design could be taught and given equal standing in the study of science in the schoolhouse. Academics were alarmed, too, when President Bush placed barriers in the path of scientists who wished to conduct stem cell research and lightly dismissed the growing evidence pointing to global warming.

University personnel were also concerned when they learned that sixty influential scientists, including twenty Nobel laureates, complained that the Bush administration had systematically distorted scientific evidence to support its policy goals with respect to the environment, health, biomedical research, and nuclear weaponry. Scholars could hardly be enthusiastic about Republican leadership after the chairman of the board of directors at the Union of Concerned Scientists said that Bush's administration "engaged in practices that are in conflict with the spirit of science and the scientific method." Dr. Kurt Gottfried said the administration had a "cavalier attitude towards science" that could place the nation's long-term prosperity, health, and military prowess at risk.[103] Members of the Union of Concerned Scientists expressed concerns that were on the minds of many academics who were alarmed by the actions of the Bush team and other political leaders on the right.

Most academics find the radcon cause abhorrent. Those teachers and scholars are committed, above all, to the ideal of evidence-based judgments, not faith-based ones. Most university personnel are extremely uncomfortable with the ultraconservatives' preference for orthodoxy and their general close-mindedness. In this sense, the academics who preferred the Democrats and Kerry offered a "liberal" perspective in the best sense of the term. They were open-minded about conducting research, analyzing evidence, and drawing conclusions.

Paul Krugman, an economist, professor at Princeton, and *New York Times* columnist, addresses this issue persuasively when discussing the polls that revealed that registered Republicans and self-proclaimed conservatives constituted only a small minority of the faculties at elite universities in the United States. He notes that representatives of the right had a small presence not only among professors in the humanities and social sciences but also among teachers and scholars in the sciences and engineering. Krugman suggests that a principal reason for this pattern relates to the efforts by conservatives and Republicans to court Americans who attack science. Leaders on the right supported efforts to challenge the teaching of evolution in educational institutions. President George W. Bush declared that "the jury is still out" on evolution despite mountains of scientific evidence that support the concept. Republican senator James Inhofe dismissed the vast body of research behind the scientific consensus on climate change as a "gigantic hoax," and President Bush, too, had demonstrated little respect for climate research in his public statements. These and other antiscience positions sent a troublesome message. They indicated that the modern Republican Party is "increasingly dominated by people who believe truth should be determined by revelation, not research" and that the GOP "does not respect science, or scholarship in general." Under the circumstances, writes Krugman, "scholars have returned the favor by losing respect for the Republican Party."[104]

### Theme Five: Illustrate with Extreme Examples

Recall that Allan Bloom exposed the absurdity of black activists disrupting an economics professor's class. He reported that these students held the instructor's chairman and secretary hostage for ten hours, and their demands led to the professor's termination at the university. Bloom entertains his readers with other examples as well that illustrate outrageous behavior by partisans of the political and cultural left. He notes, for instance, that black students gained national publicity by appearing on Cornell University's campus armed with guns.[105] Bloom reports that Father Daniel Berrigan, a protest leader against the Vietnam War, said in a speech on the campus that old ladies who serve as secretaries for draft boards are the equivalent of the Beast of Belsen (referring to the commander of the Nazi concentration camp Bergen-Belsen) and do not deserve respectful treatment.[106] Regarding feminism, Bloom writes that he heard a female lieutenant colonel on the radio explaining that the only thing standing in the way of women's full equality in the military is male protectiveness. "So, do away with it!" Bloom responds with amusement.[107]

Such extreme examples of silly, even outrageous, behavior are familiar entries in the publications and arguments of the radical right. Culture Warriors delight in representing people and ideas they wish to criticize by citing extraordinary language and extraordinary actions. In the manner of religious fundamentalists, Culture Warriors characterize nonbelievers as frighteningly flawed—they ask readers and listeners, essentially: "Can you believe this? What will those crazy people of the left think and do next?"

The right's dualistic worldview tends to blur distinctions among supposed enemies. Liberals and radical leftists look similar in this dichotomous scheme. When there are two essential categories for consideration, the right and the wrong, those who stand outside the faith, whatever their differences with each other, look equally threatening.

Hilton Kramer and Roger Kimball, skilled practitioners of this radcon strategy, offer demonstrations of the approach throughout their edited book, *The Betrayal of Liberalism: How the Disciples of Freedom and Equality Helped Foster the Illiberal Policies of Coercion and Control* (1999). Kramer had been an art critic for many years with *The Nation,* and he also commented on art for the *New York Times.* Kramer worked with Kimball as chief publisher and editor of the *New Criterion.* Kramer, Kimball, and their contributors provide one example after another of guilt by presumed association with radicalism. Each of the assembled authors conflates liberalism with extremism and exhibits no embarrassment when drawing the connection. Throughout the essays, individual contributors to the book offer specific complaints about liberals and then quickly slip into descriptions of radical thought and radical behavior. The authors leave a strong impression that modern liberalism in the United States has morphed into the philosophy and politics of the far left.

The title of Kramer and Kimball's book is deceiving because it suggests, on its face, a concern about saving liberalism from reckless individuals who betrayed it by advocating illiberal practices. Many liberals would agree with that conclusion. This is not the contributors' actual theme, however. Instead of defending liberalism, as the title implies, the authors attack it relentlessly and suggest that liberals have become radicals who no longer express American values. Liberalism, they argue, has become an alien concept in U.S. society.

In their introduction Kramer and Kimball demonstrate the technique of associating liberalism with extremism. They associate liberalism with socialism, communism, and religious fanaticism. "Socialism was an ideal toward which all liberal sentiment was inevitably inclined" in the years before World War II, the editors claim, and they charge that many liberals of that time believed the Soviet Union was, despite its many faults and failures, the most "loved and the most advanced society in the history of the world."[108] When describing attitudes in the 1960s, Kramer and Kimball report that liberals found heroes in Fidel Castro, Ho Chi Minh, and Che Guevara. This newer generation of liberals, they say, was "as susceptible to totalitarian temptation as their elder counterparts had been in the 1930s."[109] Kramer and Kimball assert, too, that during the 1960s liberals expressed interest in controversial national leaders, including communists (e.g., Fidel Castro and Mao Zedong) and religious revolutionaries (e.g., Iran's Ayatollah Khomeini). They connect 1960s liberalism as well to the neo-Marxist intellectual Herbert Marcuse (who claimed that democratic institutions, including freedom of speech and assembly, represent alibis for oppressive state power). The French intellectual Michel Foucault appears in this indictment as well. He was a favorite of American liberal intellectuals, the authors claim, and Foucault displayed interest in LSD and sadomasochism (in gay bars, no less).[110] Without a tinge of embarrassment about these claims, Kramer and Kimball associate diverse examples of thought and behavior with liberalism (often by implication), even though liberals tend not to be genuine enthusiasts of Castro, Zedong, Khomeini, Marcuse, Foucault, and other figures whom they discuss.

The editors demonstrate their greatest chutzpah in presuming guilt by association when charging Hillary Rodham Clinton (First Lady at the time) with radical sympathies. Kramer and Kimball focus on a speech that Clinton delivered at the University of Texas in 1993. In this supposedly controversial address, Clinton offered words of inspiration to the students by calling for a "new politics of meaning." Her idealistic appeal promoted altruism. Clinton's message was similar to the kind delivered by many visiting dignitaries who challenge college students to make worthwhile contributions to humankind. Clinton said, "We need a new definition of civil society which answers the unanswerable question posed by both the market forces and the governmental ones, as to how we can have a society that fills us up again and makes us feel that we are part of something bigger than ourselves."[111] How radical!

Kramer and Kimball note that Clinton borrowed the politically correct words, "new politics of meaning," from the writings of "left-wing activist" Michael Lerner. Lerner, a rabbi based in San Francisco, is a political commentator and editor of a left-wing Jewish magazine, *Tikkun*. Although a Zionist, Lerner had opposed Israeli control over Palestinian territories, a position that has brought him sharp criticism from nationalist and right-oriented Jewish leaders who support the policies of Israel's Likkud Party. Michael Lerner has gained a reputation in the United States as a promoter of ecumenical activities who urges his fellow Jews to reject ethnocentric attitudes. He is, in sum, a quintessential liberal Jew.

Kramer and Kimball charge that Lerner had made wacky recommendations about public issues in some of his commentaries. He argued, for instance, that corporate executives should not be allowed to close their manufacturing plants without obtaining a social-environmental impact statement on the human consequences of their actions. For Hilton and Kramer, this provocative recommendation shows that Lerner is an "academic totalitarian." And to think, the First Lady took his ideas quite seriously![112] Of course, it did not matter to Kramer and Kimball that Hillary Rodham Clinton had not endorsed all the details of Michael Lerner's political agenda and had only invoked a few words from his many publications. The editors readily assumed that a reference to Lerner's thought—even this brief one—suggested broad agreement with the writer's diverse perspectives. In attacking the First Lady for employing this language, Kramer and Kimball put on a stunning example of the Culture Warriors' practice of guilt by association.

Furthermore, while Lerner stood further to the left than Kramer and Kimball would like, he was hardly a wild-eyed extremist. Michael Lerner has written several books that advocate peaceful relations between blacks and Jews in the United States and between Israelis and Palestinians in the Middle East. One of them, *The Politics of Meaning* (which was the object of Hillary Clinton's reference and Kimball and Kramer's wrath), offers upbeat, positive messages. The book's subtitle is *Restoring Hope and Possibility in an Age of Cynicism*. In view of the cynical reading Kramer and Kimball gave Lerner's publication, it appears that the two Culture Warriors should have studied Lerner's message more carefully.

They might have learned some valuable lessons for life from Lerner's more cheerful perspective.

Contributors to Kramer and Kimball's *The Betrayal of Liberalism* follow the editors' lead by offering their own abundant loose associations of liberalism with extremism. Essayist Roger Scruton, a British philosopher and broadcaster noted for his public support of traditional fox hunting, claims, for example, that the curricular proposals made by liberals "will in time destroy our universities." Keith Windshuttle, an Australian historian who has decried the leftward-leaning interpretations of academics, lambastes liberals for leveling damning indictments against Western culture (liberals, he claims, dismiss that culture as imperialistic).[113] Robert Conquest, a former communist who achieved distinction as a historian of Stalin's crimes in the Soviet Union, asserts that many liberal academics are apologists for the Stalinist regime and other repressive governments. John Silber, the longtime president and later chancellor of Boston University who was noted for an imperial style of academic leadership, also regrets developments of the 1960s. He recalls earlier times of confrontation on his campus when Marxists, socialists, and other radical groups tried to seize control of faculty search committees, scare the Reserve Officer Training Corps (ROTC) away from the university, and prevent individuals from giving speeches on the campus.[114] Silber, an experienced administrator, is, at least, more skillful than the other authors at concealing his purposes. He presents lots of ugly examples of totalitarian-style behavior on campuses that suggest connections between liberalism and radicalism, but Silber acknowledges that anyone who joined the campus thought-police in those lively days of campus revolution could not genuinely be called a liberal.[115]

Culture Warriors often suggest liberalism leads to radicalism by pointing to a particularly egregious example of totalitarian-style behavior on the college campuses. They identify an outrageous attempt to interfere with freedom of expression on a campus and then hint, often by innuendo and sometimes through a direct charge, that liberals are intolerant of "politically incorrect" views from the right. These ultras frequently report on incidents in which militant leftist groups attempted to harass or silence conservative speakers or deny students opportunities to read the works of conservative writers. Almost effortlessly they slip back and forth from discussions of radical, censorious behavior to comments about liberalism. Dinesh D'Souza, the right-wing author described earlier, is a master of this technique of associating radical *behavior* with liberal *thought*.

In *Letters to a Young Conservative* D'Souza attempts to make liberals look like disgusting enemies of free speech. D'Souza describes interruptions he experienced while delivering a lecture on a college campus. Some people in the auditorium, who belonged to an international socialist group called the Spartacus League, resisted his conservative message and tried to deny the microphone to him. They waved placards that identified D'Souza as a "RACIST AGENT OF U.S. CAPITALISM AND IMPERIALISM." One extremist in the crowd yelled, "You'll be lucky to get out of here alive." Then a large disheveled woman screamed, "We don't need a debate! Stop this man from speaking!" When the campus police dragged her from the room, the woman shouted, "I'm being censured!" D'Souza drew an extraordinary conclusion from this confrontation with censorious radicals. He asked, "Is this what liberals stand for?" Then the author responded confidently, "Today, alas, it is."[116]

Obviously, American liberals would be greatly surprised to learn that the boisterous socialist protesters from the Spartacus League who tried to block D'Souza from addressing a crowd spoke for liberalism. Most liberals view such behavior as despicable. They would condemn it as blatantly opposed to the principles of a free society and contrary to the ideals of a university. For D'Souza, however, this incident revealed the essence of modern liberalism. Describing himself as a bold defender of freedom against tyrants in academia, he delivered the familiar heroic narrative of his faith.

Dinesh D'Souza makes many other references to academic intolerance in his book, hinting that campus liberals are advocates of political censorship. He argues that "classical liberals" of earlier times believed in free speech and asserts confidently that today "the left does not believe in free speech."[117] D'Souza describes a number of instances in which groups and individuals on college campuses displayed intolerance toward lecturers who expressed views of the right. Political correctness, he suggests, remains a powerful force in campus life. Like Kramer and Kimball, D'Souza draws attention to the intolerance of Herbert Marcuse, the neo-Marxist philosopher who attracted a following on college campuses in the 1960s. Like angry members of the Spartacus League, Marcuse wanted to restrict speech for people who expressed ideas he opposed.[118] Nowhere in this discussion does D'Souza acknowledge that Marcuse was not a favorite of liberal professors in the 1960s or today. Nor does he recognize that liberals generally find offensive the other censorious actions he cites, such as the efforts of left-wing campus activists to silence Jeane Kirkpatrick, President Ronald Reagan's ambassador to the United Nations, when she tried to speak at a university. D'Souza leaves the impression, too, that liberals applauded the actions of campus leftists who attempted to prevent a speech on campus by Adolfo Calero, a Nicaraguan Contra leader. After describing these regrettable efforts to deny freedom of expression, he readily associates the mentality and behavior with liberalism. Like Kramer, Kimball, and many other radcons, D'Souza knows how to play the game of guilt by association.

### Rule Six: Lambaste Identity-Conscious Minorities

Allan Bloom engaged in one of the favorite practices of the militant right when he singled out blacks and women for particular criticism. Many Culture Warriors echo Bloom's complaints about race- and gender-based politics, and they add a good deal of complaining about gays as well. They speak often about groups who appear to think of themselves first as minorities and only secondly as full-fledged Americans (the association of women with minorities is, of course, semantic, for the group constitutes a numerical majority of the population; the term *minority* applies to a group's sense of suffering from a denial of rights). Participants in the culture wars frequently argue that minorities' campaigns for recognition and protection of race, ethnic, or gender interests do not truly advance the cause of equality.

Identity politics promote separatism, they argue. Blacks who indulge in ethnocentric appeals undermine assimilation, integration, and unity. Far too many African Americans want special, privileged treatment that other Americans are not qualified to receive. Affirmative action, they say, has no place in an equality-conscious society.

Culture Warriors also denigrate feminists as radicals who revolt against nature and undermine the security of the American family. They dismiss feminist claims about sexism as the ranting of psychologically discontent and abrasive individuals who have failed to find personal happiness in traditional male-female relationships.

Until recently many Culture Warriors lambasted gays as well for engaging in identity politics, and their literature included critical remarks about homosexual lifestyles (the matter did not attract much attention from Allan Bloom, for he was gay). In view of recent shifts in public opinion and a Supreme Court decision that affirms rights for gays, many but not all culture-minded conservatives have changed their focus. Instead of suggesting a general disapproval of gay practices, they have pulled back to what looks like a more defensible position in view of shifts in mainstream public opinion. Culture Warriors now treat opposition to same-sex marriage as a desperate finger-in-the-dike approach for saving civilization, protecting morality, and affirming family values.

When writing and speaking about African Americans, Culture Warriors often criticize blacks for identity consciousness but give almost no attention to the historical conditions that have energized their attitudes. Conservatives often complain about separatist inclinations but say little about the history of slavery, racism, and discrimination that fostered group-interest politics. Many commentators from the radical right generally disapprove of blacks' attempts to emphasize a distinctive culture and distinctive needs. They counsel blacks to consider themselves primarily as Americans, not as *African* Americans. The Culture Warriors disapprove of blacks' efforts to lobby for their particular interests. Corporations or other economic groups may lobby for their private interests, conservatives acknowledge, but African American engagement in such activities receives the right's stern criticism. Blacks should approach most political issues as individuals, these conservatives recommend, rather than as representatives of a racial group with distinctive cultural and economic needs.

Culture Warriors focus on negative characteristics of identity politics and give almost no attention to positive ones. Dinesh D'Souza, the noted polemicist of the right discussed earlier in this chapter, provides a good example of this approach in *What's So Great about America* (2002). D'Souza is sanguine in his overall conclusions about conditions in the United States. Unlike militant social conservatives of earlier years such as Weaver, Kirk, Bloom, and Bork (who lamented a decline of American civilization), D'Souza is bubbly and upbeat in his assessment of the state of American society. He says dreams come true in the United States. America is a place where the poor native-born citizen and the newly arrived immigrant have the best chances in the world to improve their lives. When D'Souza comments on the place of African Americans in this New World paradise, however, his summary turns profoundly gloomy. D'Souza's attention is riveted on the complaints that some African

Americans have leveled against U.S. society. He claims that Jesse Jackson has applied outrageous pressure tactics to force companies and the federal government to provide jobs for blacks. D'Souza notes with dismay that some African Americans claim the Scholastic Assessment Tests (SATs) are culturally biased. Race-minded people seem to blame every problem faced today by African Americans on slavery and racism, he fumes. Angry black militants demand "reparations" for America's record of exploitation, discrimination, and oppression, D'Souza reports. Then, evidently to protect himself from charges of presenting a completely negative view of a minority, D'Souza cites some examples of successful blacks. He points out that many immigrants from the Caribbean and Africa are doers, not complainers. They focus on the future instead of the past.[119]

Dinesh D'Souza fails to recognize that the angry viewpoints expressed by various American blacks do not represent the totality of African American opinion these days, and they certainly do not substantially represent the modern "liberal" position with which he associates the ideas.[120] In D'Souza's scheme virtually all African American and liberal commentators on race demand support for Jesse Jackson's PUSH organization, view college entrance exams as notoriously slanted in favor of whites, attribute virtually all of African Americans' problems to slavery and racism, and call for all U.S. taxpayers to pay billions in reparations to aggrieved blacks. An association of those attitudes with liberalism exists in the simple imagination of Dinesh D'Souza rather than in the complex realities of liberal politics.

While D'Souza complains frequently about blacks' attitudes and behavior, his assessment of their current opportunities is blissful. He suggests that problems associated with racial inequality have been mostly overcome. "The laws were changed, and blacks achieved their goal of full citizenship," D'Souza reports confidently. He acknowledges that "enforcement remained an issue," but concludes that the fundamental goals advocated years before by the noted African American leader W. E. B. Du Bois have now been "largely achieved."[121] With that cheerful note, D'Souza recommends that blacks try to improve their individual lot in a society that seems largely free of racial obstacles. This pleasant assessment of American society's current situation, like that of many other Culture Warriors, suggests that race is no longer a relevant issue.

Despite D'Souza's assurances, the issue of race has remained on the minds of many social conservatives in modern times. It was on display when some right-wingers rallied around Alabama governor George Wallace's campaigns for the presidency. Richard Nixon referred subtly to race when he used code words such as "law and order" to excite the fears of urban- and suburban-based whites. Republicans have drawn tremendous support in recent years from white southerners and northern white ethnics who gave them a "backlash" vote. Many of these individuals had been Democrats but switched to the Republicans because they thought the Democrats were responding too eagerly to the interests of African Americans (especially through support for busing and affirmative action). Republicans have tried to disguise their racial appeal to whites by parading a few African Americans before American television audiences at opportune moments. These symbolic gestures were especially evident at the GOP national conventions, where party planners situated blacks prominently near the TV cameras.[122]

It would be a mistake, however, to assume that militant conservatism is attractive only to whites. Elements of the Stealth Libertarian, Culture Warrior, and Hawkish Nationalist perspectives of the militant right sometimes attract prominent African Americans as well. These individuals are drawn to the conservatives' strong convictions and penchant for philosophical discourse. Black conservatives, like many other figures on the right, favor fundamentalist-style certainties. When they talk about societal problems, they express confidence in right-oriented interpretations and frequently display strong suspicion of liberal perspectives. Some of them are outspoken critics of affirmative action. Their ranks include prominent and talented commentators on national and international affairs, such as Thomas Sowell, an economist at the Hoover Institution who is a prolific author; Glenn Loury, an economist at Boston University who has made numerous appearances on television; Alan Keyes, a former State Department official who had his own radio show; Walter Williams, an economist at George Mason University who sometimes served as substitute host on Rush Limbaugh's radio talk show; and Stephen Carter, a professor at the Yale Law School who has achieved distinction as the author of both nonfiction and fiction books. Also noteworthy is Supreme Court justice Clarence Thomas, who though generally reticent about his views in public gives expression to conservative sympathies in rulings in the Court's cases.

The Culture Warriors' portrayal of feminism tends to be quite critical. While liberals generally view the rise of gender consciousness and the

feminist movement as natural responses to the record of inequality, social conservatives often portray feminism as an irrational and dangerous
movement that threatens the American people's traditions and values.
Culture Warriors describe feminists as extremists who express views that
reasonable, mainstream Americans reject. The Warriors' political narratives offer virtually no examples of statements by intelligent, balanced,
and responsible feminists. The women cited in their commentaries tend
to be hard-core extremists who hate men, despise families, and wish to
escape responsibility for raising children. In view of these characterizations it is not surprising that right-wing narratives portray these women
as serious threats to the family and motherhood.

George F. Gilder published one of the Warriors' most notable early assaults on feminism. Gilder championed ideas about markets as well as social issues while serving as program director at the Manhattan Institute,
contributing editor for the *National Review,* and speechwriter for leading
Republicans. In *Sexual Suicide* (1973) he blames women for the growing
incidence of divorce in the 1960s and early 1970s. The women's movement aimed to emancipate Americans from the family, he charges. Feminists wanted to make marriage more open, flexible, and subject to cancellation. Their campaign threatened a greater incidence of divorce, which
was "already opening up all over the country and spewing forth swarms of
delinquents and neurotics, or swarms of middle-aged men and women
looking for sexual utopia that is advertised everywhere."[123] Feminists
sought to make marriage and family life more optional, bisexual, and an-
drogynous. These so-called reformers claimed they were trying to hu-
manize men, Gilder notes, but, in fact, they were emasculating them.[124]

Feminism's challenge to American society is no small matter, Gilder
concludes. Its radical obsession with individualism and equality could
lead to a crisis in procreation in which Americans might not be able to re-
produce themselves.[125] In this and in other examples of horrible scenar-
ios, Gilder and other right-wing ultras try to paint frightening pictures of
feminism's impact on American life.

Rush Limbaugh is, of course, among the most famous denigrators of
the feminist persona. His descriptions of feminists often sound like
entries in a book on freakish behavior. In *The Way Things Ought to Be*
(1992) Limbaugh refers to feminists as "femi-nazis" and attempts to
protect himself from critics by declaring that hard-core militants are
different from other well-intentioned "but misguided" women who call

themselves feminists.[126] Limbaugh claims that the feminist movement started out as a genuine and sincere effort to improve conditions but later morphed into a loud, militant campaign of femi-nazis.[127] Then, in a book published a year later, *See, I Told You So* (1993) Limbaugh changes course and suggests that the supposedly small hard-core, radical group is not simply on the margins of the women's movement. Instead, he places them at the center. In the 1993 publication Limbaugh claims that radical women *set the agenda* for the feminist movement. Militants are "the people who define modern feminism," he asserts.[128] They are its head and heart.

According to Limbaugh, the feminists have a frightening plan for change. They want to make men fearful of expressing amorous interest in women. Some female militants seek to criminalize the process of courtship. They want men arrested for sounding a wolf-whistle at comely women.[129] Others want to entrap men when they engage in a carnal relationship. Limbaugh notes that a feminist professor at the University of Michigan law school called for an expansive definition of rape. "Politically," said the female professor, "I call it rape whenever a woman has sex and feels violated."[130] Such a definition could, of course, leave millions of men vulnerable to charges of sexual attack. After reviewing this troublesome example, Rush Limbaugh slips quickly into a discussion of transsexual behavior. He describes a "lesbian" who became the tenth wife of a gay con-man bigamist and an originally male transsexual who took injections of liquid silicone to enlarge his buttocks.[131] Limbaugh's previous treatment of feminism as a circus sideshow of freakish behavior makes the transition to transsexual extravagance seem quite natural.

Wacky feminism is also a principal subject of discussion in Phyllis Schlafly's *Feminist Fantasies* (2003). Schlafly was a longtime leader of the radical right's antifeminist crusade. She attracted attention from Republican leaders in the 1950s when she ran unsuccessfully for Congress. In the 1960s Schlafly wrote a best-seller that championed Barry Goldwater's campaign for the presidency, *A Choice, Not an Echo*. Early in the 1970s she organized the Eagle Forum to promote conservative perspectives, especially on women's issues, and she became one of the conservatives' most influential campaigners in their efforts to defeat of the Equal Rights Amendment. Schlafly also became a noted tribune for militantly anticommunist positions on Cold War issues and a critic of various plans for U.S. negotiations with the Soviet Union.

*Feminist Fantasies* offers a lengthy catalog of horror stories about feminist activities and hardly a word of appreciation for the efforts American feminists have made to improve the lot of women in recent decades. For instance, Schlafly judges Title IX, the federal program designed to enhance the presence of women in sports, a mischievous initiative. It served "as a machete to destroy the sports at which men excel," she reports. The law resulted in drastic reductions in the size of men's varsity wrestling and gymnastic teams at U.S. colleges.[132]

*Feminist Fantasies* claims the women's movement seeks a radical agenda that aims to transform traditional views of marriage and motherhood. Schlafly states confidently that "feminists strove to eliminate the role of stay-at-home wife by making it socially disdained, economically disadvantaged, and legally shorn of traditional protections."[133] She charges feminists and their political allies with making relentless attacks on traditional marriage. Feminists, she says, promote serial marriages and encourage women to romp around in sexual adventures in the manner of men who participate in causal sex.[134] They think "it is demeaning to women to care for their babies, and therefore the role of motherhood should be eliminated and daycare should be a government responsibility so that women can fulfill themselves in the paid labor force."[135] The feminists' ultimate goal is to achieve complete equality with men in every way, Schlafly concludes. They "want to gender neutralize society so they can intimidate and control men."[136] Marriage is endangered in Schlafly's disturbing analysis. Her narrative suggests that feminists are creating a social crisis by challenging the American people's core values.[137]

When Culture Warriors speak of women's attitudes about careers, they often assume the damning posture displayed by Phyllis Schlafly. Legitimate expressions of concern for women's opportunities hardly merit their attention. Instead, Culture Warriors focus on highly questionable examples. They cite particularly radical and eccentric forms of feminist behavior and treat those samples as if they were typical. Like religious fundamentalists, Culture Warriors often describe the "other" who stands outside their faith in sharply negative, emotion-laden, and simplistic terms.

These descriptions of feminism have little to do with the actual attitudes of most modern-day feminists. The women's movement has evolved considerably and cast aside the draconian choices implied in the agendas of some of the early radical feminists. Back in the 1960s and 1970s some American women participated in the "mommy wars," debating whether it was best to commit themselves to careers or to raising children. Beginning around the 1980s, however, many who expressed feminist interests rejected the militant agendas that looked upon family life and child-rearing with condescension and even scorn.[138] These individuals promoted a different kind of feminism, one that offered "choices." They said women should decide for themselves whether to forge a strong career path or to concentrate on household responsibilities, motherhood, and marriage. These moderate feminists understood that women often choose both paths rather than one or the other. Developing a comfortable balance between duties in the workplace and the home has always been a major challenge.[139] Some women deal with these difficulties by shifting the emphasis as their children pass infancy, attend school, and go off to college or a job. "Choice feminists" stress the importance of tolerance and respect for all women as they make these difficult decisions, especially in cases where the woman is well-educated and faces good opportunities to build a professional career.

This tolerance applies to the women described by Louise Story in a 2005 article in the *New York Times*. Story found that many women in America's elite colleges, including universities in the Ivy League, were choosing to get married, stay home, and raise a family—despite their excellent prospects for moving into leadership roles in business, government, and academia.[140] Linda R. Hirshman, the strong-minded feminist who coined the term "choice feminism," complained about such individuals, arguing that they hurt overall opportunities for women by abandoning the track that leads to power.[141] Interestingly, liberal women criticized Hirshman for defining feminism in an authoritarian manner and defining success only in terms of gaining money, power, and status in career pursuits.[142]

Modern feminism has morphed into a complex and varied perspective that involves many different opinions. It is not a phenomenon that is well understood by the Culture Warriors who are trapped in old and simplistic visions of the kind of people Rush Limbaugh likes to call "femi-nazis."

### Rule Seven: Identify Enemies with Clarity but Treat Solutions with Vagueness

Allan Bloom's exposition of conditions that are troublesome and despicable in modern America is explicit and focused, but his recommendations for remedying the situation are quite vague and indeterminate.

Bloom leaves no doubt about the forces that produced degeneration. "Value relativism," rock music, sexual promiscuity, multiculturalism, and other fashions have undermined morality and civility, he charges. They have brought down high culture, elevated low culture, and weakened the fabric of American civilization. Bloom's view of the troublemakers is clear in his writings: his enemies were black and feminist militants, the academic left, university administrators without convictions or backbone, and curriculum reformers.

Allan Bloom was much less willing to suggest solutions to these problems. Of course, he advocated a strong place for Great Books in the university curricula, but a return to traditional instruction in the core courses could hardly serve as a broadly satisfactory response to the many difficulties that he identified. Throughout Bloom's lengthy exposition he sidesteps a discussion of proposed solutions. He expresses passionate discontent with modern ideas and practices but leaves readers with only obscure recommendations about how they could return to Truth.

This inclination to avoid discussion of remedies is a familiar characteristic in the writings and speeches of the Culture Warriors. They are animated in identifying problems that trouble them and point clearly to liberals as principal culprits, but they offer few proposals for dealing specifically with the problems. Right-wing ultraconservatives provide a sharp picture of what they hate, but a hazy view of the better world they wish to bring into view.

This nebulousness serves a useful purpose, for it saves Culture Warriors from acknowledging the reactionary implications of their outlook. The Warriors often describe social problems in frightening language but resist identifying specific solutions for them. This strategy conceals the censorious nature of their judgments and the intrusive character of their likely solutions. Responding directly to Bloom's disgust for rock music, for example, might lead to censorship of some musical entertainment. Challenging the supposed "liberal" influence in America's universities can involve a political litmus test designed to promote the hiring of conservatives. Public disgust for these and other measures aimed at correcting ills described in the frightening commentaries of Culture Warriors would likely hurt the right in the political arena. Consequently, most Warriors bemoan the nation's social problems rather than offer specific remedies for them.

The Culture Warriors' political campaigns often appear to be aimed at arousing the True Believers in their camp rather than convincing the broader population outside their ranks. Rightist leaders evidently recognize that some of their outlandish proposals cannot win public approval, yet their failed efforts to turn radical ideas into legislation can excite enthusiasm from the faithful. Republican leaders in Congress demonstrated that tactic in September 2004 when they demanded a vote in the House of Representatives on the question of gay marriage. The GOP representatives sought a constitutional amendment that would define marriage in terms of a relationship between a man and a woman and, therefore, deny the legal recognition of wedlock to same-sex couples. In their political speeches, the representatives hailed this effort as a means to fortify the institution of marriage in America. The country was troubled by problems of divorce and difficulties resulting from great numbers of children being born out of wedlock, they said. Family life was already in jeopardy, and it could be further weakened by public acceptance of same-sex marriages. Yet the United States Senate had already rejected the proposal for a constitutional amendment, and it was clear that social conservatives did not have enough votes in the House of Representatives to pass their bill. Nevertheless, they pressed the case against gay marriages, hoping to arouse the interest of numerous Culture Warriors across the country shortly before the 2004 national elections. It did not matter that their proposals would not truly remedy problems associated with the modern American family or that their legislation had virtually no chance of passage in the Congress. The symbolic gesture of anguish, disgust, and protest sufficed as a way to deal with the cultural right's vague lamentations about social problems in America.

Thomas Frank, author of *What's the Matter with Kansas?*, notes that this kind of symbolic protest often serves to direct the frustrations of poor and middle-class Americans against an imagined elite of powerful liberals. Kansas senator Sam Brownback offered a representative example of this perspective when he claimed that the liberal elite was scheming (along with supporters in the courts) "to redefine marriage and impose a radical social experiment on our entire society."[143] Like Brownback, other leaders on the right told the conservative faithful that America's common people were being trampled upon by know-it-all intellectuals. This strategy helped to mobilize their political forces. "Losing is prima facie evidence that the basic conservative claim is true," Frank explains. It proves, in the eyes of the faithful, "that the country is run by liberals; that the world is unfair; that the majority is persecuted by a sinister elite." Notions about a liberal elitist conspiracy could excite a vigorous right-wing presence at the polling places on the day of elections, and that was the main purpose of the rhetorical posturing.[144]

The familiar litany of complaints about liberalism that Allan Bloom detailed in *The Closing of the American Mind* is, of course, grossly distorted, yet it finds expression in numerous political tracts and speeches of the Culture Warriors. Employing several or all of the seven major elements of this genre, cultural conservatives assail liberalism as a principal source of America's social problems. Like Bloom, they blame liberalism for contributing to a state of social crisis. They criticize liberal "relativism" and demand Truth. Warriors point to the 1960s, particularly, as the time when liberal ideas began to create troubles, and they identify liberals with positions of power and influence in the nation's universities. Culture Warriors often cite extreme examples of radical behavior when criticizing liberals. Many of them lambaste identity-conscious minorities (who they associate with liberalism). Finally, they identify liberal enemies clearly but offer only vague and often unworkable solutions for dealing with the diverse social problems that they attribute to liberalism.

The world of the Culture Warrior seems strange, indeed, to the outsider. Critics of the Warriors' perspectives find their descriptions of America's social tensions grossly exaggerated and filled with fantasy. They view the right's anxious claims about the growing power of radical professors, militant blacks, crazed feminists, anarchic counterculturists, and strident multiculturalists far-fetched, even laughable. Regarding the conservatives' preoccupation with the 1960s, these critics are apt to respond: get over it—the 1960s passed long ago. Yet for lots of people inside the modern conservative movement, these frightening visions are considered seriously. Like nervous fundamentalists who embrace religious traditions and fear change, many on the right share an apocalyptic vision of a society in deep crisis as it embraces modernity.

## CHAPTER SIX

# Hawkish Nationalists

Liberal Democrats, and quite a few moderate Republicans as well, were shocked in the three years after September 11, 2001, when they saw President George W. Bush's administration quickly turn aggressive and militaristic in U.S. relations with the world. The most dramatic example of this surprising shift in foreign affairs concerned the war with Iraq. The Bush administration showed contempt for traditional European allies in the buildup toward war, acted unilaterally in making important decisions, and opted for an unusual preemptive strike against the Iraqi regime. The United States went to war without support from the United Nations. U.S. troops occupied Iraq with only token assistance from an unimpressive "coalition," and U.S. leaders defended this extraordinary intervention as an admirable enterprise that could bring freedom and democracy to Iraq's oppressed populace. Americans who were critical of these developments were amazed to see that cautious policies that involved broad-based international cooperation, which had been promoted during the previous fifty years, could be abandoned so easily and brazenly.[1]

A central question that fascinates anyone who examines America's rapid shift in the early twenty-first century to a swaggering, unilateral, and hawkish foreign policy concerns the rather placid way many Americans reacted to the change. A substantial group—often a majority in the first years after September 11—accepted and defended the extraordinary deviations from mainstream U.S. foreign policy. Why didn't more citizens complain about the Bush administration's actions in view of this momentous change and the difficulties that developed from American occupation of Iraq? Why did many Americans continue to believe the administration's mistaken claims about Saddam Hussein's readiness to use weapons of mass destruction, including nuclear weapons, when abundant evidence appeared in the news indicating that the Iraqi government had not done much recently to produce WMDs? Why did a substantial proportion of the citizenry continue to believe the Bush administration's claim that Saddam's government was involved in the events of September 11, even though no compelling evidence of a connection emerged?[2] Why, in fact, did George W. Bush remain strong in the public opinion polls throughout the presidential campaign of 2004 even though his policies in Iraq appeared to be failing miserably in that year?

While there are many possible answers to these questions, one in particular is at the foundation of the substantial right-wing allegiance to this misguided foreign policy. Many who defended the administration in spite of the mounting evidence were devotees of a political faith. These True Believers were not willing to adjust their fundamentalist outlook on international issues. They had accepted the messages delivered by "preachers" of conservative sermons in the manner that enthusiastic religionists acknowledge scripture. Partisans followed respected teachings of their creed; they were not inclined to question them. They viewed people who challenged the president as mischievous liberals that refused to accept received wisdom. America's radcon populace remained loyal to the president and did not take seriously the poignant criticisms of U.S. foreign policy presented at home and abroad. Giving serious consideration to those well-publicized objections would seem like questioning the fundamental integrity of their political religion. Eventually, of course, some of that vigorous support from the right began to break as international troubles mounted, but the right's displays of discontentment were much slower and much weaker than those expressed by representatives of other political perspectives. The faithful remained devoted to their doctrines and interpretations long after applications of them appeared to be terribly flawed.

The radical right's outlook on foreign policy had not emerged suddenly in reaction to the events of September 11. Hawkish Nationalists had been developing and fine-tuning their perspective on foreign affairs for many years. Key elements of their emerging faith had been established by various groups within the GOP, such as the New Right, the evangelicals, the paleoconservatives, and the neoconservatives. In recent years the neoconservatives emerged as a particularly influential group within George W. Bush's administration. Various partisans on the right differed greatly on important questions about America's role in the world, but they managed to form a rather uniform front in support of radcon positions.

Hawkish Nationalists prefer leadership in international matters by the Defense Department rather than the diplomatic wing of the U.S. government, the State Department. They are hard-liners who often call for a muscular foreign policy. These nationalists distrust international alliances and often dismiss liberals who recommend negotiation as appeasers and wimps. They advocate tough stands when dealing with America's adversaries. Hawkish Nationalists tend to think in terms of military solutions to international problems, and they are generally enthusiastic supporters of U.S. armed intervention in international disputes. These nationalists tend, also, to argue that Americans should look after their own interests first and treat concerns of the international community as matters of secondary importance. They frequently advise U.S. leaders to step away from international accords and participation in global organizations, including the United Nations. Many of them stress the importance of national sovereignty. They worry that cooperation with global institutions will undermine U.S. interests. Generally, Hawkish Nationalists favor unilateral activity in foreign affairs rather than multilateral action.

Obviously, some hard-line conservatives do not support these positions. Just as many market- and culture-oriented radicals of the right do not agree with each other's agendas, a number of individuals in the modern conservative movement are not enthusiastic about myopic and bellicose stands on international questions. Quite a few paleoconservatives are unhappy about the extensive international commitments advocated by neoconservatives. The paleos often lean toward isolationism. They are suspicious of the neoconservatives' plans for nation-building and democracy-expansion. Libertarians are often critical of the Hawks' enthusiasm for U.S. engagement in military conflict. They worry about high taxes and expanded government, developments that frequently result from mobilization for war. Also, some conservatives acknowledge that international coalitions were useful in the West's historic confrontations with communism. They wish radical leaders on the right would demonstrate a stronger spirit of cooperation and less eagerness to "go it alone" in dealing with international crises.

Despite these and many other disagreements on the right, Hawkish Nationalists are able to operate with relatively little interference from fellow conservatives who do not accept their premises. Market, culture, and military-minded groups within the GOP have learned to mute their criticisms of each other in order to achieve goals that are dear to each. An unspoken truce often operates among the various "sects" of the hard right.[3] When dealing with foreign affairs, partisans of the radical market, culture, and nationalist views sometimes voice disapproval of security policy, but these objections are rarely sharp or sustained. Hard-line rightists certainly do not split as severely *in public* over controversies about international relations as liberals do.

When an individual on the right launches a serious indictment of a radcon leader's policy, as Pat Buchanan did in his 2004 book (*When the Right Went Wrong: How Neo-Conservatives Subverted the Reagan Revolution and Hijacked the Bush Presidency*), the reaction in conservative circles is quite feeble. Buchanan, twice an unsuccessful candidate for the presidency, had been a speechwriter and adviser to Richard Nixon and Spiro Agnew. He became a prominent journalist and television personality known for advocacy of paleoconservative positions, including opposition to immigration and multiculturalism. In international matters, Buchanan tends to promote nationalist positions, expressing suspicion about the effects of free trade and U.S. diplomatic and military commitments abroad. He sharply questioned President George W. Bush's military invasion and occupation of Iraq. Nationalist, market, and culture conservatives hardly acknowledged Buchanan's warnings, and they certainly did not join him in a robust verbal assault on the Republican president's policies. No doubt, some of those mute conservatives found Patrick Buchanan's criticisms of immigration, Jews, and international trade too controversial for comfort and preferred not to identify with him publicly. But the more significant factor behind these frail responses to Buchanan's indictments related to the right's preference for united fronts. President George W. Bush had honored diverse market, culture, and defense ideals of the right's faith. Enthusiasts of the creed were not about to turn on him. Partisans in each group were reluctant to campaign against a president who had been responsive to their particular needs—especially when the matter in question was not essential to their own principal agenda.

During the 2004 election year, conservatives, including William F. Buckley, Tucker Carlson, and George Will, expressed resistance to the president's Iraq policies along with Buchanan, but their response was, again, muted. They did not wish to level strong criticism against a president who had preached and practiced their faith in connection with many other subjects. Nor did Buckley, Carlson, and Will turn their case into a noble cause. Rather than mount an energetic campaign to change America's course, they appeared eager to put their discontent on record so that they would not be held accountable if their nation's troubles in Iraq continued to mount.

Consequently, the radical right often shows impressive unanimity on foreign policy issues despite its many internal disagreements. Hawkish Nationalists usually get what they want when Republicans are in power in Washington, D.C. They can promote aggressively nationalist and hawkish policies while hearing only frail and limited expressions of discord from within the ranks of the militant conservatives. Various right-wing groups go along with each other to get along. Right-wingers compromise when dealing with concerns of their colleagues in order to achieve respect for their own particular orthodoxy. This mode of operation leaves Hawkish Nationalists relatively free to pursue their political agenda. Facing little pressure from ideological compatriots to rein in their extremism, Hawkish Nationalists are inclined to offer highly simplistic and partisan judgments about complex international issues. In conferences and publications they work in an echo chamber. Strongly partisan views receive applause from colleagues instead of tough questions. Right-wing commentators, especially those communicating the movement's views in the mass media, repeat and amplify favored arguments rather than dispute them. This modus operandi is certainly not conducive to a vigorous and challenging dialogue on the subject of U.S. foreign policy.

The tendency of the radical right to associate criticism of its viewpoints with liberals also serves to stifle dissent. Hawkish Nationalists often treat those who question them strongly like heretics who fail to recognize the essential truths of the faith. They demonize liberals, depicting them as dangerously idealistic individuals whose naïveté can seriously undermine national security. Some particularly strident conservatives take this perspective to its logical conclusion. Almost effortlessly they elevate the stakes in debates over foreign policy and suggest that liberals are the country's principal internal "enemy." Liberals' attitudes and policies, they claim, leave the United States weak and vulnerable to attack from foreign adversaries. By preaching a Manichaean vision to the faithful, Hawkish Nationalists encourage conservative partisans to react emotionally against criticisms. They tend not to reflect on the wisdom of questions raised by their critics. When objections appear to come from errant people, they are approached with fear, not curiosity.

Partisans of the right often present grossly distorted portrayals of liberals. They associate them with radical ideas, dismissing liberal criticisms of national policies as the railing of extremists. Liberals look like pacifists, appeasers, and cowards in much of this discourse. Quite often the rhetoric portrays opponents as anti-American. The language of indictment makes liberals appear receptive to just about every criticism of policy leveled against the United States. In many of the radcons' accounts, liberals seem to believe outrageous complaints about heinous American actions abroad. Liberals are depicted as impressionable and acceptant when hearing U.S. policies associated with imperialism, capitalist exploitation, and genocide. Some commentators on the right, such as William J. Bennett, Dinesh D'Souza, Ann Coulter, and Michael Savage, go to the extreme of suggesting that liberals are a threat to national security. Right-wing radio hosts are particularly fond of taking a phone call from an individual who makes outrageous statements and then characterizing that caller as a "liberal." Sean Hannity demonstrated the practice on his radio show in January 2006 when talking about Osama bin Laden's release of a recording in which the al-Qaeda leader warned America of more attacks but also offered the possibility of a truce. Hannity asked the caller if he wanted to negotiate with bin Laden. The individual said he did, and then Hannity gave the man a lecture about Neville Chamberlain's foolish appeasement policies when dealing with Adolph Hitler in the late 1930s. Hannity asked why "liberals" take such naïve positions on foreign affairs, treating the man's outrageous remarks as representative of liberals' ideas. Disregarding the actual position of liberals (they were not eager to negotiate with the infamous terrorist), Sean Hannity blithely smeared millions of Americans through his facile association.

As in much of the right's rhetoric, strident critics of liberalism practice a strategy of escalating charges when writing and speaking about international problems. They often begin their commentaries with references to the thoughts and behavior of *radicals* and then slip quickly into discussions about *liberals'* ideas and behavior. Observations about the radical left and liberalism are mixed together loosely in a fashion that makes the two political perspectives appear similar and almost interchangeable. Consider the language of one of the radical right's most prolific interpreters of recent history and politics, David Horowitz. In *Unholy Alliance: Radical Islam and the American Left* he identifies the questions his inquiry "seeks to address":

> Why has the American Left made alliances of convenience with Islamic radicals who have declared war on the democratic West and whose own values are reactionary and oppressive? Why have American radicals actively obstructed the War on Terror, thereby undermining the defense of the democracies of the West? Why have liberals opposed Operation Iraqi Freedom, whose goals are the overthrow of tyranny and the establishment of political democracy and human rights—agendas that coincide with their own? Why have Democrats turned against the policy of regime change, which they had supported during the Clinton Administration in both Kosovo and Iraq? Why has the Democratic Party declared political war on the president's war and thus made foreign policy a point of partisan conflict for the first time since the end of World War II? What does this fracture mean for the future of America's War on Terror?[4]

In the space of a paragraph Horowitz has moved comfortably from warnings about Islamic radicals to warnings about American radicals, and then on to warnings about the ideas and actions of Democrats. These three groups appear connected. Horowitz's brief message serves wonderfully to introduce a mode of interpretation that he repeats in various other places in his book.

Many on the right find the extraordinary charges of figures such as William J. Bennett, Dinesh D'Souza, Ann Coulter, Michael Savage, and David Horowitz to be over the top, but as in other examples of dealing with their overheated colleagues, they offer little or no resistance to the hyperbole. Objections to some of the outrageous viewpoints of fellow conservatives are usually couched in soft and cautious tones. When they are expressed, the venue is usually an internal meeting or publication of the right, not a public meeting that brings the disputes fully into national view. Also, few conservatives are courageous enough to voice strenuous objections to radically nationalist and hawkish policies. They do not wish to be associated in right-wing publications and broadcasts with the "enemy," the much-despised liberals.

As Stefan Halper and Jonathan Clarke reveal in their intriguing examination of the recent shift toward a radical perspective in U.S. foreign policy, neoconservatives have been the most articulate and productive promoters of this outlook. Their arguments, presented in numerous publications over the past thirty years, frequently resemble patterns of the militant persuasion identified here. Halper and Clarke describe this neoconservative outlook as a "new orthodoxy" that supports moralistic approaches to dealing with international questions.[5] Neoconservatives, they report, attack "moral relativism" and insist on sharp characterizations of international disagreements. They view foreign affairs in terms of white and black, good versus evil, "us" versus "them." Neocons appear to know what is right; they act as if they invented "moral clarity."

Halper and Clarke say the neoconservatives exhibit a general suspicion of multilateral approaches to foreign policy. They distrust both allies and potential adversaries and place limited confidence in treaties with each. Neocons prefer leadership from the Defense Department rather than the State Department. They claim previous policies aimed at détente failed to achieve important U.S. goals. Neocons demonstrate great interest in military approaches to international issues. Power derived from the strength of U.S. armed forces is a precious instrument of foreign policy, they counsel, and it works best when the United States is on a war footing and the Defense Department's spending budgets are hefty. Of course, defense spending may be questioned as wasteful if no serious enemy is in sight, but neocons have an answer to that objection. They discern many threats and many potential enemies. Challenges to America's security and preeminence appear to lurk around almost every diplomatic corner.

Some observers describe this group as "Hard Wilsonians," because neoconservatives often support Woodrow Wilson's goal of promoting and expanding democracy in the world, but with more military clout, pressure, and unilateral leadership than the idealistic U.S. president of the early twentieth century recommended. Unlike the "realists" in today's foreign policy debates, who have tried to give Wilsonian ideals a pragmatic base, neocons often support expansive and extensive foreign commitments by the United States. They tend not to heed the warnings of critics who urge caution when Americans take on far-reaching missionary goals such as exporting democracy around the world or remaking the Middle East in terms of American social and political ideals.

Halper and Clarke show that neoconservatives demonstrate enthusiasm for bold measures in U.S. international relations and confer little respect on those who question their elaborately fashioned blueprints for foreign policy. In fact, many of them are skilled wordsmiths, experts at debate, and masters of the biting indictment. Eloquently, they express contempt for individuals who question their ambitious prescriptions. The neocons are especially harsh when characterizing Americans or foreigners who object to their interest in making military power the leading instrument of U.S. foreign policy. They often berate Americans who question their ideas, calling them appeasers, pacifists, and "McGovernites." Neocons are likely to question the patriotism of their strong critics. They are also likely to dismiss those who complain about U.S. actions in foreign countries as naïve and weak. Often they describe international leaders who do not agree with their perspective as competitors, not allies, of the United States.

Halper and Clarke point out that for many years, neocons were on the outside, looking in at Republican as well as Democratic administrations. Only a few of them reached top positions in the federal government during the years of Ronald Reagan's leadership, and some criticized George H. W. Bush for giving inadequate attention to their concerns when he was president in the late 1980s and early 1990s. In the Clinton years, neocons felt that they had been exiled to the periphery of political action. They wielded little influence in foreign affairs. Neocons remained active in scholarship during this period, however, publishing many articles and books, working at conservative think tanks, participating in conferences, and serving as heads of various research committees and university-based departments. When George W. Bush won election to the presidency in 2000, the neoconservatives found extraordinary opportunities for guiding U.S. policy. They appointed each other to important administrative positions. Among the leading neocons in George W. Bush's administration were the chief of staff to the vice president, I. Lewis "Scooter" Libby; special adviser to the president, Elliott Abrams; deputy secretary of defense, Paul D. Wolfowitz; and State Department officials John R. Bolton and David Wurmser. On governmental advisory bodies, note Halper and Clarke, were other prominent neocons such as

Richard Perle and Elliott Cohen on the Defense Policy Board. Neocons had intellectual support from prominent authors such as Donald Kagan, Bernard Lewis, and James Q. Wilson. In the media, pundits such as William Kristol, editor of the *Weekly Standard,* and Charles Krauthammer of the *Washington Post* often trumpeted their causes, as did Max Boot of the Council on Foreign Relations. And, of course, one of the most prolific of Hawkish Nationalist authors, Norman Podhoretz, was ever supportive (Podhoretz, former editor of *Commentary,* had been one of the intellectual pioneers of neocon thought in international affairs).[6]

Radicalism in foreign affairs was not the exclusive perspective of neoconservatives. As we will see, spokespeople for other positions of the militant right contributed ideas to this persuasion as well. Many of these individuals did not agree with specific measures advocated by the neocons. Among the prominent commentators on the right discussed in these pages that are not ordinarily identified with neoconservative causes are William F. Buckley, Jesse Helms, William E. Simon, Phyllis Schlafly, Lee Edwards, Dick Armey, William J. Bennett, Rush Limbaugh, Sean Hannity, Michael Savage, and Ann Coulter. Neoconservatives do not control all the microphones, printing presses, and policy chairs of the radcon movement, but they enjoyed extraordinary influence when George W. Bush assumed the presidency.

The following analysis focuses on six specific examples of the Hawkish Nationalist position on international issues. Each of the six subjects is quite complex, and this commentary can only address a few of the most salient problems posed by the militant right's outlook. The six examples relate to the way radcons viewed the Vietnam War, interpreted Soviet military buildups, criticized détente, celebrated Ronald Reagan's role in ending the Cold War, interpreted American reactions to the tragedy of September 11, and defended the U.S. war with Iraq and subsequent occupation.

These brief case studies suggest that Hawkish Nationalists often distort history in order to derive lessons from the past that support their interests. Radcons frequently skew evidence. They tend to privilege facts that please them and disregard evidence that undermines their theses. Exhibiting a fundamentalist mentality, they employ the teachings of their faith when confronting issues. Evidence that undermines their basic assumptions tends not to disturb them. Hawkish Nationalists hold their ground, convinced that their beliefs are fundamentally true.

Of course, this tendency to favor useful information and turn away from contrary evidence can be found in many analyses of foreign affairs, liberal as well as conservative ones. No interpreter of international subjects is completely objective. All commentators accentuate facts that bolster their primary arguments. The right's pattern of interpreting history is particularly egregious, however, because it involves unusually gross distortions. Radcons exhibit a troublesome tendency to approach controversial questions with strong presuppositions. They often start with conclusions (based on their beliefs) and then conveniently muster evidence to gird those assumptions. Hawkish Nationalists frequently rely on faith rather than fact when drawing lessons about the history of U.S. international relations. As political fundamentalists, they are also inclined to characterize the "other" in extreme, frightening terms. Ultimately, their quasi-religious posture contributes to close-minded handling of complex issues. Hawkish Nationalists tend to approach foreign policy problems with doctrines rather than questions.

## Framing the Vietnam Conflict

The radical right's hawkish perspective on foreign policy is evident in its views of the history of U.S. involvement in the Vietnam conflict. When trying to make sense of the American people's painful experiences with war and protest in the 1960s and early 1970s, Hawkish Nationalists give much more energetic sanction to U.S. actions in Vietnam than do liberals. Many on the right refuse to accept the judgment of numerous historians that U.S. military intervention in Southeast Asia was terribly mistaken. These radicals tend to blame liberals for the anti-war extremism of the era, claiming that liberals undermined U.S. military efforts. They claim Americans and their Vietnamese allies might have won the fight if liberals had stood up to communism in Southeast Asia with a greater sense of commitment. Instead of staying the course in what was ultimately a worthwhile fight for freedom, Hawks argue, liberals criticized the war in fundamental ways and sowed doubt among the American people. Other Hawkish Nationalists acknowledge the validity of some principal criticisms of U.S. policies in Vietnam, but they tend to focus their attention on the home front rather than the war front when drawing lessons from the history of American disputes about the war. Expressing disgust with the way some antiwar demonstrators embraced radicalism, they blame liberals for the excesses. Liberals, they say, indicted U.S. policies and military activities in provocative language and thereby encouraged impressionable young activists to make extremist statements and engage in militant behavior, especially on college campuses.

One of the most comprehensive early statements of this radcon interpretation of America's actions in Vietnam came from a pioneer of the neoconservative movement, Norman Podhoretz. He, like many neocons, moved over the years from a hawkish position in the Democratic Party (supporting Democrat Henry "Scoop" Jackson) to a Republican-oriented one. Podhoretz, the son of Jewish immigrants, received a degree at Columbia University and a master's at Cambridge University. He was close to many of the talented Jewish New York intellectuals of his day but eventually broke ranks with leading figures in the group, including some of his former friends. Podhoretz served for many years as editor of *Commentary*. In that post he turned the magazine toward conservatism. Later he became a senior fellow at the Hudson Institute. Ever the polemicist and convinced of the correctness of his own views, Podhoretz achieved distinction as a strong voice for neoconservatism.

In two books, *The Present Danger* (1980) and *Why We Were in Vietnam* (1983), Norman Podhoretz defends aspects of U.S. policy in Vietnam. He says American military intervention aimed to secure the freedom of the Vietnamese people. Podhoretz draws attention to the oppression that accompanied a communist victory over South Vietnam in 1975, claiming that the tragedies experienced by millions of victims in Southeast Asia might not have occurred if American intellectuals had displayed greater appreciation of stakes in the fight. At some points in his discourse, Podhoretz suggests U.S. intervention may have been mistaken, but then he outweighs those sentiments with abundant commentary that treats American intrusion as noble and worthy.

Like many Hawkish Nationalists, Podhoretz directs much of his criticism toward events at home rather than abroad. The villains in his commentaries are not only extremist antiwar demonstrators but also the college professors who raised strong objections to U.S. policies in Vietnam. Podhoretz claims they were an influential group in the period. Their opinions on the war carried tremendous cultural weight, he argues. Often those academics encouraged radicalism by indicting U.S. actions on moral grounds. They also stimulated radicalism by their relative silence when agitators denounced U.S. actions in Southeast Asia as criminal, Nazi-like, and even genocidal. Academics, especially the liberal ones among them, refused to distance themselves from this hyperbole because they hated the war, writes Podhoretz. Their coddling of the militants contributed to a national mood of self-doubt and self-disgust.

Podhoretz's books leave the impression that many critics of the Vietnam War harbored cynical and ugly views of the United States. Antiwar activists thought "the United States, not the Soviet Union and certainly not Communism, represented the greatest threat to the security and well-being of the peoples of the world," Podhoretz charges. These critics believed that "we were and always had been on the wrong side of the worldwide struggle."[7] Some critics of the war, such as a contributor to the *New York Review of Books,* maintained that the United States was in Vietnam "to impose its national obsessions on the rest of the world."[8] In presenting these and other citations Podhoretz associates disagreement over the war with fringe viewpoints. In a highly selective manner, he cites extreme examples of antiwar rhetoric and then hints that the comments reflected mainstream antiwar opinion, including the liberals' discontent with U.S. policies in Vietnam. His principal lesson from America's Vietnam tragedy was not the familiar one characterized in numerous liberal interpretations of the war years. Rather than focusing his case on criticism of the policies that drew the United States into a mistaken intervention, Podhoretz complains about various groups at home that questioned the war.

George Will, a hawk in many of the disputes about U.S. policy in Vietnam as well as other debates about U.S. policies abroad, also has offered hostile characterizations of opponents of the war. Will, a skilled writer who enjoys showing off his erudition by peppering his comments with obscure words, studied at Trinity College of Oxford University and at Princeton University. He worked as editor at the *National Review,* wrote a biweekly syndicated column for the *Washington Post,* and made regular television appearances on ABC as a commentator on politics and culture. Will continues to entertain his readers with scathing indictments of liberal ideas, embellished with exquisite English.

In his 1982 book, *The Pursuit of Virtue and Other Tory Notions,* Will berates liberals of the Vietnam era for losing sight of their earlier anticommunism. He notes that in the opening years of the Cold War, liberals had recognized communism's wickedness and dangerousness, but that understanding seemed to fade away during the angry period of protest against

U.S. policies in Vietnam. In the years of tumult and protest, liberals attributed U.S. intervention in Southeast Asia to "Cold War paranoia." They ridiculed the domino theory and gave little attention to the suffering of the Vietnamese people after the fall of South Vietnam to the communists, he argues.[9] Many "still believe that a 'lesson' of Vietnam is that U.S. policy toward Communist aggression should be benign neglect," he writes.[10] When considering *The Deer Hunter* (1978), a movie that some critics called "reactionary" because it portrayed Vietnamese communists treating American POWs in a brutal manner, Will takes aim at the movie's detractors. By attacking the film in this outrageous manner, he argues, these critics revealed "how much their opposition to American policy was rooted in anti-Americanism and a romantic assessment of Asian Communism."[11] Like Norman Podhoretz, Will's sweeping indictments bunch radical and mainstream liberal objections to the war indiscriminately. This tactic leaves the impression that many people who raised objections to the Vietnam conflict were enamored of the communist enemy and were contemptuous toward the United States.

James G. Watt, the born-again Christian who aroused great controversy when he served as secretary of the interior in the Reagan administration, gave expression to claims that resembled Podhoretz's and Will's arguments when he asserted that liberals had expressed an excessively tolerant view of South Vietnam's fall to communism. Watts claimed the "American liberal Establishment" failed to appreciate the horrors visited upon the South Vietnamese after communist totalitarianism took hold. In his book *Courage of a Conservative* he notes that the North Vietnamese victors arrested people associated with the old government and, in an Orwellian practice, sent many of them to reeducation camps. "American political conservatives had warned all along that this would happen," Watt asserts, but liberals did not believe them. Naïvely, they thought mass oppression and executions were "no longer part of the Communist pattern."[12]

These stories about liberal indifference to communist dominance in Vietnam were balderdash, as were the suggestions that the principal critics of U.S. policies toward Vietnam were radicals and extremists who hated America and were motivated by romantic notions about communism. Yet commentators such as Podhoretz, Will, and Watt delivered these warped interpretations of recent American history as if they represented acknowledged truths. The right-oriented commentators focused on the radical nature of some antiwar protests. They showed little interest in reporting that Americans in the political mainstream, not strident militants, were the most prominent and influential agitators against the war. These writers treated the tumultuous period in American history as a time of protest gone wild, and they acted as if liberals were ultimately to blame for the excesses. In fabricating this myth, they engaged in flights of fantasy. These Hawks subscribed to oft-repeated distortions about liberalism in the 1960s and 1970s. Many figures on the right echoed these charges. The claims began to sound like dogma to the faithful. Repeated references to the ideas in speeches and political tracts made this familiar fiction look like fact.

While many early leaders of the neoconservative movement, such as Irving Kristol, joined Podhoretz in presenting strong rationales for U.S. military intervention in Vietnam, others, such as Nathan Glazer, criticized the war but balanced his objections with complaints about antiwar protesters.[13] Glazer served as an editor at the conservative journals *Commentary* and the *National Interest* and as a professor at the University of California–Berkeley. He has published numerous books and articles that challenge aspects of multiculturalism, affirmative action, and welfare programs. In his remarks about the Vietnam War Glazer gives evidence of a stand that emerged prominently in the neocons' rhetoric of later years: he charges professors and students in the nation's universities with tilting too heavily toward the views of the New Left. Glazer writes that liberal professors needed to object to the antiwar movement as well as the war. He claims that liberal intellectuals went too far toward appeasing radical students who were indulging in revolutionary rhetoric. The militants were not just opposing U.S. activities in Vietnam, Glazer warns; they also sought a fundamental reordering of American society.[14] Like many other critics on the right who drew attention to such statements, Glazer has had difficulty distinguishing emotional outbursts of the moment from truly radical positions taken by people committed to a lifetime of ideological militancy.[15]

The claims by these conservatives about liberals fostering radical thought and protest during the years of discord over U.S. policies in Vietnam are absurd. Most liberals did not sanction hate-filled condemnations of U.S. foreign policy, and most did not support the radical condemnations of American history and American values. They usually did not endorse the angry claims about American complicity in imperialism, exploitative capitalism, and genocide. Nor should their moral objections to the war be identified almost exclusively as the primary stimulus to campus radicalism. The war itself was the main catalyst for radical protest.

It is, of course, true that some opponents of the Vietnam War indicted the United States unfairly or did not adequately recognize the tragic consequences of a communist victory in Vietnam, but these expressions did not reflect a liberal mentality. They were expressions of radicalism. "Radical" needs to be understood in a specific historical context, of course. During the highly controversial Vietnam War, some people, particularly the young, articulated sharply critical views of American society. They denounced the United States as a "criminal" nation, called U.S. policy "imperialist," and suggested that America was the greatest threat to world peace. Whenever a large-scale military engagement becomes tremendously unpopular, some among the thousands who oppose the policies indulge in such hyperbole to express their wrath. Those who made these statements in the 1960s and early 1970s were, for the most part, situational radicals. They responded to the tensions of the Vietnam controversy with strident rhetoric. The great majority of these individuals had no lengthy record of interest in the politics of the radical left, and, indeed, once the Vietnam controversy passed into history, many of them lost interest in causes of the far left.

In a lengthy analysis of the antiwar movement in the United States during the era of the Vietnam War, Charles DeBenedetti nicely summarizes the distinction between liberal and radical participants in that movement. It is a distinction hardly recognizable in the commentaries of Hawkish Nationalists, since they prefer to conflate liberalism and radicalism. "Whereas liberal peace advocates sought through informed criticism to strengthen America's international leadership for peace," writes DeBenedetti, "radicals considered the U.S. government as culpable as any other power for the inequity and instability in the world." DeBenedetti reports that liberals argued for policy change in Washington, while radical pacifists "called for the transformation of the very structure of wealth and power in America and the world." DeBenedetti's most important point of comparison relates to the way the two groups viewed the political structure. "Whereas liberals called for electoral action and citizen lobbying," he writes, "radicals demanded a personal commitment to nonviolent direct action and civil disobedience against unjust social structures."[16] DeBenedetti's analysis demonstrates that it was liberals rather than conservatives who were at the center of the campus disputes with radicals during the time of Vietnam protests.

As Kenneth J. Heineman shows in his analysis of "campus wars" at American universities, radicals often attacked liberals in the debates over devising strategies for opposition to the U.S. military actions in Vietnam. Liberals tried to rally students around the political campaigns of Eugene McCarthy and Robert F. Kennedy. Radicals were more enamored of confrontational protest strategies. They promoted draft resistance, attacks on ROTC organizations, and confrontations over military research projects on the campuses. In the course of describing disputes that rocked the campuses in these years of angry debates, Heineman reports on the efforts of a liberal professor to employ protest strategies of "realism and moderation" while radicals promoted a "cult of extremism." The radicals, Heineman notes, complained both about the war and about the liberals who did not agree with their tactics.[17]

Throughout the debates related to U.S. actions in Vietnam in the 1960s and early 1970s, liberals considered a greater range of judgments about U.S. policies than did partisans on the right. Liberals participated in vigorous exchanges about the appropriate courses of action, demonstrated more readiness to question national leadership in the war, and split from each other on related political issues to a much greater degree than hawkish partisans of the right. Dissent found more vigorous expression in the liberal camp than in conservative ranks during the years of American intervention in Vietnam. This contrast is significant, for a related pattern can be seen in the way conservatives and liberals have dealt with many other controversies in U.S. foreign policy, including the recent disputes regarding war with Iraq and the subsequent occupation of Iraq.

During the years of American combat in Southeast Asia, liberals were greatly divided on the war issues. Many became strong critics of President Lyndon B. Johnson's policies and contributed to the various movements for peace, and they eventually urged Johnson's resignation. Others remained supportive of the Johnson administration and, later, the policies of President Richard M. Nixon. A large group of liberals rallied around the presidential candidacy of an old favorite of the center-left, Hubert Humphrey, even though Vice President Humphrey refused to criticize his boss, President Johnson. Some liberals supported the Democratic Party's hawks, particularly Henry "Scoop" Jackson, a hard-nosed Cold Warrior. A number of these figures later joined the neoconservative movement and the Republican Party. By the early 1970s, the forces of liberalism had splintered tremendously over the war in Vietnam. Those disagreements were understandable and appropriate in view of the public's growing sense that Americans had walked into a dangerous quagmire in Southeast Asia.[18]

Liberal positions evolved over time and were constantly in flux. When the communist threat in Vietnam first became front-page news in America's newspapers, many liberals expressed sympathy for the South Vietnamese who had to deal with this challenge. Liberals were certainly not indifferent about a communist victory, as Podhoretz and others suggested in their criticisms. During the early years of U.S. engagement in Vietnam, a majority of liberals supported America's war effort. Military intervention seemed justified to protect allies in Southeast Asia and to contain communism. This enthusiasm for military operations began to diminish as evidence surfaced revealing divisions within Vietnamese society and the failure of U.S. efforts to prop up noncommunist governments.

Arthur Schlesinger Jr.'s changing opinions during the war provide an example of the kind of transformation that affected a number of liberals. Schlesinger, a prolific and popular historian often identified with liberalism, had been an adviser to President John F. Kennedy and wrote a notable book about JFK's time in the White House, *A Thousand Days*. When the Vietnam issue became volatile in the spring of 1965, Schlesinger supported the policy of the Johnson administration. He defended the president's idea of sending more soldiers into combat operations in Vietnam, and in a teach-in he disputed those academics who opposed U.S. military escalation. Within a year, though, Schlesinger developed strong doubts about America's course in Vietnam. He concluded that the United States was slipping into a "hopeless situation." Schlesinger believed America's response to events in Southeast Asia were out of proportion to anything the nation could achieve in Vietnam. Schlesinger also worried that divisions over the Vietnam War were tearing America's social fabric at home. Many of the nation's youths were becoming disillusioned about their country and its leaders. Protests were turning angry and sometimes violent. By the end of the 1960s he saw unilateral military withdrawal from Vietnam as the "only sensible position" to take on the war.[19]

Many, but not all, liberals sensed that the Vietnam War's cost in blood and treasure did not match the likely benefits. These liberals could not see the "light at the end of the tunnel," a metaphor employed at the time that succinctly identified a source of public discontent. News reports from Southeast Asia did not appear to support President Johnson's original assumptions about the potential for Americans to secure peace and democracy in the region. Liberals did not wish to abandon the South Vietnamese people, but they believed the time had come for the Vietnamese to achieve self-government without a huge American presence. The United States could help them with economic and military assistance, but U.S. personnel could not stay indefinitely in South Vietnam and continue fighting in large numbers to maintain the country's independence.[20]

Liberals, then, evinced a much more open-minded approach to the Vietnam controversy than hawkish conservatives, including the many that wrote and spoke about the war long after its end. Most liberals strongly preferred a noncommunist solution for South Vietnam and supported large-scale U.S. military assistance to accomplish that goal. When information emerging from Vietnam suggested that the nation's initial goals were becoming difficult to achieve or nearly impossible to realize, most liberals demonstrated a readiness to question their original assumptions in the light of new evidence. Their position was dynamic. They were willing to change.

As George C. Herring demonstrates in *LBJ and Vietnam: A Different Kind of War,* the man who had led the nation into military action in Vietnam was, by contrast, far less capable of making a major turn. President Johnson was intolerant of dissent expressed by members of his leadership team. He was harsh with Undersecretary of State George Ball when the latter raised serious questions about policy, and other aides saw that demonstrations of chutzpah in the manner of George Ball could lead to greatly diminished influence in the White House. Often Johnson exploded in anger at officials when he thought their actions had left him uninformed or lacking control in decision making. Some of Johnson's advisers and staff wanted to criticize military options more openly as U.S. troubles in Vietnam grew, but they sensed that Johnson did not like to hear challenges to his policies.

By 1968 it was becoming abundantly clear that the United States had stumbled into a terrible situation in Vietnam. Problems with the terrain, the climate, weak allies, and a tenacious foe left Americans trapped in the "fog of war." To many Americans, this war seemed formless. Leaders in the U.S. military could not find distinct battle-lines or identify distinct objectives, notes Herring. A Marine general's observations about this situation related to the larger problem of U.S. armed forces in Vietnam.

"Soon after I arrived in Vietnam," said General Lewis Wall, "it was obvious to me that I neither had a real understanding of the nature of the war nor any clear idea of how to win it."[21]

The example of LBJ's inability to shift course suggests that liberals had good reason to question the Democratic president and seek to place someone else in the White House. Senators George McGovern of South Dakota and J. William Fulbright of Arkansas criticized the president and his policies in strong language, and Senator Eugene McCarthy boldly campaigned against Johnson in the primaries. After McCarthy almost beat the president in the New Hampshire race, Robert F. Kennedy, who had a larger base of support, announced that he, too, would seek the presidency. Kennedy suggested that he would change course in Vietnam. Today, as liberals look back on the history of those tumultuous years, many of them are proud that Democrats were active, not passive, in the face of the nation's serious difficulties. They are pleased to recall that liberals took dynamic positions in the circumstances, evolving in their stands on the war as they recognized that some of their early assumptions about its nature did not hold up.

In contrast, the position of Podhoretz, Will, Watt, and other Hawkish Nationalists was essentially static. These individuals covered their flanks by admitting the war was tragic and mistaken in some ways but went on to denounce many of the people who raised serious questions about it. Hard-liners remained locked in a semidefensive outlook on the Vietnam conflict, both during the war and in the years when Americans were looking back to interpret its history. Others on the right, as in the case of some neoconservatives, acknowledged that the war was mistaken, but they, too, diminished the impact of their criticism by lambasting liberal professors and student radicals who raised their voices in protest. In these instances, the right's reporting on events of the late 1960s and early 1970s sounded like an early chapter in the history of America's culture wars. Right-wingers indicted the messengers for thinking and behaving in uncivil ways, casting their basic message in negative light.

Overall, conservative Americans held to a hawkish position on the Vietnam War much more than liberals. Philip Gold, a longtime conservative who taught at Georgetown University and spent years as a Marine Corps intelligence officer, argues persuasively that those partisans of the right betrayed their own principles when they defended the Vietnam conflict with gusto. Instead of recognizing the problems that were resulting from massive U.S. intervention in the affairs of Vietnam, they promoted jingoistic statements such as "Stand up to the Commies" and "Why not victory?" In the 1960s, writes Gold, "any conservatism worthy of the name would have opposed the Vietnam War as imprudent, unnecessary, and tragic." Yet many on the right would not take that stand. Memories of the traditional conservative caution about foreign adventures expressed by Robert Taft and other Republican leaders of years before had faded on the right, and "irresponsible zealots" carried the day. During the years of U.S. military engagement in Vietnam, when the nation needed to hear serious critiques of U.S. foreign policy from the right, conservatives offered little but gung-ho calls for more military action, observes Gold.[22]

Philip Gold does not employ the word *fundamentalism* to identify the right's mentality on Vietnam in the 1960s, but he might have found that notion useful for characterizing the way many defenders of the war responded with little demonstration of a questioning, critical spirit. With faithlike devotion to their leaders' preaching about policy, they chanted support for war.

This pattern of refusing to adjust ideas in reaction to new evidence emerging on the ground in Vietnam was evident not only in the way the militant right interpreted the history of the war years but also in the way right-wingers conducted themselves during the period of the war. Obstinacy was particularly evident in the offices of the right's principal journal of the time, the *National Review*. That magazine's editors became concerned about the U.S. military's problems in Vietnam, but they would not entertain a major change of editorial position on questions about U.S. involvement. To present strong criticism of the war would, they thought, undermine the U.S. military's position in the fighting and give leftist opponents of the conflict points in the policy debates. A change would also appear to contradict the conservatives' fierce resistance to communism.

Instead of questioning the war forcefully, the *National Review's* editors criticized Lyndon Johnson's administration because of the manner in which it fought the war. They complained that Johnson was not fighting to win. These editors said the president was hurting the country's military effort by refusing to allow American soldiers to move across the demilitarized zone and into North Vietnam (Johnson and others opposed such action because it could provoke communist China, bringing it into the war in the manner that China intervened in South Korea in the early 1950s.) Taking the fight to the enemy could produce maximum advantage, the *National Review*'s editors maintained.[23] They chose to fight over tactics rather than challenge fundamental assumptions about the appropriateness of continued U.S. combat in Vietnam.

Like many on the right, these individuals did not let facts emerging from the U.S. experience in Vietnam shake their justification for the war. They adhered to an old script that sanctioned U.S. involvement and maintained that the United States must stay the course. Hawkish Nationalists were not willing to subject themselves to the messy, divisive politics of liberalism, where doubts about LBJ's troubled strategy of military intervention (and later Nixon's) received much fuller expression in public forums. Many on the right acted similarly after the United States overthrew Saddam Hussein in 2003. When that occupation began to go badly, they were reluctant to entertain serious questions about an intervention they had celebrated in their heroic narratives. The facts emerging from Iraq did not easily shake original assumptions about the wisdom of the mission just as the facts emerging from Vietnam did not shake the opinions of an earlier generation of right-wing hawks.

## Interpreting the Cold War

A related commitment to ideological "scripture" can be seen in the way many Hawkish Nationalists interpret the history of the Cold War. They subscribe to a myth about two important aspects of President Ronald Reagan's handling of the Russians. First, they claim the Soviet Union was busily expanding its military and political influence in the world in the late 1970s and early 1980s. These activities, they say, posed a huge threat to the United States. Partisans on the right present this interpretation forcefully even though many experts who have examined this history raise questions about their assumptions. Second, Hawkish Nationalists argue that the United States' massive arms buildup in the 1980s was the key factor in bringing down communism in the Soviet Union. This, too, is a point of contention among the experts, but it is an unassailable idea for True Believers on the right. Both of these judgments about the Cold War serve to justify the Reagan administration's large-scale spending on the military. Both have become part of the received wisdom of America's hard-line conservative faith. Authors from the radical right treat their favored history lessons as fundamentally valid.

They see controversies associated with this history as resolved. Hard-liners exhibit little or no interest in looking at countervailing interpreta-tions or adjusting their conclusions in the light of contrary evidence. They rest their case on faith rather than open-minded inquiry.

Norman Podhoretz provided a comprehensive template for this interpretation much as he had articulated a representative outline of the radical conservatives' favored take on the Vietnam War. In *The Present Danger: Do We Have the Will to Reverse the Decline of American Power?* (1980) Podhoretz offers a hawkish response to news about the Cold War that many others on the right, particularly neoconservatives, voiced in the following years. Virtually every action taken by the com-munists seems hostile and dangerous in Podhoretz's interpretation. Each challenge requires vigorous military preparation by the U.S. armed forces. Whereas many other commentators on Cold War matters were promoting international cooperation, Podhoretz and his fellow radcons displayed suspicion. By portraying the international situation in frightening terms, they created the rationale for a massive buildup in U.S. military forces and a much more aggressive and risky strategy for dealing with the communists.

In *The Present Danger,* Podhoretz writes about an apparently threaten-ing Soviet military buildup during the late 1970s and expresses concern that Americans had become too comfortable in their dealings with the Soviet Union. Talk of coexistence and détente convinced U.S. leaders to let down their guard, he argues. The U.S. military was in decline at the very time that Soviet land, air, and naval forces were engaged in large-scale building programs. A new tilt in the balance of power favoring the Soviets could signify the "final collapse of the American resolve to resist the forward surge of Soviet imperialism." This failure might lead, in turn, to the "Finlandization of America." The United States could suffer politi-cal and economic subordination in the face of greatly superior Soviet power in the way that weak Finland had suffered for years at the hands of the Russians.[24] Already communists working for Moscow were gaining control in developing countries around the world such as Laos, Ethiopia, Mozambique, Afghanistan, and Cambodia, Podhoretz notes.[25] Also, Cuban troops were in Angola as surrogates for the Russians.[26] Furthermore, the Soviet Union's recent advances into Afghanistan "represented a new stage of Soviet expansionism."[27] Communists seemed to be gaining, not losing strength.

Podhoretz sees troubling evidence of American indifference to the USSR arms buildup, and he accentuates this interpretation with alarming data. He writes that the United States was not beefing up its armed forces adequately to confront the communist challenges. The United States was cutting defense spending. Podhoretz claims that the Soviets spent three times as much as the United States on defense in the late 1970s. In 1979 alone the Soviets outstripped the United States in military allocations by as much as 50 percent. This evidence came from a CIA report, says Podhoretz, while noting that historically the intelligence agency's estimates tended to be low. Soviet military expansion might be much greater than the CIA report suggested.[28] Despite this disturbing evidence, writes Podhoretz, Jimmy Carter and his secretary of state, Cyrus Vance, had promoted the misconception, inspired by talk of détente, that leaders of the two countries shared "similar dreams and aspirations."[29] In a chapter called "Thinking the Unthinkable" Podhoretz supports President Reagan's call for more U.S.-built nuclear armaments, and he criticizes the "Culture of Appeasement."[30] The author refers to an earlier time in history when accommodation failed terribly. The Europeans failed to satisfy Adolph Hitler when they gave in to his demands. A generation of Europeans raised on pacifism was unprepared in the 1930s to deal with a tyrant. Podhoretz wonders if antinuclear propaganda would leave the United States similarly unprepared.[31] He was pleased, though, that Ronald Reagan presented a solution to the problem. Podhoretz thought President Reagan's Strategic Defense Initiative "really does hold out the rational hope of an eventual escape from the threat of nuclear war."[32]

Many radical conservatives joined Podhoretz in promoting this interpretation of expanding Soviet power and American weakness. They also endorsed Podhoretz's acclaim for Reagan's muscular response to the supposed crisis. This view of history is subject to considerable debate, however. A great deal of evidence undermines the right's familiar explanation of events. Assumptions that gird the radical conservatives' interpretation have come under vigorous questioning. Yet for right-wing hawks the favored historical narrative remains a matter of faith. They do not welcome a lively debate about it. Hawkish Nationalists have heard the principal claims about Soviet advances in the Cold War repeated numerous times by their fellow True Believers. Rather than display curiosity about the validity of this familiar sermon, they insist that all join in shouting, "Amen!"

Claims by the radcons regarding U.S. military weakness and Ronald Reagan's energetic response to it served their politics well, but they based these assertions on highly questionable judgments about Soviet military threats. Their conclusions about communist intentions and military preparedness often sprang from beliefs, not evidence.

The hawks who resisted Richard Nixon and Henry Kissinger's policy of détente with the Soviets found a unique opportunity to press their case during the brief administration of President Gerald Ford. As the 1976 election campaign approached, Ford found himself in danger of losing his party's presidential nomination. Ronald Reagan, a former movie star and ex-governor, was looking strong in the public opinion polls and proving competitive in the GOP primary races. Reagan's appeal related, in part, to his claim that the Nixon-Kissinger policy of détente had allowed the Soviets to make strategic gains. Ronald Reagan claimed détente left the United States in a second-rate position. Ford needed to cut off Reagan's challenge by throwing a sop to the Republican Party's hard-line conservatives. Gerald Ford was also under pressure from conservative groups that supported Reagan's hawkish approach to U.S. dealings with Moscow. Ford reacted to these intraparty difficulties by abandoning public references to détente and asking his CIA director, George H. W. Bush, to look into the claims that recent CIA estimates of Soviet capabilities were inaccurate. Bush, in turn, acted in a way that satisfied militants of the time. He appointed a committee of hard-liners to examine the evidence.

A group known as "Team B" composed the assessment of Soviet intentions and capabilities that greatly exaggerated the communist threat. The "team" was supposed to engage in a competitive analysis of evidence with the CIA's Team A, using the same confidential information, but Team B was stacked from the beginning with hawks. Its leading participants had already indicated a strong preference for asserting that the Soviets were involved in a dangerous military buildup. Harvard professor Richard Pipes, with a reputation for fierce criticism of the Soviets, headed Team B, and Paul Wolfowitz, deputy secretary of defense in the second Bush administration, played a key role. Wolfowitz got his job on the committee in large part from a recommendation by Richard Perle, also a hawk, who later served as an important adviser on foreign policy for George W. Bush's administration. Donald Rumsfeld, who was Gerald Ford's secretary of defense and later held the position under George W. Bush, gave strong support to Team B's effort.[33]

Team B's report, arguing that the Soviet Union was engaged in an unparalleled military buildup, was based on presumptions rather than fact. In 1978 the U.S. Senate Select Committee on Intelligence indicated that the selection of members for Team B led, as could be expected, to a highly biased interpretation. The team's conclusions featured exaggerated estimates of Soviet capabilities and threats. Evidence of this bias and flawed analysis continued to mount in later years. In the mid-1980s the CIA quietly decreased its estimates of the accuracy of Soviet intercontinental ballistic missiles (ICBMs) by about half, and in 1989 the CIA reviewed its history of threat assessments and concluded that reports for the 1974–1986 period "substantially overestimated" Soviet power and threats every year.[34]

Nevertheless the ideas of Team B received a good deal of publicity in the late 1970s and after. The panel succeeded in getting substantial coverage of its conclusions in the American press and on television. Later, when Ronald Reagan campaigned for the White House, he used some of the messages from Team B's report to claim that the Soviet threat was substantial and that American readiness to meet the dangerous challenge was embarrassingly poor. The conservative candidate demanded huge increases in U.S. defense appropriations. After Reagan became president, he promoted an extraordinary $1.5 trillion increase in U.S. military spending. That program of expenditures, based on dubious conclusions about what the enemy was up to, placed a tremendous burden on American taxpayers and the U.S. economy.

Like Norman Podhoretz, who warned about impending dangers from a Russian buildup, many radcons joined Team B in sounding the mantra that Soviet power was ascendant and U.S. military strength was on the wane. These individuals delivered startling statistics that seemed to show that the United States suffered from military inferiority. Richard Viguerie, an effective organizer of fund-raising and membership drives for the New Right, presented this frightening perspective in a 1983 publication in which he warned, "The Red Chinese and Soviet influence, already dominant in many parts of Africa, is expanding at a rapid clip while U.S. influence wanes."[35] Another New Right spokesperson, Brigadier General Albion Knight, talked about a massive buildup that was producing "the largest military and naval force in history."[36] He claimed the Soviets had already obtained clear strategic nuclear superiority over the United States. The Russians built stockpiles while violating international treaties, said Knight, and "we are now strategically inferior to the Soviet Union."[37] Knight rattled off facts and figures that suggested comparisons between a slumbering weakling and an emerging giant. The Soviets led the United States by 5–1 in the production of tanks and aircraft, he claimed, and by 30–1 in constructing strategic bombers. They also had an 11–1 advantage in building nuclear ballistic and cruise missile submarines.[38]

Détente—the policy of diminishing Cold War hostilities through negotiations and arms treaties with the communists—became an object of scorn for many members of the radical right. They considered communist claims of interest in détente a dangerous ruse that could draw Americans into a false sense of security. The Soviets appeared to promise a new era of cooperation, but these partisans warned that the enemy really intended to exploit U.S. weaknesses once the American people's guard was down. William F. Buckley communicated this suspicion when he described coexistence with the Soviet Union as a form of "satanic utopianism." Cooperation was "neither desirable nor possible, nor honorable," Buckley insisted; "we find ourselves at war with Communism and shall oppose any substitute for victory."[39]

Several radicals had attacked Republican president Richard Nixon (and his key foreign policy adviser, Henry Kissinger) for promoting détente. Howard Phillips, one of the most energetic and successful early organizers of the New Right, blasted Nixon for "presiding over the most significant decline of American power in our history." Phillips, a Harvard graduate, had been an important figure in the Republican Party during the Nixon years but quit the party after he criticized the president for failing to challenge Lyndon B. Johnson's Great Society programs. Phillips applied his concerns to the three major conservative themes: criticizing liberal social stands (as in the matters of abortion and gay rights), opposing taxes, and promoting Cold War stands on defense issues. Regarding Nixon's foreign policy, Phillips said the president's crime was to work out the first SALT treaty of 1972 with the Soviet Union that aimed to limit strategic offensive missiles.[40] Jesse Helms, North Carolina's far-right senator, also raised complaints about the SALT treaties that were designed to limit the buildup of strategic arms (i.e., nuclear missiles). Helms said that Henry Kissinger, who steered Nixon toward negotiations with the communists, effectively wiped out any possibility of American superiority over the Soviets.[41] Jesse Helms warned that détente could work like the Trojan horse for the Russians, alluding to the gift the Greeks presented to their enemies during wartime. The people of Troy fell for the trick, Helms noted, just as Americans of modern times foolishly believed the Soviet leaders' promises that détente could usher in a new era of safe and peaceful relationships.[42]

William E. Simon, who served as treasury secretary in the Nixon and Ford administrations and later became president of a major right-oriented foundation, supported these suspicions about the Soviets during the late 1970s when Jimmy Carter was in the White House. In his 1980 book, *A Time for Action,* Simon wrote that U.S. leaders should not try to buy off the Soviet bullies, for that approach would only prompt them to push for greater advantages.[43] Under President Jimmy Carter, the nation had deferred development of the MX missile (then later revived it) to promote the SALT II negotiations, and Carter canceled the B-1 bomber, slowed development of the Trident submarine, and shut down production of the Minuteman missile.[44] These decisions greatly damaged the nation's strategic position, he claims. Now the Soviets outnumbered the United States in strategic missiles, tanks, combat airplanes, and naval vessels. They led in ICBMs and submarine and sub- and land-based missiles.[45] The policy of Mutual Assured Destruction (MAD) suggested "Orwellian logic," Simon argues, because it involved a "lunatic posture of creating a balance of power against ourselves."[46] The Soviets enjoyed a growing military edge that helped them to flex their muscles and "extend their influence in every quarter of the globe," he writes.[47] The USSR had sent troops to Afghanistan and Africa to carry out an aggressively imperialistic strategy. Simon finds communism at work in the religious revolution of Iran, too, claiming that a Marxist political group influenced Iran's Islamic regime.[48]

Neoconservatives who were in the course of switching from Democratic Party loyalties to Republican ones also hammered Henry Kissinger and his plans to promote détente with the Soviets.[49] They said Kissinger was too soft in handling the enemy. Later Kissinger described the neocons who had moved from the liberal to the conservative camp after the end of the Vietnam War as men who "had the passion of the convert and few incentives to recall their own contributions to the collapse of international restraints."[50] Not surprisingly, in his book *Years of Upheaval,* Kissinger describes the U.S. efforts to achieve détente, which he often led, in favorable terms. He points out that advocates of détente aimed to resist the Soviets' expansionism but also opened opportunities to negotiate with them on concrete issues. This policy stressed both deterrence and a readiness to explore possibilities for coexistence. In view of the many nuclear weapons in U.S. and Soviet hands at the time, Kissinger judges détente worthy of serious consideration. Yet the neocons often opposed it. They "did not believe America could remain vigilant while seeming 'progress' was being made under the aegis of détente," writes Kissinger. Neoconservatives insisted on ideological militancy and verbal hostility. Negotiations with the Soviets seemed futile to them; only a confrontational mode worked in their minds.

Henry Kissinger does not characterize détente's opponents in those years as political fundamentalists, but he employs related language. Speaking about the most prominent and powerful figure attacking détente in the Congress, Henry "Scoop" Jackson, Kissinger uses harsh words to identify the neocons' hero and his nemesis. "Jackson was an absolutist," writes Kissinger; "he saw issues in black and white." Henry Kissinger thought of himself as a "gradualist" who aimed to bring sustained improvements in Cold War relations over an extended historical period.[51]

The claims by Hawkish Nationalists in the 1970s that America was slipping quickly in military prowess while the Soviet Union was jumping ahead of the United States in defense matters made lively reading, but those charges greatly simplified, exaggerated, and distorted the evidence of recent history. Conservatives' attacks on détente, claims about emerging Soviet military superiority, and assertions about expanding communist influence across the globe were supported with highly selective readings of the evidence. Hawkish Nationalists' claims about the liberals' positions on Cold War issues were also strongly biased and often dead wrong. The familiar right-wing narrative about this era of the Cold War, advanced notably by Norman Podhoretz and imitated and supplemented by many other writers, is dramatically different from interpretations advanced by many scholars who have conducted research on the period. The viewpoints of these professionals are varied and complex, and certainly there has been much disagreement among the informed chroniclers of the Cold War years. It is worthwhile, though, to consider some of the principal conclusions that historians, political scientists, and journalists have presented. They contradict the interpretations confidently advanced by hard-line conservatives.

Many professionals who have investigated this history agree that the U.S. position of military power was *not* slipping toward inferiority by the last quarter of the twentieth century, as the hawks claimed, and that the Soviets were *not* emerging at the time as the country with the globe's dominant military force. Also, U.S. negotiations with the Soviets during the period made the world safer and represented a wise course of action. Treaties and settlements worked out by the parties did not represent appeasement or produce American weakness, as described by partisans of the militant right. In fact, the "soft power" of the United States—the global influence of its way of life—was growing substantially in this era in relation to the communists' appeal. American influence was not declining, as hard-liners of the right claimed. Furthermore, America's liberals were not naïve about the threat of communism and certainly were not eager to throw caution to the winds when negotiating with the Soviets. Liberals, too, were committed to the spread of capitalism, democracy, and civil liberties across the globe, but they were less likely than militant conservatives to suggest bellicosity was the best means to achieve national interests.

During this period, severe critics of détente were distinctly in the minority. U.S. efforts to work out new agreements with the USSR had widespread bipartisan support from both liberal Democrats and Republican mainstreamers. President Nixon and his national security adviser (as well as secretary of state beginning in 1973), Henry Kissinger, were among the primary architects of the policy in its early years. They earned the enmity of the radical right for promoting negotiations with the Soviets and the Strategic Arms Limitation Talks (SALT). Phyllis Schlafly, who had been a major promoter of Barry Goldwater's presidential candidacy, and Chester Ward offered a particularly biting view of Henry Kissinger and his treaty-making with the communists in *Kissinger on the Couch* (1975). Schlafly and Ward, strident critics of disarmament and the United Nations, write that the SALT I treaty "enshrined and publicized to all the world the strategic inferiority of the United States to the Soviet Union." Henry Kissinger suffered from "megalomania," they suggested, and possibly he was "nuts."[52]

Détente did not constitute a form of "appeasement," as many Hawkish Nationalists characterized it, and it did not signify approval of the communist system or a surrender of all hope that communism would soon disappear from the face of the earth. The policy represented, instead, a realistic assessment of the military prowess of the great powers, and it emerged from a sensible appreciation of the inherent dangers of nuclear warfare. Both the Americans and the Soviets had thousands of nuclear weapons available at the time. A saber-rattling relationship between the West and the East threatened to take the world to the brink of nuclear destruction. American and Soviet experiences with the Cuban Missile Crisis of 1962 showed how easily a few aggressive movements by the superpowers could lead them in the direction of Armageddon. Attempts by U.S. and Soviet leaders to arrange an approximation of nuclear parity known as Mutual Assured Destruction offered a responsible approach to a dangerous situation. The world became safer, not more dangerous, because of the advances realized through détente. Radical conservatives were dangerously mistaken in their interpretation of events.

While facts associated with these matters seemed complex to most observers, they appeared enticingly simple to partisans on the right who opposed détente. They considered questions and doubts about the true state of Soviet military strength and threats unworthy of serious consideration. Hawkish Nationalists found confident and frightening claims about Soviet progress much more appealing. An alarmist picture of ascending Soviet military power and global influence fit nicely into their favored narrative. This interpretation justified President Ronald Reagan's massive expenditures on military equipment. Radicals knew the end they wanted to achieve—the return of a belligerent anticommunist stand similar to that of earlier Cold War days—and they were prepared to massage the facts of recent history to bolster their thesis.

## Explaining the Soviet Demise

In addition to promoting a largely fictional narrative about emerging communist power and influence in the 1970s and 1980s, militant conservatives often promoted a highly simplistic interpretation of the demise of Soviet-led communism. They endorsed a favorite theory about the causes of Soviet collapse, making matters of conjecture sound like the gospel truth. As in many other right-wing interpretations of international issues, Hawkish Nationalists cherry-picked evidence that complemented their arguments while ignoring details that contradicted them.

The radical right's heroic story about Reagan's "victory" in the Cold War is familiar to Americans. According to this popular narrative, the president's tough talk and tough action knocked down the longtime communist menace. Ronald Reagan readily denounced the Reds and eagerly confronted them with superior military forces. Acting from strength, conservatives argue, Reagan convinced the Soviets to put up a white flag of surrender. They gave up communism and the Cold War. President Reagan's toughness paid huge dividends.

Lee Edwards, a historian of the conservative movement and a long-time activist on the right, offers a representative treatment of this familiar interpretation. Edwards has written biographies of Barry Goldwater, Ronald Reagan, and Edwin Meese III (Reagan's attorney general). He has also written numerous articles for conservative publications and has appeared frequently as a spokesman for the right on television talk shows.

Lee Edwards presents Ronald Reagan as the hero of late Cold War history in *The Conservative Revolution*. He gives the president high marks for demonstrating aggressive leadership in the 1980s. "Clearly containment was not working," Edwards judges, "or at least it was not working fast enough." He suggests that important changes in the Cold War came mostly from the actions of the Americans, not the Soviets. "The time had come, Ronald Reagan decided, not merely to contain Communism but to defeat it."[53] No longer would the United States stand by while the USSR armed and financed terrorists and subverted democratic governments. Reagan predicted correctly, Edwards observes, that "the march of freedom and democracy . . . will leave Marxism-Leninism on the ash heap of history as it has left other tyrannies which stifle the freedom and muzzle the self-expression of the people."[54]

Lee Edwards argues that Reagan took many effective actions designed to weaken the Soviet Union. On one front the president engaged in an economic war that destabilized the Soviet's financial situation. The president also gave overt and covert aid to groups that opposed Soviet expansion, such as the mujahideen in Afghanistan and the contras in Nicaragua. In a variety of ways, some of them obscured from public view, Reagan chiseled away at the Soviet Union's foundations of power. Also, Reagan attempted to delegitimize communism by speaking harshly about it in public, writes Edwards. Reagan's denunciations received considerable attention from the international media. Reagan told Mikhail Gorbachev to "tear down this wall" at Berlin's Brandenberg Gate, and he referred to the communist regime as an "evil empire."

Most important, Edwards recounts, Ronald Reagan sponsored what was widely referred to as Star Wars, the program that called for orbiting military stations in space that could defend the United States by shooting down enemy missiles with laser beams and other high-tech devices. Many liberals criticized the president for this initiative, notes the author, but he argues that Reagan's decision to fund initial development of the Strategic Defense Initiative (SDI) proved to be a brilliant maneuver. The Soviets, who were already badly stretched economically by the war in Afghanistan and the general arms race, needed to commit extraordinarily large funds to compete in this new field of technological endeavor. Through Reagan's commitment to SDI, the president "convinced the Kremlin it could not win." Star Wars challenged Mikhail Gorbachev profoundly and forced him to sue for peace. The Soviet Union quickly lost its satellite empire in Eastern Europe, reports Edwards, and in 1991 communism collapsed in Russia. Thanks to Reagan's tough actions, European Marxism was, indeed, buried in the ash heap of history.[55]

Several other writers have approached this subject from diverse political perspectives but have generally given factual support to those who wish to celebrate Reagan's effectiveness in forcing the collapse of the Soviet Union. Peter Schweizer's title gives away the upbeat tenor of his interpretation: *Reagan's War: The Epic Story of His Forty-Year Struggle and Final Triumph over Communism*. Schweizer is a fellow at the conservatively oriented Hoover Institution on War, Revolution, and Peace at Stanford University. The author concludes with a glowing description of the former president's "final triumph" over communism: "It provides us with wisdom and hope for the struggles of today and tomorrow," he writes. "Reagan's hope that we be guided not by fear but by courage and moral clarity is as apt today as it was during the Cold War."[56] In related ways Jay Winik maintains that the Reagan administration hastened the breakup of the Soviet Union, paving the way for a decisive victory in the Cold War. Winik praises not only Ronald Reagan but his neocon advisers, such as Richard Perle (a strong supporter of SDI), Elliott Abrams, Max Kampelman, and Jeane Kirkpatrick. Winik is on the staff of the University of Maryland's School of Public Affairs and has been an adjunct fellow at the Hudson Institute. He is considered a favorite historian of President George W. Bush and Vice President Dick Cheney. President Bush took Winik's book about the Civil War, *April, 1865,* to Camp David shortly after the 9/11 tragedy, and Cheney invited Winik to dinner, at which time the two discussed lessons of history that may offer insights for dealing with terrorism.[57]

Often, Hawkish Nationalists selectively drew upon facts about Cold War developments in the 1980s so that they could create a heroic narrative about Ronald Reagan's importance in pushing the Soviet Union toward its doom. Reagan won the Cold War, Senator Jesse Helms asserted. Through Reagan's military buildup, commitment to SDI, and tough talk he brought down the communist empire. Forceful language made a big difference in clarifying the issues, writes former Republican House leader Dick Armey. Reagan touted the moral and practical virtues of freedom loudly and self-confidently. The world had not heard such plain speaking for a long time, Armey declares: "Ronald Reagan simply said what all Americans outside the looney Left and the liberal establishment believed."[58]

Rush Limbaugh offers a related view of Reagan's heroic role in recent history in *The Way Things Ought to Be* (1992). The right-wing talk-radio host, who attracted a huge audience by the 1990s, maintains that Reagan's aggressive politics challenged the ideological foundations of the Soviet Union. The president made extraordinary progress toward bringing the Cold War to an end by threatening to deploy SDI, writes Limbaugh in the fashion of Lee Edwards. Star Wars had its effect without actual deployment, he notes with apparent glee. Limbaugh claims that the very idea of the United States possessing a powerful deterrent proved too much for the Soviet leaders. In the course of building this argument, Limbaugh could not turn away from the opportunity to laugh at liberals for making incorrect judgments. He recalls that critics of Star Wars complained about the tremendous cost of the high-tech program, yet it aided Reagan in realizing his goal and without huge expenditures. The Soviets believed Reagan intended to build SDI, and that expectation, in itself, forced them to accept defeat.[59]

Without Ronald Reagan in the picture, Limbaugh concludes, the Soviet Union would not have not have collapsed. Mikhail Gorbachev, the Soviet leader, does not, however, receive much recognition for contributing to the change. Limbaugh asserts that the fall of communism "would have happened whether Gorbachev was around or not, although Gorbachev should be given credit for not resisting it at the end with military force."[60]

Hawkish Nationalists frequently offer a favored narrative about the end of the Cold War that is similar to the themes presented by Edwards, Armey, Helms, and Limbaugh. Interpreters from the right celebrate Ronald

Reagan's exploits and give little or no attention to other explanations for the collapse of communism. They do not exhibit much curiosity about the interpretations favored by many foreign policy experts, specialists in Russian affairs, historians, and other research-oriented professionals. Hawkish Nationalists tend to consider the case closed. Only one historical narrative is compelling to them—the one that conveniently supports tenets of their political faith.

When writing or speaking about this history, few on the radical right address an important question about the supposed role of U.S. military prowess in bringing down the Soviet Union. They do not ask why leaders of the powerful communist state allowed their empire to collapse without strong military resistance. When forced to confront this query, the hawks usually offer vague references to the tremendous expense the Soviets faced when trying to keep up with U.S. military technology. This explanation could be a factor, but it certainly does not suffice as a complete answer.

Clearly, the Strategic Defense Initiative played some role in the Soviets' calculations in the 1980s, but no military development in the competition between the United States and the USSR delivered a deadly blow to Soviet power. The communist regime had at its command thousands of nuclear missiles and warheads in the 1980s. No American counterforce of the immediate future, not even a sophisticated and well-developed Star Wars program, could completely negate the threat of that lethal arsenal. Furthermore, SDI remained in the experimental stages in the Reagan era; it was still years away from only small levels of deployment and certainly far away from substantial development. The Soviets possessed impressive bargaining power in their relations with the United States thanks to their large nuclear stockpile. Even a remarkably successful SDI system that could knock out 90 percent of incoming missiles would not protect U.S. cities from disaster in the event of nuclear war. Reagan's commitment to SDI could not force the Soviets to give up communism.[61]

Three other explanations for the ending of the Cold War deserve important consideration in an analysis of the causes of change. The first two get short shrift or no attention at all in the Nationalists' typical narrative of the historic events. The third one gets some attention, but radicals are reluctant to embrace it because the idea undermines their favored story in defense of Reagan's military buildup. The first factor concerns Mikhail Gorbachev's role in fomenting change (much of it through unintended consequences rather than specific planning). The second factor relates to the appeal of capitalism, democracy, and freedom in the modern world. The people of the USSR became more acquainted with this appeal by the 1980s, and it appears to have made a significant impact on them. Finally, and ironically, President Reagan deserves credit in this counternarrative, not for his tough tactics in the early Cold War years but for his openness to negotiations with the communists, especially during his second term in office.

Most scholars credit Mikhail Gorbachev as the principal catalyst behind developments that led to the demise of communism in the Soviet Union. They note that the Soviet premier intended to reform the state but instead awakened a revolution against it. The changes Gorbachev fostered greatly weakened the communist system. When this fragility became apparent, Mikhail Gorbachev did not promote the draconian measures earlier Soviet leaders had employed to crush resistance. Gorbachev allowed the people of the Soviet republics to choose their future, and those people readily opted out of the communist system. Without the threat of violence, his regime looked like a paper tiger. It collapsed quickly and rather peacefully.

Gorbachev's individual importance in this rapidly altering history became immediately apparent (except to Hawkish Nationalists, who tended to view him as a secondary player in the unfolding drama). Within a short time after taking office in 1985, Gorbachev promoted major changes. His program of glasnost (public truth-telling) opened dialogues about improving life in the Soviet Union and the affairs of state. Perestroika (restructuring) was designed to make the economy more modern and efficient. These measures aroused expectations, especially when the citizenry recognized that Gorbachev was not simply creating a false impression of change. Russians and citizens in the satellite states sensed that the Soviet premier's programs actually allowed greater expression of opinion and encouraged new efforts to modernize the Soviet Union. The people saw that they could articulate their ideas and feelings openly, and soon they exploited that opportunity. Publicly, they showed disgust for the communist system, especially young adults in the Soviet bloc nations. Gorbachev hoped glasnost and perestroika would help to make communism more acceptable to the public, but he found, instead, that his reforms facilitated the efforts of many discontented citizens to reject the system altogether.

Mikhail Gorbachev also made history by working to defuse the dangerous Soviet-U.S. arms race, an accomplishment that is recognized by scholars of history far more than it is acknowledged by Hawkish Nationalists. The Soviet leader pressed for new understandings in negotiations at Geneva, and later submitted a vast plan for dismantling nuclear weapons in a meeting at Reykjavik, Iceland. At first that proposal attracted a friendly reception from President Reagan, but exchanges between the two leaders and their negotiating parties quickly became tense. Especially troubling were difficulties over the SDI (Reagan wanted to proceed with an initial testing of the Star Wars program; Gorbachev wanted to halt American development and deployment of the system). Nevertheless, Gorbachev continued pushing for agreements after Reykjavik, and in late 1987 he traveled to Washington, D.C., to sign a treaty between the United States and Soviet Union to destroy weapons (the agreement aimed to eliminate intermediate nuclear forces). Then, in 1988, Gorbachev announced that the USSR would unilaterally begin overall force reductions in Europe and would withdraw military forces from Afghanistan. It is difficult to believe that such significant changes could have occurred within three years of taking office if another leader had been at the Soviet helm.

Gorbachev also took the extraordinary action in May 1989 of announcing that the Soviet Union would no longer use force to prevent democratization in its satellite states, and this message had tremendous repercussions. By November of that year, citizens of East Germany tested Gorbachev's promise by scaling the infamous Berlin Wall. Communist guards did not fire on the people who sought refuge in free Berlin. This event inspired actions by citizens in other Soviet bloc nations. Even Romania, which for years had been caught in the iron grip of a brutal dictatorship, fell quickly. Romanians executed their hated leader. Again, it is difficult to imagine that all of this could have happened rapidly in the late 1980s if the reform- and peace-minded Mikhail Gorbachev had not been the USSR's leader. For radical conservatives, though, Gorbachev is not the major catalyst for change. Their eyes are on the White House. The right's historical drama about the end of the Cold War puts the spotlight on President Reagan.

The second major factor that gets short shrift in the Hawkish Nationalist narratives about factors behind the ending of the Cold War relates to the appeal of capitalism, democracy, and freedom. U.S. scholars and journalists as well as Russians themselves have commented on the way Western lifestyles undermined the Soviet people's support for their regimes. Jeans, baseball caps, rock music, McDonald's hamburgers, Coca-Cola, and other attractions of Western culture weakened the public's allegiance to communism. It was not so much a fear of American military might that made the East jettison communism; it was the appeal of consumer goods in the possession of Americans and other Westerners. The East's attraction to the free enterprise system (and to American culture) ought to excite great interest among conservatives. Yet it doesn't, for they emphasize the "push" of American military spending and planning rather than the "pull" of the West's economic and cultural attractions.

It is, in fact, ironic that radical rightists do not give more credit to the second interpretation, because it relates to strengths of the free world that have long been prominent in their anticommunist rhetoric. Radcons often celebrate the ideal of a free people operating in a market-based economy, but they do not adequately recognize the importance of that notion in undermining the stability of Soviet communism. Once again, the Hawkish Nationalists' commitment to a myth of their political faith leaves them unprepared to view history with genuine curiosity. They will not consider interpretations that detract from their favored images of Ronald Reagan, armed with SDI, slaying the Red Dragon. The right gives short shrift to a perspective that places more emphasis on peaceful factors in the fall of communism than to elements related to war making.

The counternarrative favored by historians and other professionals draws attention to the difficulties communist leaders faced when trying to keep their people behind a wall of censorship. It notes that for much of the twentieth century, Moscow's bureaucrats were largely successful in hiding details about Western affluence, democracy, and freedom from the people of the Soviet Union. They could keep their public rather isolated from developments in communities beyond communist borders, and leaders employed the mass media to advertise their own economy as an admirable engine of progress. In the years immediately after World War II it was easy to maintain this deceit, because the nearby capitalist world did not appear to offer much competition. Western Europeans had been terribly battered by the recent war, and many of them suffered from miserable poverty. Then an economic takeoff developed in the 1950s. A glaring distinction between market-oriented societies and command-oriented communist societies became increasingly evident in subsequent decades.

This interpretation, which conflicts with the familiar theme about the influence of Reagan's sword-rattling, notes the impact of the modern communications and transportation revolutions. It suggests that these important developments had the effect of informing many people behind the Iron Curtain of the momentous changes that were occurring in the West. A greater availability of films, videos, and television programs exposed citizens in Russia and the satellite countries to the comparatively higher quality of life in Europe and the United States. Travelers from the communist countries jetted to Paris, London, and New York and returned with observations that exposed the great communist lie. These visitors brought back a troublesome message based on personal experience. They said the Soviet Union was not superior to the West, as they had been taught. The Soviet economy and quality of life were glaringly inferior. Once Gorbachev lifted the lid on expression through glasnost, news of these stunning advantages and disadvantages spread quickly and widely.

The concept of freedom plays a significant role in this counternarrative, yet Hawkish Nationalists give the interpretation relatively little weight when explaining the causes of communism's collapse and the conclusion of the Cold War. Again, they refuse to embrace an analysis that pulls the spotlight off of Ronald Reagan. The counternarrative suggests that an expansion of communications in communist countries involved more than just talk about consumer goods. News from the West brought impressive evidence about the advantages of democracy and freedom. Those who visited the United States and Western Europe could report that citizens in the West enjoyed significantly greater opportunities to participate vigorously in their countries' politics than did citizens of the Soviet Union. The "dictatorship of the proletariat" looked, in practice, like a dictatorship of the bureaucrat. Furthermore, the totalitarian Soviet government had a horrible record of neglecting human rights. Some of the notable outrages against dissidents included arrests by the secret police, placement in gulags, and mass executions. This information began to come into public view during the years of Nikita Khrushchev's leadership in the Soviet Union during the 1950s and 1960s, and it received much greater and freer public discussion under Gorbachev's program of glasnost (and in the premier's speeches). The beacon of freedom had become much more visible to people behind the Iron Curtain by the 1980s.

A third factor that serves to undermine the favored radical narrative about the end of the Cold War concerns President Reagan's actions. At first glance, this approach seems to bolster the right's argument about the impact of Reagan's posture as a Cold Warrior who boldly denounced communism and spent freely on military programs, but upon closer examination, the interpretation serves to undermine this simplistic viewpoint. The third explanation for the demise of the Soviet Union stresses Reagan's adaptability in dealing with the Russians. The right tends to minimize this factor when developing its narratives about the fall of communism. Hawkish Nationalists prefer to speak and write about a fighting Reagan rather than a negotiating one.

President Reagan made an impressive change in direction in his dealings with the Soviets during his second term. When Gorbachev began offering an olive branch, Reagan, the man who had seemed eager to greet the Soviets with weapons instead of treaties, reached out and accepted the premier's peace offerings. Secretary of State George Shultz supported these moves. At a Geneva summit meeting in late 1985 the president had an opportunity to meet the Soviet leader, and he quickly sensed a difference from the old-style Russian leadership. Reagan reported that Gorbachev seemed to be a man you could do business with (Margaret Thatcher had said the same thing earlier).[62] At the Reykjavik meeting a year later, Reagan responded positively when Gorbachev surprised him with a proposal for bold reductions in nuclear armaments. Late in the meeting Reagan asked, "Why don't we just get rid of all nuclear weapons? Just get rid of them all." The Soviet leader replied, "Yes, let's do that."[63] Reagan's openness to discussion kept the dialogue moving—even to the point that it alarmed some of his aides who urged more caution. To be sure, Reagan continued to hear advice that represented the thinking of the old-fashioned hard-liners (his defense secretary, Caspar Weinberger, was particularly resistant to negotiating with the Soviets, a position that sometimes exasperated Reagan). At least Reagan was willing to explore the possibility of conducting meaningful exchanges. If Weinberger or some of the other Cold Warriors associated with the administration had been president, it is likely that the progress made in the late 1980s toward bringing nuclear weaponry under a greater degree of control could not have been achieved.[64]

Reagan sounds too much like a liberal in this historical interpretation to please the Hawkish Nationalists. They are not eager to celebrate the president's flexibility, his readiness to change course in the face of new evidence, or his openness to working deals with the communists in order to make the world more secure.[65] Many on the right stick to their previously prepared historical sermons. Through a rigid allegiance to hardliners' interpretation of events, they fail to give adequate recognition to one of Ronald Reagan's greatest achievements as president. As Strobe Talbott, Bill Clinton's deputy secretary of state, has remarked, "The truth is a better tribute to Reagan than the myth."[66]

Raymond L. Garthoff challenges that myth in his well researched book, *The Great Transition: American-Soviet Relations and the End of the Cold War* (1994). Garthoff concludes that the people who see Reagan's saber-rattling as the key to the West's victory in the Cold War are essentially wrong. The West did not win, as is widely believed, "through geopolitical containment and military deterrence," he asserts. "Still less was the Cold War won by the Reagan military buildup and the Reagan doctrine, as some have suggested." Instead, Garthoff traces "victory" to the arrival of a new generation of Soviet leaders who "realized how badly their system at home and their policies had failed." Mikhail Gorbachev renounced the idea of Marxist-Leninist-Stalinist world conflict, says Garthoff. He, above all, paved the way for change by accepting "the interdependence of the world, of the priority of all-human values over class values, and of the indivisibility of common security." In the final analysis, writes Garthoff, only a Soviet leader could have ended the Cold War peacefully at that time, and Gorbachev was the individual who set out specifically to bring it to an end.[67]

Another sophisticated interpreter of the way the Cold War ended, Don Oberdorfer, gives credit to the far-sighted men sitting on *both* sides of the U.S.-Soviet negotiating table. Mikhail Gorbachev is a major player in the drama described in Oberdorfer's impressive study, *From the Cold War to a New Era: The United States and the Soviet Union, 1983–1991*. Gorbachev is "a great historical figure," the author concludes. Though flawed in some ways, the Soviet leader grew in stature and maturity. Ultimately he "was the central figure in the transformation of his country and its relations with the world."[68] Reagan, too, made significant contributions. Through self-confidence and eagerness to negotiate with leaders of the "evil empire," he "played a major part in what took place."[69] Oberdorfer also gives major credit to key advisers who worked alongside these two world leaders. Gorbachev's foreign minister, Eduard Shevardnadze, "is a remarkable figure meriting a place of his own in the annals of his time," writes Oberdorfer, because he showed the vision necessary to work large changes.[70] On the American side, it is evident that Ronald Reagan benefited greatly from the advice of his able secretary of state, George Shultz. Reagan, says Oberdorfer, "knew that he wanted a less dangerous relationship with the Soviet Union, but he did not know how to go about achieving it." Shultz enabled the president to realize his goals. The secretary of state provided a persistent and practical drive to improve relations with the Soviets and the organizational skills to mobilize members of a fractious U.S. government to interact with them in a systematic way.[71] Thus four men, not one, emerge as significant figures in this story of the Cold War's end.

It should be emphasized that an open-minded perspective on this history does not require complete denial of the importance of Reagan's arms buildup. Clearly, it helps when a nation negotiates from a position of strength, and Reagan tried to bring the country toward that condition in the 1980s. Whether the extraordinarily high levels of defense spending that Reagan demanded were necessary to enhance the nation's bargaining position with the USSR is a matter of debate. Perhaps more moderate but nevertheless significant improvements in military preparedness and technological know-how could have aided U.S. diplomacy just as well. Hawks tend to consider every dollar essential of the billions spent for defense in the 1980s. In comparison, many professionals who address this history from outside of the conservative movement, including liberals, are doubtful that the expenditures produced the wonderful results confidently claimed by the radcons. Liberals and others believe the spending spree Reagan sponsored to buy military hardware and technology was not as important in contributing to the collapse of the Soviet Union as were other factors. These more open-minded interpreters note that the gigantic military expenditures contributed to a glaring budget deficit, and this financial problem became a major source of troubles for the U.S. economy.

Inside the radical right, then, familiar stories about the conclusion of the Cold War represent sermons delivered by pastors of the political faith. These interpreters treat history as a sort of divine tale about a brave and godlike individual who brought salvation to his people by displaying strength and courage. The familiar narrative about Reagan's exploits reads like Biblical commentary about a heroic figure, and radcons often treat people who challenge this epic tale as heretics who fail to recognize the veracity of the scriptures. Their outlook contrasts dramatically with the perspective of those who approach history with inquisitive and critical minds.

## Identifying the Enemy after 9/11

Al-Qaeda's airplane attacks on the World Trade Towers in New York City and the Pentagon in Washington, D.C. (in addition to a fourth hijacked plane that crashed in a Pennsylvania field) on September 11, 2001, aroused a tremendous sense of unity in the United States. Americans felt a common vulnerability to terrorism and were determined to respond strongly to the huge challenge. In the first days after news about the events of September 11 sent shock waves across the nation, the American people seemed as one. Democrats and Republicans came together to express grief and anger. Differences between the two parties looked much less important than the bond Americans shared in mourning the innocent victims and showing determination to confront and defeat their dangerous enemies.

It seems hard to imagine that a political group in the United States would exploit the national tragedy of September 11, but that is exactly what many leading conservatives did. They attempted to direct the American people's attention in the terrible crisis to the liberals. Both by innuendo and through direct accusation, prominent figures on the right claimed that liberals represented America's Achilles' heel in the struggle against terrorism. In much of this commentary the threat from al-Qaeda appeared to be of secondary interest. From the perspective of the right, the big menace was an internal one coming from America's left.

William J. Bennett offers a comprehensive example of this perspective in *Why We Fight: Moral Clarity and the War on Terrorism* (2002). As was noted earlier, Bennett had served in leadership positions in Republican administrations and had achieved popularity as the author and editor of books about virtue and morality (his reputation for moral leadership came under question, however, when the public learned that he was an inveterate gambler who lost a great deal of money in gaming).

In *Why We Fight* Bennett focuses particularly on the reactions of Americans to the shock of 9/11 rather than to the matter of dealing with terrorists abroad. He applies a technique of guilt by association when identifying people who, he thinks, lack a proper moral vision for America's war on terrorism. He cites evidence of highly emotional, provocative, and controversial statements by some Americans in response to the attacks of 9/11. Then, in a facile manner, Bennett implies that mainstream liberals were sympathetic to these controversial statements and outlooks. Bennett does not use the term *liberal* throughout his discussion. Rather, he directs his criticism primarily at intellectuals and educators. Bennett knows his audience, though, and his message is clear. Radical statements made against the United States in the context of the 9/11 tragedy, he suggests, morphed out of a liberal perspective on international issues. At the source of many problems Americans face in the age of terrorism, he implies, are *liberal* intellectuals and *liberal* educators.

It was relatively easy for Bennett to uncover a few extremist statements to build his case for conservative outrage. Of the millions of comments Americans made in their anguish over the attacks of 9/11, some speakers directed criticism toward the United States. These individuals claimed the nation would not have been targeted by terrorists if its record in global affairs had been more honorable. Some of these speakers and writers complained about exploitative capitalism, the politics of oil, environmental wreckage, or cultural hegemony. Others pointed to historical examples of U.S. aggression in foreign affairs, including covert operations. Some denounced the placement of U.S. troops in foreign counties. These critics, for the most part, did not blame the United States completely for the attacks of September 11, but their claims were surely controversial under the circumstances. In the tense and angry days after 9/11, these individuals directly challenged the assumption held by most Americans that terrorists did not have a good reason to hate the United States or attack its citizens. In the context of the times, those who played a blame game, pointing fingers at the United States, were taking a great risk of inciting anger.

Politically savvy commentators on the 9/11 tragedy appreciate the Biblical message that suggests there is a proper time and a place for everything. They understand that the first days following the destruction in New York City, Washington, D.C., and Pennsylvania were less appropriate times for engaging in critical discourse about controversial aspects of U.S. foreign policy than later periods. The individuals who raised these complaints immediately after the tragedy seemed clueless about human psychology and American politics. Many Americans thought their critique of U.S. relations with the world in the aftermath of such heinous crimes sounded like attempts to diminish the guilt of the terrorists. Understandably, irate citizens and pundits lambasted the commentators for suggesting U.S. culpability.

Only a few among the millions who spoke about the meaning of September 11 claimed, in a sense, that the United States "had it coming," yet William J. Bennett tried to gain political capital from these provocative statements. Like many other conservative commentators, Bennett suggested that these criticisms reflected the basic outlook of the left. He did not treat the insensitive statements as occasional outbursts by marginal individuals who displayed a penchant for inviting controversy. For Bennett, the comments represented opinion from a vast group of discontented Americans who felt contempt for their country. There was an opportunity to exploit the situation irresponsibly, and Bennett seized it.

William J. Bennett attributes the exaggerated statements in his book to highly placed individuals. "Educators," "intellectuals," "relativists," "nonjudgmentalists," "pacifists," members of the "peace party," and representatives of the "adversary culture" were the culprits, he argues. The troublemakers were not simply on the fringes. America's "unpatriotic," he asserts, "are culturally the most influential among us."[72] They are present in the universities and other respected institutions, he writes. Although these people were not numerous in comparison to the total population of the United States, they had power through sheer cultural weight and prestige, and "at least until September 11, 2001, the flag-wavers among us represented a large but dissenting minority."[73] Bennett claims that influential educators and intellectuals were engaged in a "relentless critique of American reality and American ideals." These offensive people considered the noble impulse to love one's country "a suspect category."[74] For forty years, Bennett attests, educators and intellectuals "had been saying the United States was no better and might even be worse than its enemies; that Western 'civilization,' sometimes mockingly put in quotation marks, was a mask under which one perfidy after another had been visited upon the poor nations of the world; that good and evil themselves were matters of perspective if not of mere opinion."[75] The left interpreted American history darkly, Bennett writes in *Why We Fight,* demanding apologies for land grabs against native populations; despoliation of the environment; mistreatment of blacks, Mexicans, and women; and the thievery by robber barons.[76] Bennett worries that generations of

American children had been raised on the principle that the United States was "always wrong."[77]

Bennett peppers his analysis with references to outbursts made by university students and professors who criticized the United States in connection with September 11. He reports that a New York University student said, "This is all [America's] fault anyway," and shortly after September 11 a professor at a teach-in at the University of North Carolina in Chapel Hill argued that the United States should apologize to the widows, orphans, and impoverished victims of American imperialism.[78] Bennett observes that some university-based commentators refused to sanction military action after the September 11 tragedy. A Columbia University sophomore said, "I don't think the solution to violence is more violence," and a mother in Maine argued that "killing people won't prove anything. It's just more of the same."[79] Bennett complains that pacifists were "impugning our right to defend ourselves."[80] He is horrified to see many timid, confused, and appalling responses to 9/11. "Why, I wondered," writes Bennett, "were not more of us angry?"[81]

If William J. Bennett thought the American people were not adequately angry in the aftermath of September 11, he must have been holed up in a cave in the days after the tragedy. Citizens of the United States, including "leading educators and intellectuals," to use Bennett's language, were clearly outraged and eager to see American forces find and kill the terrorists. Anyone present in the country during those days of shock, fear, and rage can recall the power of that emotional response. The Americans' spirited demand for military action was impressive. William J. Bennett, however, chose to view responses to September 11 one-dimensionally, with a lens only on his right eye. Instead of seeing a united people ready to act in concert against a dangerous enemy, Bennett saw a divided nation. He claimed that champions of negativism had been undermining the American people's patriotism and resolve for years. Influential academics as well as intellectual and cultural malcontents had been preaching self-hatred, he charged. Now, in a moment of national crisis, the American people were too weakened by the resultant self-doubts to put up an effective struggle against wicked enemies.

Bennett's claims are so patently ridiculous that it is reasonable to suspect that he did not truly believe that the controversial remarks and actions he referenced had much relevance to the actual state of affairs in America after 9/11. The conservative author and former government official is much too politically astute to believe such nonsense. It is far more likely that Bennett framed his arguments to appeal to the conservative faithful. He knows that audience well, having published best-selling books that attracted a strong readership on the right. Bennett crafted his rhetoric to please a right-wing audience that loves to hear about the thoughts and activities of supposedly heinous professors and intellectuals.

Bennett's disturbing portrayal of a divided and weakened America had little to do with actual conditions in the United States after September 11. The American people were not substantially split in their reactions to the attacks. Bennett's assignment of blame to educators and intellectuals was just as preposterous as the attempts by a few cynics to blame American capitalism, imperialism, and aggression for the terrorist attacks. In both cases the choice of targets revealed more about the speakers' agendas than about recent history. Furthermore, the ugly implication of Bennett's diatribe against academics and intellectuals is clear. In an indirect manner he suggested that the attitudes of liberals constituted a principal source of the nation's weakness in the face of terrorist threats. The problem, Bennett hinted, was not with educators and intellectuals generally but with *liberal* educators and *liberal* intellectuals specifically.

Whereas William J. Bennett targets academics and the intelligentsia, Sean Hannity aims his attacks much more directly against "liberals" (Hannity uses the term frequently throughout his publications and in his comments on television). Hannity attended but dropped out of New York University and later established a successful career as a radio commentator. He draws huge audiences for his syndicated radio shows and appearances as host on the Fox News Channel's *Hannity and Colmes*. Hannity often makes liberals and Democrats the target of his complaints. The subtitles of two recent books by Hannity suggest that he is more interested in writing about the liberal threat than the one from al-Qaeda. In fact, the major arguments in these publications imply that the liberals' challenge to America is grave and the American people desperately need to be rescued from their evil grip. *Let Freedom Ring* (2002) indicates through its subtitle that the great task ahead for America is *Winning the War of Liberty over Liberalism.* A later publication, *Deliver Us from Evil* (2004), looks at first glance like a primer on ways to evade the wrath of suicide bombers and other jihadists, but the subtitle reveals Hannity's continuing obsession with a different, more local enemy. Safety from that "evil," he says, will depend on *Defeating Terrorism, Despotism, and Liberalism.*

Years ago, books with such outlandish titles were appropriately consigned to the shelves containing kook literature about imagined conspiracies. These days, however, books about saving the country from the evil of liberalism are at the top rungs of the best-seller list. Hannity's two publications have situated him among America's best-grossing authors of nonfiction (his writing seems inappropriately catalogued; it belongs in the fiction list). The conservative talk show host's publications nicely serve the liberal-baiting crowd. Many readers on the right find Hannity's claims about fighting a "war" against the "evil" of liberalism appropriate language for characterizing the nation's current struggle (they have certainly encountered similar language in many other popular books). The favored tracts demonize liberals. Some of the books identify liberalism as a horror tantamount to other evils from history such as despotism, communism, and terrorism.

Sean Hannity says that Americans are vulnerable in their confrontation with terrorism because they have been "softened" by the allure of modern liberalism.[82] "For the past half century," he observes in an alarming history lesson, "liberals have been engaged in a dangerous and destructive effort to morally disarm our children." Liberal educators, he says, have undermined American youngsters' faith in their nation by teaching them to hate the United States. Why, during a time of war, Hannity asks, should we entrust the education of our children "to people who loathe and ravage so many of our core values."[83]

As in Bennett's book, Hannity's verbal assault operates on the assumption that leftist ideologues are imbedded in the schools and colleges of America, where they brainwash innocent and impressionable students. To support this claim, Hannity, like Bennett, features stories about professors who have made extraordinarily critical statements about American activities abroad. Hannity cites, for instance, the example of an instructor at Columbia University who announced at a teach-in that he hoped American soldiers who participated in the occupation of Iraq would face a million Mogadishus (referring to a 1993 incident in Somalia when eighteen U.S. soldiers were killed during a military operation). Hannity also criticizes radical statements made by MIT's Noam Chomsky and other university-based commentators.[84]

Sean Hannity argues that the liberals are "appeasement-minded" and in no position to stand up strongly to Osama bin Laden and the al-Qaeda terrorists.[85] Appeasement doesn't work, he tells readers. Toughness succeeds. The contrast is evident in history, from the success of Winston Churchill compared to the failure of Neville Chamberlain, from the success of Ronald Reagan compared to the failure of Jimmy Carter, and from the recent successes of George W. Bush compared to the failures of the modern Democratic Party.[86] Sometimes Hannity employs the terms "appeasement" and "pacifism" interchangeably. He complains that Bill Clinton's "appeasement virus" infected the world and then easily slips into a scolding of liberals for promoting a pacifistic outlook that does not take into account the harsh realities of human nature. Bin Laden and the al-Qaeda operatives are brutal murderers, he reminds readers, and no program of appeasement or pacifism can succeed in dealing with them.

As the author moves deeper and deeper into this interpretation based on familiar conservative dogma rather than the realities of American liberalism, his charges against the supposedly dangerous ideological enemy on the left become increasingly fantastic. After Hannity has demeaned liberals as the scum of national politics, virtually any accusation about their perfidy appears to complement his call for rescuing America from the left's evil grip. Hannity claims that liberals are "moral relativists" who reject absolute standards of right and wrong and, therefore, can offer little more than a meek response to September 11. Liberals do not view bin Laden and his followers as depraved murderers, he asserts. Instead, they see the terrorists as men "driven to their bad acts by the injustices of Western society."[87] Liberals are sympathetic toward the terrorists much as they are sympathetic toward murderers on death row in the United States, Hannity tells readers. The left displays concern for the perpetrators of violence rather than the victims of violence, he claims.[88] Liberals lack a proper philosophical and religious sense of right and wrong, and, consequently, they lack the will necessary to bring evildoers to account. The left mocks President George W. Bush for seeing the world starkly in black-and-white terms, yet that is exactly what Americans need in their president during a time of crisis.[89] In sum, liberals project dangerous views for a country facing terrorism. They "must be confronted and defeated," says Hannity, "if America is to lead and succeed in the twenty-first century."[90]

The leap from Bennett's and Hannity's popular diatribes against liberal thinkers, educators, and politicians to the still more outrageous ranting of rabidly conservative radio and television pundits such as Michael Savage and Ann Coulter is not great. The escalation in language from Bennett to Hannity to Savage and Coulter is largely one of degree, not of kind. Savage and Coulter take fundamental arguments in the Bennett and Hannity theses—that liberals and their fellow leftists have often turned the American people against their own society—and push that argument to its logical conclusion. Savage and Coulter portray liberals as more perfectly formed devils, the purveyors of dastardly deeds in America. Liberals are the enemy in their diatribes, the practitioners of treason. It these forms of political fundamentalism, the representatives of Satan are clearly identified.

Michael Savage, a popular right-wing radio host who published *The Enemy Within: Saving America from the Assault on Our Schools, Faith, and Military* (2003), gives the verbal assault a particularly shrill and mean-spirited quality. Savage, whose original name was Michael Alan Weiner, grew up in the Bronx but has spent much of his life in northern California. After studies at the University of California–Berkeley, he became a promoter of alternative medicine. Savage published widely as a herbalist and nutritionist. Eventually he discovered the power of radio and the profits that come with fame as a right-wing media personality. Using the pseudonym Michael Savage, he gained a national reputation for delivering biting radio-based critiques of liberals. He also complained frequently in his broadcasts about feminists, gays, immigrants, and academics. Savage had a brief run with his own TV show on MSNBC, but his controversial remarks helped to terminate the program. He alienated a gay caller, saying, "Are you one of those sodomites? . . . You should only get AIDS and die, you pig!"[91] Savage continued on the radio, and in recent years that show has attracted up to eight million listeners.

Whereas Bennett implies that liberal ideas weaken the nation and Hannity claims it directly, Michael Savage writes in a blunter fashion. Savage's blistering attack gets off to a lively start at the beginning of the book, when he associates liberals with sinister conspirators who plot against the state's interests. His sermon on their threat begins with a lengthy sentence from Cicero. Savage notes that the Roman orator warned about a type of person who "rots the soul of a nation, he works secretly and unknown in the night to undermine the pillars of the city, he infects the body politic so that it can no longer resist. A murderer is less to fear."

Michael Savage mixes comments about the "extreme left" and the "radical left" with claims about liberals in a fashion that makes these groups appear to be virtually the same.[92] In the course of lashing out against America's supposed internal enemies, Savage spews out one wild accusation after another. He binges on hate. The author claims liberal judges give child pornographers and drug dealers special protection. The left-wing establishment believes that a "corrupt, racist American state deserved to be attacked and destroyed," Savage reports. "That is their *modus operandi*." Liberals are eager to push "failed socialist ideals on America," he tells readers.[93] They want to "put a Democrat-socialist in power."[94] Most important, in the war on terrorism, liberal "turncoats" and their sympathizers are so filled with anti-American hatred that they are willing to sabotage President Bush's fight for freedom in Iraq. The modern-day descendants of Benedict Arnold who have criticized President Bush's fight against terrorism "with their subversive tongues" are "openly anti-American," Savage charges.[95]

Ann Coulter, a sexy-looking and vituperative speaker on television talk shows, is as irresponsible as Michael Savage in describing liberals as enemies of the nation. Coulter, an attorney, attracted attention when she delivered stinging criticisms of President Bill Clinton when revelations appeared concerning his affair with Monica Lewinsky. Coulter has been pushed aside by various publishers and TV executives because of her outrageous statements, but she has managed to remain a powerful voice in public affairs nevertheless. Like Michael Savage, Coulter gives greater attention to a supposed threat from the American left than to the threat represented by terrorists outside the country (at least in terms of the number of angry words she applies in her comments about the challenges Americans faced after 9/11). Coulter clearly identifies the principal danger, as she sees it, in the title and subtitle of her book: *Treason: Liberal Treachery from the Cold War to the War on Terror* (2003). Like Bennett, Hannity, and Savage, Coulter finds the nation weakened by a cancer of liberalism. Her descriptions of liberals support the claim of "treason," since she charges liberals with working constantly against the nation's interests. Liberals "always manage to take the position that most undermines American security," she reports.[96] "Whenever the nation is under attack from within or without, liberals side with the enemy."[97] Furthermore, liberals "malign the flag" and "ban the pledge" of allegiance. They "hold cocktail parties for

America's enemies," Coulter asserts, but it is difficult to criticize these practices. Liberals see to it that "no one is allowed to cast the slightest aspersion on their patriotism."[98]

The dramatic remarks made by Bennett, Hannity, Savage, and Coulter may seem over-the-top—just the ranting of marginal extremists. Some observers assume that sensible Americans readily dismiss the strident rhetoric of these verbal provocateurs. Many people do, but the audience for these diatribes is nonetheless huge. Publications by the four ultras were abundantly and prominently on display in bookstores throughout the United States in the years after the 9/11 attacks. These publications sold much more briskly than many of the more moderate and scholarly books on American responses to international issues.

One might expect America's conservatives to feel embarrassed by these scurrilous accusations about their political opponents. It is not unreasonable to expect them to denounce Bennett and Hannity (and, especially, Savage and Coulter) as radical demagogues who have gone to extremes in their criticisms of liberals. Partisans of the conservative movement who are committed to intelligent discourse on the important political issues of the day ought to take strong measures to separate their cause from such tirades. Sober-voiced conservatives should treat the authors of these hate-mongering books as pariahs, much as William F. Buckley did in the 1950s when he tried to disassociate the fledgling new conservative movement from the paranoid rhetoric of the John Birch Society. Public denouncements are not particularly evident, however. Occasionally a few conservatives show discomfort with these and other figures who treat liberals as serious threats to the nation, but they usually do not engage in a vigorous campaign to disassociate themselves and their political organizations from such comments. For the most part, leaders on the right do not engage in severe criticism of these angry exercises in liberal bashing. Most conservatives apply Ronald Reagan's "Eleventh Commandment" in these situations. Just as Reagan promised not to question fellow Republicans in public, today's right-wing leaders tend not to criticize their strident colleagues under the lights of the national media.

Conservatives who are uncomfortable with these caustic attacks on liberals may also fear the consequences of public dissent. To raise questions about the excesses of Bennett, Hannity, Savage, and Coulter may draw the wrath of True Believers. Questioners are likely to find invitations to conservative think tanks, cocktail parties, and weekend retreats quickly withdrawn. Opportunities to publish essays in journals of the right can disappear. The faithful will eagerly kill a messenger bringing unwanted news. Hannity, Savage, and Coulter are not pariahs of the right, even though they ought to be. They have not been banished from the political church because of their excesses. These authors and commentators are, instead, influential preachers who draw large followings from sects within the expansive faith of militant conservatism. Of course, some of the more staid and educated thinkers on the right view these strident figures as akin to the fire and brimstone leaders of religious revivals, and they tend not to take a personal interest in their sermons. Hannity, Savage, and Coulter are, nevertheless, generally tolerated and welcomed in the diverse and broadly ecumenical cathedral of modern conservatism. Establishment figures on the right understand that these angry orators strengthen the resolve of followers at the grassroots. Bennett, Hannity, Savage, and Coulter operate like revivalists who promise fire and brimstone to their audiences. They effectively arouse many partisans in the movement for a spirited crusade against the liberal devil.

## Confronting the Prospect of War and Occupation in Iraq

The tragedy of 9/11 led quickly into another tragedy for Americans, this time in Iraq. As Richard A. Clarke, George W. Bush's former antiterrorism czar, reports in his book, *Against All Enemies: Inside America's War on Terror* (2004), shortly after the shocking event, leaders in the White House, including President George W. Bush, jumped to the unwarranted conclusion that Saddam Hussein's government had something to do with al-Qaeda's attacks. The president visited Clarke's office at the time and demanded that he and his team quickly gather information about possible links between al-Qaeda and Saddam Hussein's government.[99] President Bush's actions gave evidence of a mindset that drew the United States into a gigantic quagmire in the Arab nation, as the former treasury secretary in George W. Bush's administration, Paul O'Neill, indicated in a book released in 2004 by journalist Ron Suskind, *The Price of Loyalty*.[100] Bush and his advisers were determined to make war on Iraq. In fact, they were moving in that direction well before September 11.

As George Packer observes in his informative analysis of the U.S. pursuit of war and occupation in Iraq, the neocons who advised George W. Bush to intervené militarily acted in supremely self-assured ways. Richard Perle, an influential adviser to the Defense Department, "personified the neoconservative insurgent, absolutely confident of himself and his ideas," writes Packer.[101] A government official described Paul Wolfowitz, Donald Rumsfeld's deputy at the Defense Department, as a man of good qualities but also as one with "an unfortunate ability to delude himself because he believes so passionately in things."[102] Packer says the key people who worked under Rumsfeld took it "as an article of faith" that the nation's prospects were good for replacing Saddam's Hussein's regime with a peaceful, stable, democratic government. Critics of the Bush administration called this belief their "theology," and Packer suggests "they weren't completely wrong" when employing the term. He says that neocon "theology" operated with blissful disregard for evidence. "This faith defied both history and the live evidence on CNN," writes Packard.[103] A Lebanese professor who worked in the UN offices in Baghdad offered Packard an invidious comparison. Ghassan Salame thought the neoconservatives were not like the Americans he had met earlier who took pragmatic, problem-solving approaches to policymaking. Neocons "are new Americans," he said, "unknown Americans, Americans with ideology, with a master plan, with friends here, not open to everybody, with interests—somehow missionaries."[104]

The president and his advisors deserve blame for the trouble that resulted, but others need to be held accountable, too. Bush and his wayward team could never have dragged the nation into a mess in Iraq if America's conservatives had projected a more open and critical attitude during the year and a half after September 11, 2001. When the country marched to the drumbeat of the war-planners, True Believers on the right, in large part, cheered the mobilization and shouted down those who suggested that military intervention and occupation might represent inappropriate or ineffective solutions to the problems at hand.

Before the United States launched its war against Saddam Hussein on March 19, 2003, the case for engagement was shaky at best, and many Americans outside the conservative camp were opposed to immediate action. They offered numerous reasons for opposing President Bush's call for war. Some wanted to give the United Nations inspectors more time to look for chemical, biological, and nuclear weapons. Quite a few suspected there were no WMDs in Iraq because the inspectors' work to that point had not turned up evidence of a large-scale program. There was, then, no justification for war. Many commentators suggested they might sanction war after many months if the evidence of dangerous weapons programs surfaced. Others wanted U.S. actions against Iraq to progress under the auspices of the United Nations. The absence of French, German, Russian, and Chinese support for immediate military engagement troubled them greatly. Some insisted that war was completely inappropriate because the situation did not involve a direct threat to the United States. Quite a few Americans were opposed to the concept of a preemptive war—military intervention to prevent the possibility of future threats. Some critics of war believed U.S. forces would win an easy victory over Saddam Hussein's army, but they thought a victor's occupation of Iraq could prove very difficult. If Americans broke the country, they said, Americans would have to fix it, and that effort would require a huge commitment in treasure and blood.

These and other reasons for opposing military action against Iraq in March 2003 impressed lots of Americans, but the arguments made little impact on the thinking of most of the nation's radical conservatives. When the United States went to war and in the period of U.S. occupation of Iraq, most partisans of the militant right accepted the president's rationale for armed intervention and occupation. The possibility of unintended consequences did not trouble them nearly as much as it affected Americans who stood outside the radcon movement. These distinctive mindsets can be seen in a comparison of the way two of the nation's most prestigious newspapers dealt with the international crisis in the weeks before the invasion began. The *Wall Street Journal,* arguably the conservatives' single most influential publication, beat the drums for war consistently in its editorial pages during this period and gave virtually no space for voices opposed to war. In contrast, the *New York Times,* arguably the most influential national publication that is *not* securely in the conservative camp, featured a lively exchange of views in its editorial pages during the period. Certainly the *Times* did not provide a perfect example of journalistic excellence in this case. Its editors later became embarrassed by the prominence they gave to Judith Miller's questionable articles regarding the Bush administration's claims about weapons of mass destruction in Iraq. Editors at the *Times* also regretted giving the Bush administration's interpretation of war issues front-page coverage while relegating stories about objections to the war to the newspaper's secondary pages. Still, readers of the *Times* received much more food for thought about the choices for and against war than consumers of the *WSJ* received, especially in the editorial and op-ed pages.

A reader of the editorial pages of the *Wall Street Journal* during the first eighteen days in March 2003, before the outbreak of war, would have difficulty understanding what the opposition to war was all about. The *Journal*'s editorials and the op-ed articles by guest columnists and regular columnists pushed the case for military action relentlessly. *WSJ* staff members blasted the opponents of armed action, suggesting that critics of military action were failing to support the nation and the president in a time of crisis. The editors also argued with confidence that Saddam Hussein possessed weapons of mass destruction and represented a serious threat to world peace. The United States was going to war for purposes of "self-defense," the editors told readers. "Saddam poses a clear and present danger to Americans."[105] The editors also maintained that the Iraqi dictator harbored al-Qaeda members in his country. Saddam Hussein had links to Osama bin Laden, they assured readers.[106]

The *Wall Street Journal* sounded like a house organ of the Republican Party when it lambasted Democrats for standing in the way of President Bush's plans for armed action. After House Minority Leader Nancy Pelosi complained about Bush's Iraq policy, the editors said her critique "could have been written in Paris." Negative references to the French were frequent, since those Europeans were most directly associated with resistance to the United States in the United Nations. The *Journal*'s editors delighted in comparing troublesome Democrats to the French. Senator Tom Daschle received the treatment when he said that the United States was rushing into war instead of waiting for evidence about Iraqi arms programs. The editors cracked that he was seeking the "right of French first refusal."[107] References to the Democrats often lacked humor and packed a nasty punch, as when the editors maintained that Democrats were siding with the French and Russians and working against their American president. "No wonder voters are reluctant to trust Democrats with the responsibility for ensuring American safety and liberty," the editors observed.[108]

The *Journal*'s staff also ridiculed Democrats and others who pressured President Bush to go to the United Nations for a vote of approval in support of armed intervention in Iraq. Time was wasting, the editors warned, and continued delay might result in considerable expense. The

UN was sinking into irrelevance because of its lethargic responses to Saddam Hussein's threatening behavior. It was "proving daily that it is another League of Nations."[109]

Most of the op-ed contributors to the *Journal* demanded military intervention. They did not treat the war as a moot question, and they did not appear troubled by unforeseen complications that could result from U.S. occupation. The task ahead seemed obvious. The United States should fight Iraq immediately and remove Saddam from power. Oriana Fallaci, a controversial Italian journalist known for damning critiques of Islam, invoked an analogy from history, arguing that Iraqis would greet this action with glee. Fallaci noted that the Italians hanged their evil dictator, Benito Mussolini, once Allied troops moved into control of Italy near the end of World War II. Saddam Hussein could meet the same fate at the hands of angry Iraqis once an American-led coalition arrived.[110] Winston S. Churchill, grandson of the famous British wartime leader, called for courage to act against "this monster once and for all." He pointed to a link between al-Qaeda and Iraq and warned that Saddam Hussein "possesses" an arsenal of chemical, biological, and nuclear weapons.[111] *Wall Street Journal* columnist Daniel Henniger saw connections to al-Qaeda, too. George W. Bush needed to "stick Saddam Hussein in a hole," before more U.S. citizens died from 9/11-type tragedies involving suicide bombings, anthrax, or other horrible attacks.[112]

Several op-ed contributors joined the *Journal*'s editors in mocking the French. Some suspected the French were uncooperative for emotional rather than rational reasons. They were jealous of the Americans, Joshua Muravchik, a neoconservative at the American Enterprise Institute, concluded. The power of the United States frightened the French, wrote Muravchik, so they tried to tame that strength by resisting American war plans.[113] When the French asserted that further diplomacy was needed, *Journal* deputy editor George Melloan reasoned, they were offering only a "pathetic cover" for their unwillingness to face up to Saddam Hussein's evil ways. Melloan assured readers that the French president, Jacques Chirac, was losing support from his own people because of his failure to join Bush in taking a strong stand against Iraq. The power of the left was in decline in France, Melloan asserted with a hint of glee, and Chirac, in opposing needed action, was placing himself "on the wrong side of history."[114]

Only two *WSJ* op-ed columnists did not provide full-throated calls for war in the March weeks before the war began, yet their arguments did not suggest fully committed resistance to war, either. The secretary general of the United Nations made a vague appeal for wise decision making in a time of crisis in one article, and in the other a writer who described himself as an "anti-Saddam hawk" warned about the dangers of U.S. involvement in Iraq once the war was won. The UN secretary general, Kofi A. Annan, expressed a general hope that the "world community" would find ways to "act together." Annan called for proof that Iraq's government no longer had WMDs, and he recalled that Saddam Hussein had employed such horrible weapons twice before in his government's military activities. Annan's primary worry concerned "unintended consequences" that might develop out of the war.[115] Albert R. Hunt, the "anti-Saddam Hawk," expressed similar concerns. He warned that Americans could find themselves walking into a "minefield" in Iraq or sinking into a "black hole" if they did not establish a clear exit strategy and secure promises from other nations to share the burden of stabilizing Iraq.[116] These essayists provided the only meager examples of contrary opinion that the *Wall Street Journal* offered in its editorial pages. The thrust of editorial and op-ed commentary was overwhelmingly hawkish.

The *New York Times* presented, by contrast, a substantially greater variety of opinions about Iraq in the March days before bombs began to fall on Baghdad. Editors at the *Times* urged the president to take more time, gather additional information about arms programs, and build a stronger international coalition before taking the leap toward war, but the editors did not rule out the need for armed conflict with Iraq. If the United States and the UN could not obtain satisfactory information about Saddam's arms programs, military intervention could be necessary, they argued. Authors of op-ed pieces in the *Times* ranged broadly from enthusiastic advocates of quick military action to champions of peaceful negotiations. Readers of the *Times* were exposed to a wide-ranging debate. During the final countdown toward war, those readers encountered a rich variety of editorial opinions about choices. The newspaper's editorials appeared to move in both directions in the final days before the war, bemoaning George W. Bush's failures at diplomacy but also blaming the Iraqi dictator for creating conditions that led to America's preparations for war.

Several *Times* editorials had a critical edge regarding the Bush administration's decision making. The editors urged delay in U.S. war plans because "diplomacy should be given a chance." Saddam Hussein's government deserved a last opportunity to change course. Editors at the

*Times* chastised President Bush for trying to act alone and for looking away from the tradition of collective security that had guided U.S. foreign policy since World War II. The Bush administration had snubbed the French and arrogantly dismissed international accords, they complained.[117] The United Nations ought to complete a stepped-up search for Iraqi weapons through the employment of many more inspectors.[118]

Editors at the *Times* matched these demands upon the Bush administration with criticism of the French and the Iraqis. "This page remains persuaded of the vital need to disarm Iraq," wrote the editors. They criticized the French leader, Jacques Chirac, for making vague demands of Iraq and failing to come up with "a reasonable mechanism for judging [Saddam Hussein's] compliance." Chirac's government sent Saddam all the wrong signals. Shortly before the war began, the editors said the primary fault in the building confrontation lay with the Iraqi leader, not the U.S. president. They concluded that "Mr. Bush is right to insist that the choice between war and peace has been in the hands of Saddam Hussein."[119]

While the staff's editorials reflected a conflicted condition of two personalities—one justifying peace through work with the UN and the other justifying war if the peace option failed—op-ed articles appearing in the March 2003 days before combat showed an even greater clash of opinions. Both the *Times* regular op-ed columnists and its guest columnists offered dueling interpretations of the choices before President Bush. In some cases the writers appeared to speak directly to each other through their conflicting essays.

Among the regular columnists, Maureen Dowd, Bob Herbert, and Paul Krugman resisted the calls for war, while William Safire offered a hearty justification for military action and Thomas Friedman criticized the president's unilateral approach to foreign policy but found reason to support his decision making. Krugman worried that the United States was quickly losing friends in international relations because of Bush's headstrong and arrogant leadership.[120] Maureen Dowd, in her familiar caustic style, blasted the "brazen Bush imperialists" who were determined to impose their will on Iraq.[121] Bob Herbert reminded readers of the effects of war. "Bombs and Blood" would be evident throughout Iraq once the fighting began, and the country's innocent civilians, including many children, would suffer terribly.[122] In contrast, William Safire argued that Saddam Hussein had already started the war ten years before when he violated the terms of his government's surrender after the Gulf conflict. The dictator was very dangerous, Safire concluded, and connected to terrorism. "Either we will allow him to become capable of inflicting horrendous casualties in our cities tomorrow," the columnist reasoned, "or we must inflict and accept far fewer casualties in his cities today."[123] Thomas Friedman pushed for military action but with reservations. He worried about the president's failure to win broad international support for war. Nevertheless, Friedman praised Bush for gambling boldly. The president was involved in the greatest shake of the dice since Truman decided to drop atomic bombs on Japan and Kennedy threatened the Soviet Union during the Cuban Missile Crisis, Friedman argued. Bush's effort to bring democracy to Iraq might prove a "geographical game-changer" that "could help nudge the whole Arab-Muslim world onto a more progressive track."[124]

The closest examples of a direct debate over the issue came from a former Democratic president and a prominent Republican senator. Jimmy Carter launched the dispute in a provocative op-ed piece entitled "Just War—or a Just War?" The ex-president bemoaned America's move toward unilateral action and domineering policies, which brought international trust in the United States to its lowest level in memory. "American stature will surely decline further," Carter concluded, "if we launch a war in clear defiance of the United Nations."[125] A few days later Republican John McCain appeared to respond to Carter with a case for a just war. Economic sanctions and inspection had been in effect for years, McCain noted, yet Saddam Hussein "still refuses to give up his weapons of mass destruction." The American troops about to go into battle would be fighting for peace and security, liberty and justice, he said, and they could "take pride in their cause."[126]

The *Times* did not claim its commentaries were "fair and balanced" (to employ a phrase advertised by Fox News), but it certainly approached that ideal much more effectively than the *Wall Street Journal* in its editorial and op-ed commentaries on the question of war. In fact, readers of the *WSJ* could hardly know that there was a *question* about the subject after reading the *Journal*'s editorial pages. Furthermore, the *Times* engaged in some embarrassing public soul-searching about its reporting on the war and occupation a little more than a year after U.S. soldiers invaded Iraq. In May 2004 the *Times* editors published a note to readers that was loaded with apologies. After reviewing the newspaper's reporting on the issue of weapons of mass destruction between September

2002 and June 2003, the editors found much fine reporting but also some shortcomings that troubled them. They concluded that their staff had not adequately challenged reports about Iraq's weapons programs. Too many writers reported unsubstantiated claims made by Iraqi exiles who were eager to see the United States overthrow Saddam Hussein. The editors often "buried" reports that questioned those claims in the back pages of its newspapers. Coverage of the war and the early occupation was not as rigorous as the editors would have wished, the in-house review concluded.[127] While the *Times* editors regretted their handling of some news reporting, they did not need to express apologies for their work in providing editorial commentaries. They had, at least, presented a rather diverse collection of opinions on the relevant issues.

Interestingly, the *Wall Street Journal*'s highly partisan approach to the Iraq issue led the editors to make some foolish statements that appeared badly mistaken with the passage of time. In mid-April 2003, for instance, at a moment when military victory over Iraq seemed secure, the editors spoke condescendingly about those who had questioned the propriety of President George W. Bush's war policy. They particularly targeted "liberals," a broad term that included, in their terms, the staff of CNN and the major television networks, most academic experts, and editors at the *New York Times*. The *WSJ* editors wrote, "Liberal elites continue to wallow in pessimism about this liberation." Liberals worried about the difficulty of achieving democracy and reconstruction in Iraq, the editors noted. Liberals also feared a national uprising against U.S. troops similar to America's Vietnam experience, and they expected that Arabs would become enraged against Americans because of the occupation. Furthermore, liberals thought the war would produce thousands of Iraqi civilian casualties and refugees, and they believed the occupation would arouse saboteurs to strike at Iraq's petroleum fields, causing global oil prices to rise. These anticipated disasters had not come true, the editors noted. Thus, liberals were wrong in making pessimistic judgments. "They are flummoxed if not embarrassed by America's Iraqi victory," the editors concluded. They failed to understand the situation in Iraq because it had become a "self-insulated elite convinced of its own virtue." Liberals thought of themselves as "the anointed," and they operated "in an echo chamber that listens to and rewards one another to the point that they refuse to admit contrary evidence."[128]

Over the next year, as America's problems in occupying Iraq mounted steadily, it became clear that the editors of the *Wall Street Journal* and other conservatives like them had been the ones who operated in an echo chamber and refused to admit contrary evidence, not the liberals. Many commentators from the right had sounded the trumpets for war and shown little tolerance for individuals who raised legitimate and wise questions about President Bush's actions. A few meager voices among the conservatives coming from the libertarian and neo-isolationist camps could be heard expressing concern about the moves toward armed conflict and occupation. For the most part, though, militant conservatives championed war with Iraq and did not engage in serious debates about the difficulty of making U.S. soldiers and civilians the managers of post-invasion Iraq. Doubts about the need for war and concerns about the danger of entanglement in Iraq had not registered strongly with them, because they accepted the teachings of their orthodox political faith early in the disputes. George W. Bush was the acknowledged preacher of their political faith at the time, and he had stated clearly that his crusade was moral and necessary. The people's task, many Hawkish Nationalists judged, was to follow the president, not challenge the direction in which he was moving. This general hostility to dissent and debate helped to lead the United States into one of its greatest foreign policy entanglements of modern times.

## Dissent in Two Wars

The dangers associated with right-wing commitments to political orthodoxy are evident not only in a comparison of the *Journal*'s and the *Times*'s editorial approaches but also in a general comparison of the way conservatives and liberals confronted issues of dissent in the Vietnam and Iraq wars. In the days of the Vietnam conflict many liberal Democrats challenged the leadership of their Democratic president and his administration. In contrast, conservative Republicans have remained comparatively loyal to their president and his administration in the case of the war and occupation of Iraq. Interestingly, this contrast applies broadly to the general behavior of conservatives at the time, not just to the radically inclined ones.

This is, of course, a very broad-based comparison, and political conditions in the 1960s and the 2000s are different. American liberalism and conservatism in the 1960s were not the same as in the 2000s (in fact, conservatism in the 1960s was relatively weak compared to the movement that has achieved considerable influence in the twenty-first century). The situations in Vietnam and Iraq have presented distinctive challenges to American troops. U.S. combat fatalities grew at different rates, too. The number of U.S. deaths increased at a much higher rate in Vietnam once the United States committed openly to combat in early 1965. Although the situations were distinctive, comparisons are nevertheless instructive regarding the matter of dissent during wartime.

A notable contrast between approaches to dissent can be seen in the positions of Democrats and Republicans in the Senate Foreign Relations Committee during the Vietnam and Iraq wars. In 1966, during the early days of American fighting in Vietnam, J. William Fulbright of the Senate committee, a Democrat, boldly challenged President Johnson's policies and, thereby, helped to give legitimacy to the emerging antiwar movement. By contrast, in 2004 the Republican-headed Senate Foreign Relations Committee under the leadership of Richard Lugar of Indiana was much less provocative in responding to George W. Bush's troubled involvement in Iraq. Lugar, a former Rhodes Scholar who performed important work in support of the former Soviet Union's dismantling of nuclear weapons, entertained serious doubts about the Bush administration's strategy and activities during the occupation of Iraq, but he was not willing to take a critical stand publicly in the manner of Fulbright. Richard Lugar acted more like a team player than did the confrontational J. William Fulbright. The distinction in approaches may be attributed to the senators' personalities (Fulbright was the more aggressive figure in dealing with political controversies), but Richard Lugar's caution seems also to relate to the political environment. Senator Lugar served in a party dominated by partisans of the radcon political faith. He could not comfortably raise questions that challenged the leadership of George W. Bush, the symbolic pastor of the Republican (and conservative) political congregation. Senator Fulbright, in contrast, received applause from many liberals for challenging LBJ's war positions.

This analysis can be applied not only to the positions of Fulbright and Lugar but also to stands on the two wars taken by people at the grassroots level and in the upper echelons of party leadership. A comparison of the liberals' attitudes toward dissent in the years of Lyndon B. Johnson's presidency with the conservatives' approach to dissent in the period of George W. Bush's presidency suggests very different sensibilities about following or questioning the commander in chief. Liberals demonstrated far more willingness to challenge President Johnson's handling of an unpopular war. Conservative reactions were meek by contrast when President Bush drew the nation into a controversial invasion and occupation of Iraq.

Back in 1966 and 1967, many liberals were giving angry public expression to their discontent over the course of the Vietnam conflict, and some spoke openly about replacing President Johnson in the next election. The Democratic camp split sharply between those who opposed the war and those who chose to stay the course under Johnson's leadership. In the Senate, figures such as Frank Church, J. William Fulbright, George McGovern, Wayne Morse, Gaylord Nelson, and Stephen Young became troublesome critics of the president. As Robert Novak and Rowland Evans observe, "What had started in 1964 with the two-man opposition of Wayne Morse and Ernest Gruening and then grew to a half dozen or more in 1965, now had mushroomed to perhaps half the sixty-six Democratic senators in 1966."[129] Of course, the greatest liberal outbursts against LBJ occurred in 1968 after setbacks associated with the communists' Tet Offensive. Still, manifestations of a dump-Johnson movement were becoming quite evident during the eighteen months following the president's spring 1965 decision to send U.S. troops into combat.

The record of the conservatives' loyalty to President George W. Bush during disturbing times of trouble in Iraq stands in stark contrast to this picture of the liberals' tense relationship with President Johnson. Despite numerous setbacks in the military occupation of Iraq and abundant revelations in the press showing that President Bush had engaged in the war for questionable reasons, his conservative Republican followers remained generally loyal to him during the eighteen months after the 2003 attack on Iraq began. As mentioned earlier, by 2004 a few prominent conservatives, such as Pat Buchanan, Tucker Carlson, and George Will, had expressed worries about U.S. policies in Iraq, but their commentaries excited little support from conservatives and no serious evidence of intraparty rebelliousness at the time. Republican resistance to Bush and his policies did not emerge forcefully until the president's poll numbers dropped precipitously in 2006.

This contrast with the liberals' resistance to Johnson is particularly striking in view of the role of the news media during the two eras. Back in the mid-1960s, Americans had at their disposal comparatively few broadcast outlets to express discontent with the Vietnam War. Three major television networks devoted only a few minutes to news stories each day. Also in the mid-1960s, journalists tended to report without question much of the information passed down to them by U.S. military authorities. By the twenty-first century, however, the American people's opportunities to obtain critical commentaries through the news media had changed significantly. Evidence about political clashes over foreign policy was available from several all-day news and information channels on television, on many radio programs, and through the Internet (as well as in print journalism). Information about failures in planning the Iraq war reached the public much more easily, yet conservative Republicans were slow to react. Committed to their far-right political faith, they could not readily adopt a culture of dissent.

By early May 2004, President Bush's record of engaging the United States in the affairs of Iraq looked to many Americans like a fiasco, yet Bush continued to run strongly in the presidential race. He stood even with John Kerry in a Gallup Poll released at that time despite a plethora of recent news reports indicating that his foreign policy was in a shambles. The Gallup Poll results suggested that many conservatives probably understood the unpleasant facts of the war and occupation, but the facts didn't matter. They recognized that U.S. policies were not working, but they did not blame the president severely for these failures.

This complex reaction is evident in Gallup data from the early months of 2004. Four months before the May 2004 poll, public opinion was rather upbeat about Iraq. In January of that year, 61 percent of Gallup's respondents approved of President Bush's handling of the situation in Iraq, and only 36 percent disapproved. By May, after troublesome developments including the deaths of many Americans in Iraq, Gallup's statistics revealed a dramatic shift. Americans had turned substantially against Bush's handling of the war and the occupation: 55 percent disapproved of his handling of Iraq, and only 42 percent approved. In spite of this growing discontent, Bush's standing in the presidential contest climbed significantly. After falling behind Kerry when the Massachusetts senator emerged as the Democrats' apparent nominee in the primaries, Bush pulled up and tied Kerry in the presidential preference poll of May 2004.[130] He maintained a strong presence in the polls and won the election that November.

Many Bush supporters recognized the troubling facts of the situation but were unshaken by this evidence. In May 2004 they remained faithful to the conservative president and fearful of the prospective Democratic nominee. Obviously, Republican campaign advertising played a role in shaping their negative opinions of Kerry. Yet, despite the troublesome news from Iraq, many refused to blame their leader or seek a new direction for the country by voting for the Democratic candidate.

This record of allegiance is extraordinary when placed against the evidence of policy failures that had come to light through late spring 2004. By that time, the toll of American deaths and injuries in Iraq had mounted steadily, and the purpose of those sacrifices appeared more blurred than ever. Instead of securing stability and democracy for Iraq, the U.S. occupation seemed to provoke chaos and violence. Furthermore, the original reasons for going to war no longer looked plausible. In early 2004 David Kay, the chief U.S. arms inspector, and Hans Blix, the chief UN arms inspector, concluded that Saddam Hussein's government had not harbored weapons of mass destruction in its last years. Books released in early 2004 by Paul O'Neill (Bush's former treasury secretary) and Richard Clarke (Bush's former chief coordinator of antiterror planning) showed that the Republican administration had been determined to pick a fight with Iraq well before 9/11. These authors also suggested that Saddam Hussein did not have major ties to al-Qaeda, and his government was not involved in the terrorist attacks of September 2001. The war with Iraq was looking like a major foreign policy error and possibly a disaster of the first order, yet the president appeared unscathed. In fact, his candidacy was stronger than it had been a few months before.

Why was the faith in Bush so firm at this point in the debates over Iraq? Surely, part of the explanation lies in the details of electioneering. Once Kerry emerged as the clear target for Republican strategists, the Bush campaign team mounted a tremendous effort to characterize Kerry negatively in the national media. Republicans spent millions of dollars in television advertising during spring 2004 to define the Massachusetts senator as a waffling "flip-flopper" who took contradictory stands on major issues. Through newspaper punditry and TV appearances as talking heads, conservatives questioned Kerry's strong suit—his war record— and thereby raised questions about his supposed skill in handling national security issues. Republican campaign leaders had made a successful preemptive election strike, leaving the supposedly impressive Democratic candidate looking vulnerable.

In a broader sense, though, the persistence of support for Bush among conservatives that spring, despite mounting evidence of his foreign policy errors, related to the conservatives' fundamentalist outlook on global affairs. American conservatives' views on international relations could not be upset very easily by the messy details in news reports. The absence of WMDs, the growing chaos and violence in Iraq, the mounting death toll involving American soldiers and contract workers, the news about American soldiers torturing and abusing Iraqi prisoners, and other disturbing information undermined the conservatives' enthusiasm for U.S. occupation of Iraq, but these facts did not provoke them to question or challenge their leadership vigorously.

Hawkish Nationalists projected a Manichaean view of foreign policy disputes and were not about to abandon their vision of a conflict between good and evil when signs of specific difficulties emerged. They were privy to disturbing facts about the war and U.S. management of Iraqi affairs, but these facts did not matter. The president, a conservative Republican, was, in their view, moral and correct. The opposition leader, a Democratic Party candidate, was inherently mistaken, they concluded. Many conservatives continued demonstrating allegiance to their partisan hero and denounced Kerry, who seemed to speak for an alien vision of the world. To abandon Bush for Kerry would appear tantamount to forsaking the conservative creed and joining forces with the Democratic Party's nonbelievers. People of a political faith do not switch religions so easily.

Political fundamentalism is troubling enough in cultural and economic affairs, but it seems especially disquieting when it guides opinions about dealing with international crises. In these instances the consequences of faulty thinking can prove quite serious. Dealing effectively with international challenges requires nimble reactions. Global conditions are constantly in flux. Leaders change; nations change. Policy makers often cite analogies from history, expecting that they can draw useful lessons for the present from the record of the past. Yet when those applications do not work, policy planners need to shake loose from their presumptions. They have to seek new insights.

The record of recent decades illustrates that individuals outside of the militant conservative camp have often demonstrated that they are capable of adjusting to the changing times. When facing difficulties with the Vietnam War, many of them evolved, adopting new proposals for handling a situation that had not worked as planned. Individuals outside of the radcon camp were not fooled by the exaggerated claims of American military decline and growing Soviet superiority. Many of them welcomed détente in relationships with the Soviets, understanding that some efforts toward accommodation were necessary in the dangerous nuclear age. Open-minded individuals recognized that Ronald Reagan took some notable actions that contributed to the closing of the Cold War, but they understood, too, that explanations for the end of superpower rivalry are complex, not simple. Americans who are not enthusiastic about radcon rhetoric also appreciate the complexity of dealing with the challenges of al-Qaeda's attacks on 9/11. They are not swayed by rightists who castigate liberals as appeasers and weaklings. And, of course, Americans who do not fancy themselves as militant conservatives are generally much more willing to raise tough questions about the U.S. military engagement in Iraq. These individuals—moderate conservatives and moderate liberals, open-minded Republicans and open-minded Democrats—operate without the blinders that cover the eyes of political fundamentalists.

## CHAPTER SEVEN

# Media Wars

The hard-line conservatives' familiar attacks on political correctness in universities and other centers of cultural influence in the United States are extraordinarily amusing in view of their enthusiasm for political correctness in publishing, radio, television, and Internet communications. In recent decades the right has become expert at promoting its own point of view in these media and quite active in excluding opinions it finds unappealing. This drive for conformity is unique in the current political debates. While liberals have advocated vigorous exchanges of opinion, militant conservatives have increasingly pressed for uniformity of ideas. They have provided strong voices for political orthodoxy.

Yet some journalists often take a different approach in their discussions of conservative and liberal approaches in the mass media, suggesting that the positions of the two groups are essentially similar. They claim that sharp partisanship is characteristic of all competition in the American political arena. Ideological groups must fight tenaciously for their causes and act as if their goal is complete victory, these journalists argue. Conservatives and liberals, Republicans and Democrats, mirror each other's combativeness. The right's drive to obtain a dominant position in the battle of ideas seems, therefore, no worse than the liberals' quest for similar influence. Each side tries to overwhelm the opposition. Liberals cheer film director Michael Moore's successes in slamming the right, while conservatives applaud Rush Limbaugh's attempts to pummel the left. Liberals give each other high fives when liberal radio host

Al Franken scores points with argument and humor, while conservatives applaud Bill O'Reilly's political zingers. Sharply biased politicking is normal. It is characteristic of modern political rhetoric, say these interpreters.

Recent evidence of intense partisanship by conservatives suggests, however, that radicals on the right engage in more than just good old-fashioned and healthy political competition. These partisans appear so convinced that they are in possession of The True Word of their faith that they treat individuals who advocate different visions as heretics. They counsel extraordinary measures for dealing with skeptics, often applauding efforts to silence opponents by excluding them from public exchanges of political ideas or by attempting to block the efforts of people they do not like to reach the eyes and ears of the American public. Of course, some of the nation's prominent Republicans do not participate in these blatant attempts to crush contrary opinions. Yet they do not criticize the militants vigorously for actions that appear to undermine freedom of speech.

## The "Elite" Liberal Media

Rightists who employ rough tactics to smash political opponents usually justify their actions by pointing to a powerful and intolerant opposition that essentially forced them to take such extreme measures. These commentators are in the habit of lamenting the powerful influence of the liberal media in the United States. They claim the "left" controls major organizations that present the news. Public broadcasting on radio and television is notably liberal, they charge. The nation's major newspapers, especially the highly influential *New York Times,* are in the hands of liberals, ultras claim. Liberals also have a firm grip on Hollywood, they say, and from that position the left is able to turn mass entertainment into subtle forms of propaganda. Radcons say liberals dominate the major intellectual centers in the United States, too. Universities, foundations, think tanks, and various private research organizations are, presumably, under the left's control. Rightists depict their struggle with the mainstream media as essentially a battle between David and Goliath. In this context, confronting such powerful bastions of liberal influence requires extraordinary measures.

When claiming that liberals exercise extraordinary control over American culture, adherents of the conservative faith appear to borrow concepts from Antonio Gramsci, an Italian Marxist. Gramsci maintained that dominant classes control subordinate majorities not always by physical pressure but through "spontaneous consent." By managing the dissemination of ideas (hegemony), ruling groups convince the masses that the dominant group's values serve the interests of all citizens. Partisans of the right employ Gramsci's ideas about hegemonic influence for their own needs, making liberals look much like the powerful and sneaky capitalists in Gramsci's analyses. Of course, these messages about cultural dominance strike liberals as laughable. They can hardly believe that they wield the kind of vast cultural influence that the hard-line right attributes to them.

Gramsci's analysis suggests that powerful figures are engaged in a sort of conspiratorial effort to control the masses, and the American right promotes a similar outlook. The Italian Marxist argued that members of the elite dominate society in subtle ways. They attempt to give their outlook the appearance of common sense. It looks like the natural order of things. The masses are hardly aware that the dominant classes are controlling their consciousness. In a related way, American conservatives often argue that the liberal elite, through their great influence in the media and the universities, convince the public that their perspective on American life is the correct one. Interestingly, both Gramsci and leaders of the American right suggest similar remedies for the problems they discern in hegemony. Gramsci drew attention to the critical importance of intellectuals in bringing about a new revolutionary consciousness. He wanted to infiltrate the establishment by radicalizing intellectuals (professors, noted authors, and the like) and getting their speeches and writings into prominent places in the mass media. Gramsci also recognized that the working classes needed to produce their own intellectuals—people who spoke in a language they could understand and in ways that could excite a new awakening in the neighborhoods and local communities. Leaders of the American right have mobilized in the manner suggested by Gramsci—for very different purposes, of course. They have attempted to promote the careers of their own intellectuals so that these individuals could make a substantial impact on public opinion in the national media. Conservatives have also rallied around intellectuals who serve the masses, including popular radio and TV personalities such as Rush Limbaugh and Sean Hannity. And, like Gramsci, they have frequently warned that the job of challenging the powerful elite is tremendously difficult and requires strenuous efforts from the exploited, victimized masses.

While conservatives have employed diverse language to identify liberals who are supposedly in positions of extraordinary influence, the point of reference that became especially fashionable in the right's rhetoric during the 1980s and 1990s was the "New Class."[1] This term may have derived from the writings of Milovan Djilas, a Yugoslav dissident who criticized communism in a 1957 book called *The New Class*. Djilas described a small, powerful, and arrogant group of bureaucrats in the Communist Party who enjoyed enormous privileges and used their positions to grab the spoils of power. The concept of a New Class seems also to have sprung from the ideas of prominent commentators on changes in American academic and corporate life. Daniel Bell wrote about a new intelligentsia and a new technical elite gaining influence in an information-based and service-based postindustrial society. Another possible source for the concept comes from the leftist sociologist C. Wright Mills, who spoke of a "power elite" made up of opinion makers and various military, corporate, and political leaders.[2] Irving Kristol, an important intellectual leader of the neoconservatives, helped to give the term "New Class" currency when he claimed that this supposedly liberal-oriented group was emerging in the nation's education establishment, entertainment industry, and broadcast media. Kristol, in turn, appears to have borrowed some of his notions about the New Class from a mentor who guided him in his days of graduate studies at Columbia University. Lionel Trilling had spoken about the "adversary culture" made of up intellectuals who often operated in opposition to the prevailing values in their societies.[3]

Before long, many on the right were incorporating the idea of new, powerful, and privileged classes and groups in their political writings. Samuel Francis, a traditional conservative, spoke of a "new elite" that promoted bureaucratic forms of governance and was "animated by an ideology of manipulative, administrative social engineering."[4] Francis, a paleoconservative who expressed opposition to immigration and multiculturalism, later came under sharp criticism for making racially insensitive statements. Jerry Falwell also spoke about the New Class. Falwell, a Virginia-based preacher with a large television ministry, promoted the idea of the Moral Majority in the late 1970s and became noted for his jeremiads about permissiveness and moral decay in America. Falwell included editorial writers, columnists, artists, and religious spokespeople (presumably liberal ones) when identifying the supposedly threatening New Class. Their influence is large, he reminded supporters, and it is magnified by their ability to broadcast their ideas widely. Robert Bork, the conservative judge and legal scholar who failed to win a seat on the U.S. Supreme Court during Senate hearings, projected a similar picture. America's intellectual elite was relatively small in number, Bork wrote, but enjoyed vast power through its ability to shape the American public's ideas and values.[5]

The concept of a New Class has served nicely to arouse feelings of class resentment, since rightists characterize members of the New Class as wealthy and well-placed in high society. Norman Podhoretz, the leading neoconservative and editor of *Commentary,* describes the "New" group as prosperous and well-educated liberals who act "against a less prosperous and less well-educated" public that comes "mostly from the working and lower middle-classes."[6] William Rusher, publisher of the *National Review* for many years and a syndicated columnist and radio commentator, describes members of the New Class as a "liberal verbalist elite" that could spread its influence "through the bureaucracy, the education establishment, the media, and the major foundations." He claims this elite "has persistently led this nation from its moral and psychological moorings."[7] Rusher accentuates this picture of common heroes and elite villains by invoking an invidious comparison between producers and nonproducers. His list of productive Americans includes business leaders, manufacturers, hardhat construction workers, and blue-collar laborers. On the nonproductive list are those who work with the major news media, the educational "establishment," the federal bureaucracy, the foundations, and the research centers.[8]

Whether right-wingers called these privileged and influential people the New Class, the nonproducers, or some other pejorative term, the implications were clear. Hard-line conservatives implied that America's liberal cultural elite had become indifferent to traditional values that were important to many hard-working, middle-class Americans. Liberals, they claimed, were out of touch with the American mainstream.

The time had come, militant rightists argued, to push the haughty liberal elites off their high perches. Some, such as the neoconservatives, hoped to replace representatives of the New Class with their own partisans. The neocons went to work diligently creating their own "think tanks" and providing generous financial awards for right-oriented "scholars." They attempted to confront the challenge of liberal influence over the culture by obtaining greater intellectual legitimacy.[9]

The paleoconservative columnist Samuel Francis also sought replacement of the powerful enemy, but unlike the neocons, he offered more rhetoric than organizational skill. Francis hoped for "the overthrow of the present elite and its replacement" by right-oriented idea-makers.[10] This struggle to remove the influential class from its position of dominance was no minor affair, Francis told readers. It represented a "revolutionary goal."

Related ideas about challenging a supposedly powerful liberal elite had appeared earlier in the right's political rhetoric, but those efforts did not build into a sustained campaign. For a time in the early 1950s, Senator Joe McCarthy, the communist-baiting demagogue, employed the tactic. He lambasted Ivy League–educated liberals serving in the Truman administration, complaining that they had been born into privilege and had little understanding of the interests of common Americans. George Wallace, sounding populist themes during his campaigns for the presidency, spoke of "pointy-headed professors" and "brief-case totin' bureaucrats."[11] Wealthy conservatives such as William F. Buckley also joined the fray against the supposedly powerful liberal elite. The pundit and editor of the *National Review* joked that he would rather be governed by the first thousand names that appeared in the Boston telephone directory than by the Harvard faculty, and he hurled verbal barbs against the "intellectual plutocrats of the nation, who have at their disposal vast cultural and financial resources."[12]

It was Richard Nixon's acerbic vice president, Spiro Agnew, however, who became most impressively identified with the idea that a privileged and biased group exercised tremendous power through the mass media. When it became evident that television could play a significant role in U.S. elections, Agnew found opportunities to identify broadcast journalists and the network executives behind them as particularly frightening examples of an influential New Class. His actions developed out of Pat Buchanan's recommendation that the Nixon administration find ways to deal with criticisms of the Vietnam War that were appearing in the press and on television. Agnew agreed to perform the dirty work. In 1969 he charged the TV networks with bias in favor of the communist enemy and critics of the Vietnam War. The vice president claimed that network television news was led by a "small group of men" who "do not represent the views of America." These individuals possessed "vast power," Agnew asserted. They constituted an "effete corps of impudent snobs" and often sounded like "nattering nabobs of negativism."[13] It was time, he suggested, for representatives of the national news media to examine themselves and take steps to improve the "quality and objectivity" of their reporting. Agnew's pressure tactics seemed to make an impact. In the year following his public criticism, conservatives appeared more frequently on television and in the editorial pages of the nation's newspapers.[14]

The conservatives' descriptions of disputes about the news media tell us a good deal about the nature of modern-day political nomenclature. In the right's familiar political rhetoric, major news organizations that present two or more sides of an issue are, essentially, "liberal." Conservatives often identify newspapers, magazines, radio stations, and television networks that have built reputations for delivering generally balanced presentations of political topics as organs of the "left" or of "liberal" opinion. In contrast, militant conservatives strongly praise and provide considerable audience loyalty to print and broadcast journalism that favors the perspective of their political faith. They are comfortable with reporting that excludes or sharply limits presentation of opposing perspectives.

Although many aspects of the radical right's descriptions of liberalism are bogus, in this case, at least, the right's choice of terms appears correct. A liberal approach to news reporting truly does involve a strong commitment to balance. The liberal perspective is much more tolerant of conflicting opinions; it welcomes the presentation of diverse viewpoints. This liberal outlook contrasts notably with the radcon outlook, which favors a strongly right-oriented finessing of the news. Radical Conservatives are much more comfortable than liberals with print and broadcast journalism that features a heavy ideological slant

Ann Coulter, an especially strident radical conservative who often appears on television, summarizes many of the right's standard complaints about the mass media's handling of the news in a book that flails at political opponents, *Slander: Liberal Lies about the American Right* (2002). Voices of the left, she tells readers, can be encountered in the *New York Times,* the *Washington Post,* the *Detroit Free Press,* and the *Philadelphia Inquirer.* She also lambastes *Time* magazine for a liberal bias. Network news anchors take a beating in her analysis, too, particularly the former giants of the television industry, Dan Rather (CBS), Peter Jennings (ABC), and Tom Brokaw (NBC). Coulter speaks of a "ceaseless liberal presence" on National Public Radio (NPR). She reports with apparent glee that the Fox News Channel beat out all of the elite "liberal" media in the audience ratings. Fox had become America's number-one preference for news and commentary.

Bill O'Reilly, the popular radio and television host (who espouses right-wing causes but claims he is above ideology), joined Coulter in criticizing National Public Radio for supposed leftward bias. At one point O'Reilly told his audience about his difficulties getting an interview on NPR. He had sought an opportunity to discuss one of his books. Later, O'Reilly secured an NPR interview to talk about his newly released publication, *Who's Looking Out for You?* (2003), but he was not pleased with the experience. O'Reilly launched a sharp criticism of Terry Gross, host of the NPR interview program "Fresh Air." He complained that Gross was more interested in the O'Reilly–Al Franken disputes than in discussing his latest book. In later radio and television commentaries O'Reilly devoted considerable time to railing against Gross specifically and NPR generally. In these commentaries O'Reilly suggested that National Public Radio leaned strongly toward the liberal camp. NPR provided one side of the polemical debates, he suggested, but there was another side. "You can get Rush Limbaugh, you can get NPR," he argued.[15] Yet the two venues were quite different, said O'Reilly, because public radio received public funding from American taxpayers. That support should be cut off, he suggested, and the network should compete in the marketplace, as Fox News does.

Bernard Goldberg joined the antiliberal media bashers with biting commentaries in *Bias: A CBS Insider Exposes How the Media Distorts the News* (2002). Goldberg, a longtime TV news personality with CBS, fell out of favor with the organization in 2001. After disagreements with news anchor Dan Rather, Goldberg left his job at the network. Goldberg's book has the appearance of an exercise in revenge. He lashes out at CBS and Rather for supposed liberal leanings.[16] Like Ann Coulter, Bernard Goldberg thrills to the evidence of audience preference for Fox News. The network had become the favorite of television audiences, he reports, while the news bureaus at the three major networks had lost thousands of viewers.[17] Bernard Goldberg's book sold well to the admiring faithful, and a year later the radcon author offered a sequel, *Arrogance: Rescuing America from the Media Elite.*[18]

Coulter, O'Reilly, and Goldberg identify principal themes that have become familiar in the militant right's assaults on the news media. In numerous commentaries, hard-line conservatives argue that major newspaper, radio, and television organizations lean strongly to the left. They usually name the *New York Times* and the *Washington Post* as the most important examples of journalistic bias. National Public Radio is a favorite target in their complaints about radio broadcasting, and the news organizations of the major TV networks typically come in for attack as well. CNN is on their hit list, too.[19] During the 1990s some radical conservatives got in the habit of referring to CNN as the "Clinton News Network" because of presumed favoritism toward the Democratic president, while others jokingly referred to the organization as the Communist News Network.

## Bias and Balance

In contrast, many on the right point to the Fox News Channel as their favored news source. It is "fair and balanced," observes the cohost of one of its popular opinion programs, Sean Hannity. In contrast, he says, CNN is "failed and biased."[20] Hannity acknowledges that the Fox network broadcasts many shows that feature opinions, "but they are clearly identified as such—and, just as important, they allow both political viewpoints to be expressed." The right-wing commentator claims that a principle of objectivity guides Fox's news programs: "We report, you decide."[21] Other commentators from the right maintain that there is a slight conservative tilt in Fox's presentations, but they justify this supposedly minor inclination by asserting that the mainstream media more than compensate by operating with a substantial liberal bias. Ann Coulter, who praises the Fox News organization for fine reporting, says, "Fox News may modulate slightly to the right, but the idea that its anchors betray their political predilections more than Peter Jennings or Dan Rather is absurd."[22] Roger Ailes, head of Fox News, acknowledges a slight inclination to the right on Fox. But, like Coulter, he sees the opposition's bias as an excuse for Fox's practices. "There are more conservatives on Fox," he confesses. "But we are *not* a conservative network. That disparity says far more about the competition." Bernard Goldberg, the newscaster who attacked CBS News for a supposedly liberal bias, presents a similar argument. Goldberg acknowledges that the rightward tilt of Fox News serves as a form of compensation. After all, Goldberg argues, there are very few conservatives on ABC, CBS, NBC, CNN, and MSNBC.[23]

The notion of a nearly fair and balanced presentation of news at the Fox News Channel is laughable. Fox's nightly broadcasts typically feature lengthy lineups of prominent speakers from the right and only a few voices from the liberal camp (who are often silenced or left frustrated by the interruptions and badgering of Sean Hannity, Bill O'Reilly, and other microphone-dominating personalities). As Robert Greenwald shows in his documentary film *Outfoxed: Rupert Murdoch's War on Journalism,* presentation of news on the strongly right-oriented channel is anything but "fair and balanced." Greenwald is the producer of numerous programs for television and the maker of films critical of the 2000 election results, the post–9/11 erosion of civil liberties, and U.S. involvement in the Iraq War. *Outfoxed* shows that the Fox News Channel consistently features upbeat reports on the war in Iraq, for instance, and its hosts often question the patriotism of guests who raise questions about the war. Advocates of military invasion dominated the TV screen in 2003, and those who questioned war-making, U.S. occupation of Iraq, and the overall wisdom of the Bush policies in Iraq came under relentless attack from various Fox hosts and guests. Greenwald and his band of researchers found that Rupert Murdoch's staff members at Fox were under pressure to spin the news in ways that favored the policies of George W. Bush's administration. "Fox is a Republican, not merely a conservative network," argues Greenwald.[24]

The Fox network's strong conservative coloration of the news reflects not only the bias of its owner, Rupert Murdoch, but also of its chairman, Roger Ailes. Ailes was a longtime political counselor to conservative Republicans. He served as an adviser to President Richard Nixon and later assisted George H. W. Bush and his aides in their attacks on Michael Dukakis in the 1988 presidential race. Roger Ailes also promoted Rush Limbaugh for syndication on television. As CEO at Fox, Ailes has not maintained a posture of objectivity in his handling of political matters. He employed, for instance, John Ellis, George W. Bush's cousin, to help with the network's election night reporting in 2000 (a night in which Fox called Florida for George W. Bush in contrast to the predictions of a Gore victory by other network news organizations). Ailes also sent ideas to Karl Rove at the Bush White House shortly after September 11, 2001, providing the Republican strategist with recommendations for the administration's handling of the politics of terrorism.

Fox News is not alone, of course, in delivering a strong conservative spin on the news. The influential *Wall Street Journal*, which has a larger national circulation than the *New York Times*, features one conservative commentator after another on its editorial pages. That publication consistently boosted supply-side economics during the Reagan years, and during the buildup toward war with Iraq the *Journal* consistently promoted intervention. Another favorite of the right, the *Washington Times*, is heavily biased in its presentation of information and in its editorial features. The *Washington Times* is owned by the Reverend Sun Myung Moon, a wealthy protheocracy leader of his own Unification Church. Moon, implicated in the "Korea-gate" influence-peddling scandal in the 1970s, reports that he started the *Times* in response to Heaven's direction.

The right also has a strong presence in magazine publishing, book publishing, and the Internet. Conservative periodicals such as the *National Review, American Spectator* and the *Weekly Standard* promote diverse views of the right rather consistently and generally exclude views from the center and left. In the field of book publishing, Regnery, a Chicago-based business, has long been a favorite house for strongly right-wing thinkers. It releases a steady stream of publications by figures such as Pat Buchanan, Mona Charen, William F. Buckley, Ann Coulter, Dinesh D'Souza, Lee Edwards, Steve Forbes, Russell Kirk, G. Gordon Liddy, and David Limbaugh (brother of Rush). Regnery provides virtually no space for voices from the center or the left. This orthodox perspective on the news can be witnessed, too, on-line. One of the best examples appears at Townhall.com, a Web site run by the Heritage Foundation. Townhall lists regular columnists such as Robert Novak, Thomas Sowell, Chuck Colson, Jonah Goldberg, David Horowitz, Oliver North, Phyllis Schlafly, Emmett Tyrell Jr., and George Will. It does not offer a welcome mat to liberal columnists.

No television or radio network or publication can truly boast of complete balance, since virtually all choices about what to print or broadcast involve subjective judgments, but it is abundantly clear that the news organizations right-wingers typically criticize for bias are fairer and more balanced than the ones they praise. Most of the national news organizations that are not managed by conservative bosses try to maintain reasonably objective journalistic standards. When featuring stories about controversial subjects, their producers attempt to present conflicting points of view with roughly equal time on-camera or on-microphone for liberals and conservatives. This is pretty much standard procedure for CNN news reporting and for National Public Radio's *Morning Edition* and the evening news program, *All Things Considered*. The Public Broadcasting System's (PBS) *News Hour with Jim Lehrer* follows this format, too, and a segment at the end of each Lehrer broadcast frequently presents a clash of editorial opinions featuring dueling pundits such as Mark Shields for the liberal side and David Brooks for the conservative position.

Conservatives complain that America's most prestigious and powerful news media project a liberal bias, but the presence of the militant right in the operations of these publications and broadcast organizations belies the claim. The *Washington Post,* for instance, features, among its regular columnists, right-wing pundits such as Charles Krauthammer, George Will, and Robert Novak. The *Post* began giving prominent places to conservative essayists years ago when Meg Greenfield took over leadership of its editorial pages. At the *New York Times,* John Tierney and David Brooks have offered strongly conservative perspectives. Right-wingers are also prominent on programs of the television networks that often catch flak from conservative critics. George Will has been a mainstay as commentator at ABC News for years. Robert Novak, Tucker Carlson, and Kate O'Beirne have been regular participants on CNN programs, and Joe Scarborough runs his own ultra-right show, *Scarborough Country,* on MSNBC. When conservatives complain about "liberal" news networks, they are saying, essentially, that these organizations give considerable attention to the "other" side of political debates as well as the right's positions.

In this regard, radcons are quite correct in their use of terminology. CNN, ABC, NPR, the *New York Times,* and other news sources are, indeed, "liberal." They offer what liberals seek in the presentation of news—political dialogue representing a wide spectrum of opinion. Evidence released by the Pew Research Center for the People and the Press appears to substantiate this point. The center reports that a plurality of CNN's audience consists of Democrats while a plurality of Fox News Channel's audience is Republican. CNN, the news network conservatives are fond of describing as liberal or Democratic, is essentially nonpartisan and offers its viewers considerable exposure to both Democratic and Republican perspectives. Fox, by contrast, overwhelmingly pursues a conservative and Republican agenda in its delivery of the news and opinion.[25] The news sources favored by liberal Democrats and hard-line

Republicans offer stark choices: tolerance, openness, diversity, and balance on one side; intolerance, close-mindedness, a dominant perspective, and bias on the other.

Interestingly, news with a strongly conservative spin has become quite popular in recent years. The Fox News Channel has captured the top position in audience ratings, and right-wing commentators have gained prominent positions in the news and opinion shows on other networks. Right-wing ultras now have a much greater presence in the national media than they had ten or twenty years ago. In the so-called liberal media of CNN, NPR, the *New York Times,* the *Washington Post, Time,* and *Newsweek,* militant conservatives hold an equal and sometimes dominant voice in the debates over political issues. Three recent developments have fostered this growing right-wing influence in broadcasting and print journalism.

First, there has been a substantial conglomeration of big business holdings in the industry, and this trend has favored strongly conservative interests. Large-scale investors such as Rupert Murdoch have succeeded in building media empires, and they often cast their spell over the editorial actions of their armies of employees (as evidenced, for instance, in presentations of news and opinion by Murdoch's Fox News Channel and *New York Post*). Also, the Clear Channel Communications' radio empire of more than 1,200 radio stations has promoted the hard right's causes blatantly. Clear Channel's vice president, Tom Hicks, had helped George W. Bush become a multimillionaire in Texas. The engagement of Murdoch's companies and Clear Channel's radio empire in right-wing politics provides impressive evidence of the radicals' prominence in the offices where important media decisions are made.

It is, after all, the bosses at the news organizations, not reporters or editors, or op-ed columnists, who have the greatest influence on matters of political opinion. As Eric Alterman observes in *What Liberal Media? The Truth about Bias and the News,* these executives decide which kinds of news broadcasts will receive funding. Alterman, who taught English at Brooklyn College and wrote for the *Nation,* said, "It is they who most often select, hire, fire and promote the editors and publishers, top general managers—the journalists—who run the newsrooms." The power of money essentially determines the content of news.[26]

Second, the emerging format for television's handling of political commentary strongly favors a right-wing debating style. News and opinion programs have come into sharp competition in the age of cable and satellite television. Viewers quickly surf for different selections if they are not swiftly entertained when watching political programming. A verbal warrior with a sharp tongue and firm ideas serves best in these televised face-offs of talking heads. People of a political faith entertain and excite audiences more effectively than discerning liberals who raise questions about diverse issues and apply nuance and complexity in their efforts to come up with answers to tough questions. Ultraconservative guests on television often describe political choices in terms of white and black, good and bad. This simplistic perspective works well in the medium of television. Tucker Carlson, Pat Buchanan, Bob Novak, David Brooks, Bill O'Reilly, Joe Scarborough, and other tribunes of the right demonstrate this advantage frequently by engaging in disputes with the combative assurance of someone who knows Truth.

Finally, the radical right's badgering for "equal time" on television has helped to ensure that its orthodox perspectives achieve prominence in national discourse. Some observers have compared these pressure tactics to "working the ref" in a football or basketball game. If a coach complains often about an official's calls and succeeds in these acts of intimidation, the referee may give the offended coach some slack in the next call. Spiro Agnew employed that technique with success in the Nixon years (as noted earlier, broadcast and print news organizations began to feature spokespeople for the right soon after feeling the heat from the vice president's public criticisms). Conservative gains in Congress over recent decades and the arrival of more ultras in high administrative posts in Washington under Reagan and the two Bushes gave the right more leverage in pressuring the media to feature voices for its side in the political arguments. Consequently, as David Brock has noted, managers of the news media often feel they must provide "balance" and "equal time"—that is, attention to "both sides" of the supposedly conservative/liberal clashes.[27]

The radical right's lobbying for one of two principal seats at the mass media's debate table has had the effect of dumbing-down the treatment of important political issues. Discourse in newspapers and magazines and on television typically treats complex choices regarding domestic and foreign policy as simple judgments that must fit into the familiar right-versus-left dichotomy. Virtually everything must be structured in terms of a clash of ideas between conservatives and liberals. This format gives people of a political faith a much larger presence in the exchanges than they might ordinarily receive.

Whatever the issue, audiences now expect to see an orthodox, doctrinaire radcon representing one side in the exchanges. Opinions from the right often represent an ideological extreme, not the mainstream, but they nevertheless command 50 percent of print and broadcast op-ed coverage. It is as if a two-person debate about the world's shape needs to include one individual who contends that the earth is flat. On virtually every major subject, opportunities for sophisticated dialogue are lost in large part because of the media's requirements for ideological representation from the right (in practice, this means the radical right). A discussion about the changing role of women in modern America must include one person who will criticize career-oriented women specifically and denounce feminism generally. An exchange about global warming must include one debater who contends that there is no evidence of a change and who claims that predictions about global warming come only from the crusading of environmentalist radicals. A discussion about U.S. policy in the Iraq war and occupation needs to feature someone who claims the Bush administration was correct in its military decisions and argues that the Iraq war helped to make the United States more secure in the war on terrorism.

These perspectives of the militant right need to be heard, of course, but the quality of political dialogue is diminished when radicals manage to frame the issues on nearly every occasion. Audiences today confront simplified polemical choices instead of complex choices. Political issues are boiled down to decisions between liberals and the far right. Militant conservatives are generally pleased with this dichotomous arrangement because it gives them a prominent place at the debate table. Today they receive much greater exposure in the news and opinion media than decades ago. Liberals are generally unhappy with the format because it tends to trivialize political discussions. Important questions receive inadequate attention in the mass media, they argue, because ideologues of the far right have been able to dictate the terms of discourse.

## Propaganda Mills

Radcons have been tremendously successful in promoting their ideas in the print, broadcast, and Internet media over recent decades because of the immense influence of their "think tanks." These well-endowed institutions have proliferated since the 1960s and have had great success in communicating political ideas to large national audiences. Right-wing benefactors fund these organizations generously because they believe liberal opinion makers wield extraordinary authority in American society. The benefactors think America's intelligentsia stands firmly on the left. Liberals appear to dominate the country's universities and major government agencies. Liberals also seem to be well-represented in the national news and opinion media and in the nation's entertainment industries. The solution to this problem, these benefactors believe, is to promote the growth of a counterintelligentsia. They foster career development of hard-line conservative "experts" on social, economic, political, and international issues by awarding fellowships, sponsoring their publishing activities, and helping to secure their appearances on television and radio. Today, the results of this work by conservative think tanks are abundantly evident. The militant right now enjoys much greater prominence in the mass media than it did a few decades ago.

Of course, "think tank" is a misnomer. These organizations are actually propaganda mills. They crank out policy arguments for leaders in the Republican Party and provide conservative newspaper columnists and right-wing speakers on radio and television with selected news items and bullet points that can easily be incorporated in their daily gigs. The names of these organizations are often misleading, because the titles suggest a free exchange of ideas when, in fact, the institutions aim to produce nothing like that. For instance, the Heritage Foundation features a Web site called TownHall.com. "Town Hall" implies that the site promotes a lively venting of diverse opinions (as one might expect to find in a local community's meeting at the town hall). In this case, however, the hall appears to have been taken over by a band of demagogues. Those who control the Web site are reluctant to invite individuals who might disagree with featured sermons preached by noted pastors of the far right. If anyone was confused about the role of this "think tank," the Heritage Foundation's former vice president, Burton Pines, clarified the matter. "We're not here to be some kind of Ph.D. committee giving equal time," noted Pines. "Our role is to provide conservative public-policymakers with arguments to bolster our side."[28] (Interestingly, the Heritage Foundation, which delivers an abundance of information on behalf of Republicans, is a tax-exempt foundation.

As David Brock points out, it is not supposed to act or lobby on behalf of a particular political party).[29]

Newspapers, radio stations, and television programs provide rich opportunities for writers and speakers from the militant right's propaganda mills without any indication of the commentator's agendas. The individuals appear as "experts" and "scholars" who, purportedly, aim to throw light on various complex economic, social, and international topics. Yet these guests cannot approach their subjects with truly independent thought. Their opinions on the topics of the day are almost entirely predictable. A fellow from the American Enterprise Institute, for example, spoke on October 6, 2003, on National Public Radio's *Morning Edition* about George W. Bush's request for $87 billion in additional aid for U.S. military and economic activities in Iraq. The commentator from AEI, not at all surprisingly, defended the president's request. He argued that, relatively speaking, $87 billion was not more than the value of one large business in the United States. If the expert from AEI had argued against Bush's financial request and criticized his policy in Iraq during this radio commentary, he would probably find his work at the American Enterprise Institute quickly terminated. Another fellow from the AEI spoke to the media in 2003 about the UN's efforts to play a strong security role in occupied Iraq, a request that the Bush administration strongly opposed. Again, not surprisingly, the resident scholar from AEI supported President Bush by arguing that UN security missions had often met with failure, and the United States was likely to prove more successful at nation-building than the United Nations. If this "scholar" had claimed President Bush was wrong and Americans would do better working in cooperation with the UN, he would likely lose his research support at AEI.

When challenged about the highly biased mission of their propaganda mills, right-wingers often claim that the Brookings Institution, one of the most prominent Washington-based think tanks, is tilted toward the advocacy of liberal policies. They say organizations such as the Heritage Foundation, the American Enterprise Institute, and the libertarian Cato Institute provide balance. Walter Wriston, a former chairman of Citicorp and a member of the American Enterprise Institute's development committee in the 1980s, made the case for AEI in precisely this fashion. "Brookings is fat with liberals out of office," he charged. "AEI is the other side of the operation."[30] Bernard Goldberg, the former employee of CBS News who left the organization and charged it with liberal bias, also used the Brookings example to make a point about the supposedly liberal media. He noted that CBS News identified the Heritage Foundation as a "conservative" think tank. "But where was the idea of the Brookings Institution as 'a liberal think tank?'" he asked.[31]

This comparison is ridiculous. The Brookings Institution, a well-respected research organization, is far more committed to independent and responsible investigation than organizations such as the Heritage Foundation, the AEI, or the Cato Institute. There is no comparison. The Brookings Institution stresses bipartisanship; the others emphasize partisanship. As Eric Alterman notes, during the Clinton years the head of the Brookings Institution was a Republican, as were many of the institution's fellows. The Brookings Institution has built its strong reputation on grounds of promoting objective research. As Sidney Blumenthal observes, it has provided both Republican and Democratic administrations with experts for many years.[32] Other favorite targets for conservative claims about bias are the Carnegie Foundation and the Council on Foreign Relations, yet those organizations provided opportunities in recent years for many individuals who had been associated with the Reagan and Bush administrations.[33] As in the case of various television news networks, when radicals of the right call these institutions "liberal" they mean that they provide research opportunities for people of diverse political persuasions.

Right-wing propaganda mills usually carry names that sound imposing and suggest dedication to serious investigation of policy issues. In practice, these organizations tend to deliver one-sided diatribes and support writers and speakers who will deliver the very messages that prominent benefactors seek. Among the organizations that have received considerable support are the Hoover Institution at Stanford, the Manhattan Institute, and the Hudson Institute. The titles of these organizations often suggest (falsely) an objective scholarly mission as in the cases of the Intercollegiate Studies Institute, the Institute for Educational Affairs, and the Center for the Study of Religion and Society.

Substantial donations from right-oriented benefactors have provided the propaganda tanks with valuable sources of revenue. Paul Weyrich, Edwin J. Feulner Jr., and other New Right organizers who launched the Heritage Foundation obtained large-scale support from Colorado beer magnate Joseph Coors, as well as from other archconservatives to launch the Heritage Foundation in 1973. Various right-wing organizations and publications received millions from the donations of the Smith-Richardson Foundation, the Scaife Family Trusts, the Lynde and Harry Bradley Foundation, and the John T. Olin Foundation. The patriarch of the Scaife family was the conspiracy-minded Richard Mellon Scaife, who funded dirt-digging efforts against Bill Clinton with a $2.3 million contribution to what became known as the Arkansas Project (the effort helped to produce unsubstantiated hints about Vince Foster's suicide and suggestions about a "Troopergate" scandal).[34] Harry Bradley had been a member of the John Birch Society, and Rupert Murdoch, the media mogul from Australia, helped to launch the *Weekly Standard* and put his money behind the radcon-oriented Fox News Channel and the *New York Post*. These sugar-daddies of the right were eager backers of the True Faith. They were hardly tolerant of diverse opinions, particularly "liberal" opinions.

Uniformity of opinion also applies to the publications sponsored by conservative benefactors and foundations. *Commentary,* an important organ for the promotion of neoconservative writings, was generously funded by Rupert Murdoch and the Bradley, Olin, and Scaife organizations. *American Spectator,* a stinging organ of the right, received support from the same three groups, and *New Criterion,* also a hard-line publication, won enthusiastic financial backing from the Scaife and Olin foundations. An Olin Foundation grant of $600,000 in the mid-1980s helped to launch neoconservative Irving Kristol's publication, the *National Interest*.[35]

Individual right-wingers also benefited from the conservative movement's largesse. Myron Magnet, Norman Podhoretz, David Horowitz, John Dilulio, and others worked with generous financing when they constructed one-sided, partisan arguments for the media. The Richardson Foundation gave Jude Wanniski $40,000 to write a book that helped to make the idea of supply-side economics popular with Republicans.[36] Peter Steinfels, author of an early study of neoconservatism, reports that hard-line conservative benefactors offered thousands for a collection of right-oriented essays on the power of a liberal "new class." Contributions of up to $4,000 were available for 30–40 pages of printed argumentation. One scholar who was used to receiving between $75 to $300 for his contributions to journals said of these payments, "It certainly clears one's calendar and concentrates the mind."[37] Charles Murray, the militantly libertarian "social scientist," became a particular darling of these supporters. He received more than a million dollars over several years from Scaife and Bradley to write his controversial book, *Losing Ground: American Social Policy, 1950–1980* (1984).[38]

When questions about bias and partisanship arise, recipients of foundation support from the far right are quick to claim that they operate with an open mind. This issue became especially important in the case of John R. Lott Jr., a research scholar at the American Enterprise Institute. Lott had been associated with some of the nation's leading educational institutions: UCLA, the University of Chicago, Yale, Stanford, and the University of Pennsylvania's Wharton Business School. He came under criticism when he published the controversial book *More Guns, Less Crime: Understanding Crime and Gun-Control Laws* (1998). Criminology professionals challenged Lott's claim that concealed-carry weapons permits reduced crime. They charged him with systematically skewing the evidence reported in his book. Critics demonstrated that he selectively features statistics that benefit his arguments and consciously leaves out important evidence that undermines his case. Eventually, Lott admitted to making some errors, which he blamed on faulty editing. His critics also accused him of back-dating some corrections. Later, researchers discovered that Lott had featured reviews of his own books on the Internet under an assumed name, Mary Rush (that name was based on letters in the names of his children).

Representative (later Senator) Charles Schumer contributed to this debate in an interesting way when he noted that Lott had given thanks in his book for the "generous funding" he received from the John M. Olin Law and Economics Program. In turn, the Olin Corporation, manufacturers of Winchester ammunition and maker of the "Black Talon" bullet, provided major funding for the foundation.[39] Charles Schumer saw a conflict of interest. By funding a pro-gun study, the foundation was evidently advancing the interests of its commercial benefactor.

William E. Simon, the former treasury secretary and energy czar and president of the Olin Foundation, sent a letter to the *Wall Street Journal,* calling Schumer's charge "outrageous slander." Simon said Schumer's claim represented an attack on the "scholarly integrity" of Professor Lott. He claimed the Olin Foundation's purpose "is to support individuals and institutions working to strengthen the free enterprise system." The organization supported research activity at leading universities such as Yale, the University of Chicago, Harvard, Stanford, and the University of Virginia,

Simon insisted. "We do not tell scholars what to say," he asserted. Money for the foundation came from the late John M. Olin's personal fortune, and the workings of the institution were not associated with activities of the Olin Corporation. That manufacturing industry "never sought to influence our deliberation," Simon assured readers of the *Wall Street Journal*.[40] William E. Simon provided an additional defense of Lott's scholarship by pointing to the supposedly unbiased makeup of the foundation's board. "The trustees and officers of the foundation have been selected by virtue of their devotion to John Olin's principles," he wrote, "not by virtue of family connections." This letter to the *Journal,* Simon concluded, "clarifies the funding issue."[41]

Simon's communication to the *Wall Street Journal,* with its message about Olin's devotion to scholarly integrity, contrasts sharply with the message he presented in an earlier publication. Back in 1978, two years after he assumed the position of president of the John M. Olin Foundation, Simon gave a more candid report on the partisan purposes of the Olin charities. The foundations, he said, maintained a "philosophical restriction" on their beneficiaries. Their policy would "not result in a uniformity of intellectual product," he informed readers, because there was "an enormous diversity of viewpoints within the center-to-right intellectual world which endorses capitalism." Simon provided a rationale for the restrictive approach by claiming the "opposition," the intelligentsia of the nation that operated in the media and in the universities, was dominated by enemies of capitalism. Ironically, he said, American businesses were underwriting institutions that sought the destruction of capitalism. "The great corporations of America sustain the major universities," Simon observed, "with no regard to the context of their teachings." Major foundations "which nurture the most destructive egalitarian trends" were financing "whole departments of economics, government, politics and history that were hostile to capitalism and whose faculties will not hire scholars whose views are otherwise."[42] Simon claimed that the Ford Foundation had become "a veritable fortress of the philosophical opposition." In the intellectual centers, defenders of free enterprise were the outvoted minority, the "impoverished underground."[43]

William E. Simon proposed to change this situation by directing the Olin Foundations toward development of a "counterintelligentsia."[44] The Olin philanthropies would promote a "philosophy of freedom" rather than "experimental dabbling in socialist utopian ideas or funding of outright revolution."[45] The new brand of philanthropy "must not capitulate to soft-minded pleas for the support of 'dissent,'" he insisted. For too long, the capitalist commitment to "fairness" had led corporations to finance "the intellectual opposition" and allowed the foundations they created to be "literally taken over."[46] In short, a tough policy of philosophical restriction was necessary to "challenge the ideological monopoly."[47]

Simon's conflicting explanations regarding the objectivity of the Olin Foundation reveals a fundamental problem that applies to most militantly conservative research institutions. These organizations are not involved in genuine research. They do not support objective inquiry or promote genuinely open-minded investigations. The institutions are not "think tanks." Rather, they are propaganda mills. Their "fellows" are often True Believers or mercenaries, or both. Most of them are not actually "scholars." The researchers are generally averse to drawing conclusions that conflict with philosophies endorsed by the institutions that fund their work. If these "scholars" publicly defend interpretations that displease the institutional benefactors and managers, they will quickly lose their coveted positions.

## Muffling Dissenting Voices

When comedienne Margaret Cho made fun of President Bush's pronunciation of "nuclear" in 2004 and joked about his failed programs in Iraq, she came under angry criticism from the nation's Republicans. This harsh reaction from the right was one of several examples of nasty protest against individuals and productions of the mass media that irritated hardline conservatives. Unfortunately, the complaints evolved quickly into something more significant than simple statements of disagreement (which, after all, are perfectly appropriate, since expressions of political opposition should always be welcome in a democratic society). In several cases right-wing organizations attempted to punish those who spoke in ways they did not approve. Radical organizations encouraged boycotts of the speakers' music, videos, and films and attempted to pressure various media organizations to remove from public circulation CDs, DVDs, films, and television programs made by the offending individuals. Censorship of political communication is almost nonexistent in modern America, but these right-wing groups have attempted to promote the *consequences* of censorship by applying pressure on those who communicate ideas in the mass media. Their efforts have the effect of placing a pall on the free expression of political opinion.

Relatively few Americans saw the CBS television miniseries *The Reagans* when it was released in 2003, because a barrage of protests from Republicans and militant conservative groups evidently convinced CBS executives that the controversial series was more appropriate for a small paying audience watching TV's Showtime than a large audience watching free entertainment in a network broadcast. Reagan supporters warned leading advertisers about the series and offered hints about a possible conservative boycott of CBS programming. Their success in frightening executives at CBS revealed that intimidation works in the entertainment industry. Partisans managed to block a dramatic presentation of history that they did not like.

These actions served the cause of censorship, but critics of the television series did not acknowledge that their actions represented an assault on freedom of speech. Instead, they claimed to be advocates of "accurate" and "balanced" history. Ed Gillespie, chairman of the Republican National Committee, complained that the CBS script contains language that Ronald Reagan never actually used, and Gillespie concluded that the film's interpretation is excessively critical of the former president. He asked CBS to allow Reagan's former associates to examine the film for historical accuracy. Otherwise, said Gillespie, the network needed to place a disclaimer on the screen every ten minutes advising viewers that the drama contains fictional material.

If filmmakers followed the recommendations of the GOP's chairman, just about every historical drama would be off-limits for Hollywood and network television. "Docudrama" is, by its very nature, inaccurate and unbalanced. Dramatic representations of the past always contain what some would call inaccuracies, because the creators of these films must imagine conversations and actions that have not been recorded by historians. The films are unbalanced because artists can never represent an entire life in their stories. They must select examples, and those choices reflect opinions. Since the time of Shakespeare's historical plays, virtually all docudramas have offered hard-hitting, opinionated viewpoints.

Most film and television dramas that excite public interest in history deliver partisan portrayals of events and people. They are all "controversial" in some way. *Gandhi* portrays the famous leader of India's independence movement as a saint and overlooks his flaws. *Braveheart* glorifies Scottish patriot William Wallace's cause and makes the English look like villains. *Roots,* the influential 1970s television miniseries that aroused the American public's interest in the history of slavery, portrays most blacks as noble and depicts most whites as exploitative. Docudrama is usually not interesting or entertaining if it is not controversial. Only a few notable docudramas have attempted to present two-sided portraits that reveal both positive and negative aspects of their subjects. For instance, *Patton,* awarded Best Picture in 1970, presents the combative World War II general as a heroic figure, but the movie also reveals some of George S. Patton's shortcomings.

*The Reagans* does present a strongly critical portrayal of the former president and his wife, even though it contains a few favorable examples of Ronald Reagan's leadership, as well. It shows the president's political skills and commitment to his beliefs and gives him credit for helping to end the Cold War. It also highlights the president's forgetfulness and loose control over his staff, and it portrays Nancy Reagan as a control-obsessed First Lady who seeks advice on policy matters from astrologers. Partisans could certainly argue about the placement of this information and other details in the film. Yet they needed, as well, to acknowledge that just about all elements in the story to which they objected had been reported in news accounts, biographies, and tell-all books written by former leaders in the Reagan administration. To be sure, *The Reagans* delivers, overall, a sharply critical assessment of the late president, but artists should enjoy the freedom to express that kind of interpretation in a free society. Reagan fans, in turn, can enjoy freedom of expression in designing a strongly positive cinematic portrayal of Ronald Reagan. The effort to shut down the film's distribution on major network television is troubling.

When critics of the program heard complaints that they were trying to prevent broadcast of a work of art, they insisted that docudramas should present stories about the deceased, not living figures such as Ronald and Nancy Reagan. If that requirement applies, we will need to wait thirty or more years to see a drama about Bill Clinton or Tony Blair (or a miniseries about the life of recording artists, screen stars, or athletic heroes who are among the living). To deny the media opportunities to portray living characters in film drama is to deny artists the chance to comment on American life and politics at a time when the portrayals are likely to seem particularly relevant. An effort to close off cinematic commentary about living persons sounds like a campaign appropriate for a dictatorship, not a democracy.

The complaints leveled by Gillespie and others did not constitute a noble effort to ensure fair treatment of a historical subject. They represented a form of intimidation. These protesters did not agree with the point of view offered by the CBS docudrama, and they wished to prevent broadcast of the miniseries. Political censorship is not formally sanctioned in modern America, but the pressure tactics of Gillespie and his supporters came close to advancing the goals of a censor.

Michael Moore came under similar pressures when he planned to release his controversial film *Fahrenheit 9/11* in 2004. Moore's documentary sharply criticizes Bush's war in Iraq and raises questions about the Bush family's ties to wealthy and influential figures in Saudi Arabia, including members of the large bin Laden family. The Disney Company was to distribute *Fahrenheit 9/11,* but its bosses had second thoughts about releasing a controversial documentary during an election year (although Disney showed no hesitation in continuing its broadcasts of Rush Limbaugh and Sean Hannity on its WABC radio affiliate in New York City). Michael Moore's film won the top prize at the Cannes Film Festival, yet Disney executives considered it too hot to handle. Disney blocked its Miramax division from distributing Moore's movie. Harvey and Bob Weinstein eventually secured the rights and brought it to theaters in the summer of 2004.

Right-wing organizations quickly began campaigns against *Fahrenheit 9/11*. A group called Move America Forward went into action against Moore (this was another example of deceptive naming on the part of the right, since Move America Forward really aimed, through its censorious actions, to push the country backward). The right-wing group tried to harass theater owners by warning of mass boycotts if they showed the movie. Their tactic was similar to the one Move America Forward employed against *The Reagans*. Another far-right organization, Citizens United, criticized the television ads for *Fahrenheit 9/11,* claiming that they showed President Bush in a critical light during the key election period and, therefore, represented a violation of campaign finance laws. The head of Citizens United was David Bossie, author of an intensely anti-Clinton book and producer of the infamous Willie Horton ads that helped to ensure George H. W. Bush's smashing victory over Democrat Michael Dukakis. Bossie also had contributed the Gennifer Flowers ads that Republicans employed against Bill Clinton.

Michael Moore tried to joke about this and other right-wing assaults on his movie. With tongue in cheek, Moore said of Bossie's efforts, "I am deeply concerned about whether or not the FEC 'Federal Elections Commission' will think I paid Citizens United to raise these issues. How else can you explain the millions of dollars of free publicity this right-wing group has given the movie? I plan on sending them a very nice holiday card this year."[48] In a broader sense, though, the well-orchestrated campaigns to arouse public doubts about the movie and its maker made an impact on public opinion. The right-wing critics' assault left the impression that *Fahrenheit 9/11*'s interpretation of recent history is deeply flawed even though Moore is essentially correct in the principal points he raises in his movie.[49]

The radical right's anxiety about criticism of President George W. Bush and his war in Iraq also figured in the political assault on the country-pop band the Dixie Chicks. The trio's lead singer, Natalie Maines, found herself in a maelstrom shortly before the Iraq war began when she said during a London concert that she was "ashamed that the President of the United States is from Texas." Republicans rallied in protest against Maines, and various radio stations refused to play Dixie Chicks songs. One station arranged for a 33,000-pound bulldozer to smash their CDs, tapes, and other paraphernalia. As liberal *New York Times* columnist Paul Krugman reported, many of these protests were not rising from the grassroots. They were, instead, staged by right-wing media leaders who coveted a good relationship with the president (some of them had been gobbling up radio stations across the country since the Telecommunications Act of 1996 made larger conglomerations possible). They hoped for continued favorable treatment as they planned more acquisitions in the future. At the time further deregulation was under consideration. The rally featuring a bulldozer had been organized by Cumulus Media, and Clear Channel Communications planned many prowar "Rally for America" gatherings. The vice chair of Clear Channel was Tom Hicks, the man who purchased the Texas Rangers baseball franchise in an arrangement that brought a handsome price to George W. Bush.[50]

Artists reacted in diverse ways to intimidation. Some appeared cowed in view of the Dixie Chicks' rough treatment by the right; they did not wish to see their own sales of CDs and other products diminished sharply from political reactions. Apparently that danger was on the mind of Madonna. Shortly after negative reactions to the Chicks reached the mass media, Madonna pulled a video that contained some harsh imagery symbolic of the war in Iraq. Others defended Natalie Maines and the Dixie Chicks. Bruce Springsteen supported their freedom of expression through a comment on his Web site, and country singer Faith Hill affirmed, "She's an American. She has the right to say whatever she wants to say." Hill declared, "It doesn't matter who agrees or who doesn't agree. That's our right and that's what we fight for."[51]

Censorious pressures continued as American troubles in Iraq mounted. When Ted Koppel attempted to devote his *Nightline* program to a roll-call of the American dead in Iraq (principally by featuring head-shot images of the deceased soldiers), cries of protest emerged from critics on the right. Some ABC television affiliates chose not to broadcast the program. Later an NBC freelance cameraman named Kevin Sites came under verbal attack for showing a U.S. marine shooting an apparently unarmed Iraqi prisoner in a mosque. On the right-wing Web site freepublic.com, Sites was called an "anti-war activist," a traitor, and an "enemy combatant." All of these charges were, of course, not true. Sites chose to shut down his own blog after he received death threats from Americans who were not pleased with his camerawork in Iraq. Evidently, the facts from Iraq were unacceptable to these partisans.[52]

Militant leaders on the right have played a clever political game in recent years by constantly sounding the refrain about a new class or new elite of liberals in the mass media who supposedly control the world of news and entertainment. These claims about a powerful and dangerous enemy with hegemonic influence over the information Americans receive helps to divert attention from the radical right's own biased, distorted, and censorious treatment of information. If a true danger exists in the realm of the media's handling of evidence, it is of their making. Right-wing organizations, working through the print and broadcast media, have been addressing issues with such blatant disregard of journalistic standards that they threaten to reduce public presentation of news to mere exercises in propaganda.

In one respect, though, liberals can express appreciation to the radical right for helping to clarify differences between the two groups' points of view. Radcons frequently praise strongly biased organs of opinion such as the Fox News Channel and the *Washington Times* as worthy sources of information, while they call organizations known for much more balanced delivery of news (PBS, NPR, CNN, the major network news organizations, and the *New York Times*) "liberal." Liberals can agree emphatically with this distinction. Organizations that generally attempt to present diversity of opinion are "liberal" in the finest sense of the word.

## CHAPTER EIGHT

# The Closing of the Conservative Mind

The militant right has distorted the meaning of conservatism to the point that the term has lost a great deal of its relevance in modern-day America. Much that passes as "conservative" does not truly represent the principles of intelligent, responsible, and thoughtful conservatism. Real conservatives believe in a balanced budget, not the huge deficits sponsored by George W. Bush's administration. True conservatives recognize that some degree of government regulatory activity is necessary to promote business competition, support the health and safety of the American people, and protect the environment from serious damage. They are not Stealth Libertarians who reject government activity at almost every turn. They are not, in short, radicals with an extremist commitment to laissez-faire. Real conservatives advocate a cautious foreign policy and question America's potential for nation-building in deeply troubled societies rather than support military interventions with little questioning. True conservatives do not mount a hostile response to virtually every American effort to deal directly with the historic inequalities suffered by African Americans, nor do they look upon virtually all campaigns that draw attention to the particular problems of women as appalling examples of radical feminism. Real conservatives do not fear modernity, with the many new cultural and social fashions it fosters, nor do they simplistically blame the controversial social transformations of modern life almost exclusively on "liberals." The arguments presented by many so-called conservatives these days do not uphold solid traditions of conservatism that have commanded much respect from Americans. Rather, they reflect viewpoints of people who display enthusiasm for an extremist, fundamentalist, far-right political faith.

America's democratic spirit has been undermined in recent years by militant conservatism. The advocates of a fundamentalist-style political outlook promote belief, not questioning; conformity, not independent thinking; faith, rather than reason. Leaders of the radical right have tried to silence moderates who voiced dissent within conservative organizations, and recently they have shown signs of applying that modus operandi to the nation's political affairs. They have called individuals who questioned U.S. policies in Iraq unpatriotic and un-American. Citizens who doubted the wisdom of the far right's economic and cultural policies have been described as socialist, relativist, secularist, and anti-Christian. The radcons' most familiar invective is simply "liberal," an emotion-laden term that suggests a broad range of ugly associations. Right-wingers have engaged in venomous personal attacks against filmmakers and television producers who commented on social and political issues through their art. Crusaders of the militant right have also directed scurrilous personal criticism against Democratic politicians who resisted their agendas, and they have tried to ostracize centrist-minded Republicans who have not accepted their radical agenda.

The most fundamental problem with the militant right's political faith is its orthodoxy. Radcon ideology promotes the outlook of True Believers who are reluctant to question the basic assumptions of their ideology. Followers of a political faith are hesitant about subjecting their convictions to critical scrutiny. They accept the teachings of right-wing gurus even when they encounter disturbing facts that ought to undermine confidence in their doctrines. The radicals' faith promotes the politics of obeisance, not questioning. It encourages followers to chant the mantras of their creed rather than to seek new, independent-minded understandings. Radcon attitudes represent a dramatic rejection of the open-minded, inquisitive, and practical outlook that made the United States great over the long course of its history.

This preference for homogeneity—for one prevailing perspective rather than diverse conflicting ones—is evident as well in the way many of today's conservatives seek strongly biased presentations of the news. In the Washington, D.C., area many radical conservatives enthusiastically read a transparently partisan newspaper, the *Washington Times*.

Many business-minded conservatives appreciate the right-wing orthodoxy they encounter on the editorial pages of the *Wall Street Journal*. Millions who follow the right's hard-core faith listen to Rush Limbaugh's promotion of it on the radio or rely on another disseminator of it, the Fox
News Channel, for political information and opinions. Whether turning
to the newspaper, radio, or TV for commentary, or to information on the
Web, these partisans show a high comfort level with treatments of the
news that are strongly slanted to the right. At the same time, they express
deep suspicion of news sources that feature information and opinions
representing a broad spectrum of viewpoints. When referring to mainstream media or to the "liberal media," their favorite targets are organizations known for broad and more balanced coverage, such as the *New York
Times*, the *Washington Post*, the *Los Angeles Times*, National Public Radio,
CBS television, CNN News, and PBS television.

The radcons' suspicious characterizations of these media organizations strikes moderates as laughable. Moderates understand that at various moments these sources of news and opinion may provide information that leans in one political direction or another, but readers, listeners,
and viewers can generally expect to encounter a much greater variety of
commentary from these outlets than can be found in venues favored by
the right. Interestingly, too, moderates (including liberals) do not flock to
sharply partisan radio venues in the manner that enthusiasts on the right
tune in to conservatively oriented programs. The right's radio warriors
depend on an angry following of political fundamentalists. Limbaugh,
Hannity, O'Reilly, and their many imitators attract a sizable army of listeners that favor Manichaean descriptions of the current political scene.
These broadcasters portray dramatic clashes between saintly conservatives and mischievous liberals. Limbaugh, Hannity, and O'Reilly provide
entertainment for True Believers, not inquisitive audiences. Moderates
usually approach the news with greater intellectual curiosity. They prefer to see presentations of political opinion delivered in mixed doses so
they can become acquainted with a wide range of ideas. When they seek
news on the radio, they favor programs that feature diverse and conflicting voices on the issues such as National Public Radio's *Morning Edition*
and *All Things Considered*.

The radcons' preference for orthodoxy is evident, too, in their efforts
to denigrate opinions that conflict with their faith. Radcons have organized quickly to push contrary perspectives out of public view. As we

saw, they threatened CBS with massive boycotts when that network proposed to broadcast an unflattering drama about the life of Ronald Reagan. Their tactics succeeded in convincing the network's chief, Leslie Moonves, to schedule the drama on pay-for-view rather than through free network broadcast. Right-wing outbursts against singer Natalie Maines's critical remarks about President George W. Bush led to a campaign for the massive boycott of her trio's work that culminated when Cumulus Media, owner of radio stations throughout the United States, stopped its forty-two country outlets from playing Dixie Chicks music. Militant conservatives also launched a multifaceted assault on Michael Moore's *Fahrenheit 9/11* and managed to keep the film off of a number of movie screens throughout the United States. When Ted Koppel of ABC's *Nightline* planned to broadcast the names of 721 Americans who had died in the war on Iraq, the Sinclair broadcast group, a conservative organization whose leaders support President Bush's policies in Iraq, directed its ABC affiliate stations not to run the programs. In these and many other examples of intimidation, conservatives applauded efforts to keep viewpoints they disagreed with out of public view.

Most representatives of America's conservative elite remained noticeably mute in these instances. They did not issue loud protests against partisans' efforts to smother dissenting opinions. Despite glaring violations of principles of free speech, they offered little or no protest. Those intellectuals on the right had long before sold their souls to the Republican Party and to conservative sponsors who had generously financed their research, writing, and fellowship activity at so-called think tanks. They were not about to bite the right-wing hands that fed them. Representatives of the nation's conservative intellectual elite remained silent during a time when their compatriots were engaged in political bullying. In fact, some on the right, such as Chris Weinkopf, applauded the censorious pressures. When right-wing complaints and warnings convinced leaders at CBS to cancel their plans to broadcast *The Reagans,* Weinkopf gave the news a positive spin. Writing for a leading "think tank" of the right, the American Enterprise Institute, Chris Weinkopf declared that a "democratic argument" of the people defeated the "media elite" in the case of CBS's decision not to broadcast the program over its main network. "That's the American way," Weinkopf concluded gleefully.[1]

Support for the censorious spirit also appeared in the pages of Fred Barnes's influential publication, the *Weekly Standard,* which featured an article by Matthew Continetti about George Mason University's decision to rescind an invitation it had extended to Michael Moore to speak on campus during the 2004 election campaign. University officials had pulled the invitation to Moore after they came under fire from Republicans. Continetti endorsed the university's cancellation, even though representatives of the American Association of University Professors (AAUP) and Phi Beta Kappa honorary society objected strenuously to this apparent violation of academic freedom. Continetti suggested that Moore was unsuitable as a speaker because his price was too high. Besides, Moore was a college dropout and had no academic affiliation. The writer suggested, too, that Moore's presentation was not likely to rise to the highest standards of art and literature. Continetti expected that Michael Moore would deliver a sophomoric message to the students.

The author of this article in the *Weekly Standard* failed to recognize that students at George Mason University should have had the opportunity to listen to Michael Moore and judge the quality of the speaker's presentation for themselves. As a contributor to one of the right's most prestigious publications, Continetti (and his executive editor, Fred Barnes) should have heeded the words of the American Association of University Professors' secretary general, Roger Bowen, when dealing with this case. The AAUP leader expressed disappointment with the decision to withdraw Moore's invitation. He said the action was "inconsistent with the principle that a university is a place where all views can be heard and discussed."[2]

When one of the right's premier journals of opinion fails its readership in this manner, it is not surprising that strident commentators of radio, television, and the Internet give similar close-minded responses to issues of the day. The combative pundits of popular culture lack impressive models of independent thinking from the right's intellectual leaders. Truly critical thinking is a rare exercise in the radcon camp. When rightists confront tough questions presented by individuals delivering unpleasant information (as in Michael Moore's case), they tend to attack the messenger rather than examine the message. Radcons assert beliefs rather than question basic assumptions. Their faith in doctrinaire conservatism remains firm in these circumstances because their commitment to political fundamentalism runs deep.

Conservatism, an honorable and important tradition in American political life, developed a tarnished image in recent decades because it became associated with hard-core, extremist ideas. Moderate, open-minded conservatives sense today that leading organizations on the right do not extend welcoming hands to them. Congregants in the church of True Believers turn away people who appear to be weak at heart. In contrast, they welcome right-wing fundamentalists. Radcons are not comfortable with individuals in their movement who question the basic assumptions of their political faith. Nor are they indulgent of people who lack interest in thrashing liberals and blaming them for much of what bothers them about American life.

As long as Ronald Reagan's "Eleventh Commandment" remains in practice, the radical character of rightist politics is unlikely to change significantly. In 1966 Reagan modified the language of California's Republican state chairman, Gaylord Parkinson, when he said, "Thou shalt not speak ill of a fellow Republican." Parkinson and Reagan offered this general rule in view of the problems Barry Goldwater had faced in his 1964 presidential race. Some moderate and liberal Republicans associated the GOP contender with "extremism," and the label hurt. Reagan warned that similar criticism within the party could undermine his campaign for governor. The actor-turned-politician asked for unanimity on the right. By the time Reagan won the presidency in 1980, he had come close to achieving his wish. Most Republicans learned not to pass strong judgment on each other in public. By the time George W. Bush arrived at the White House, the right's commitment to an "Eleventh Commandment" had broadened considerably. For conservatives, the directive meant, essentially, "Thou shalt not speak ill of the radicals in our movement."

Conservatives, more than liberals, are especially challenged today to bring the right back to its more center-oriented and practical traditions. They are in a better position than liberals to gain the attention of radcons. If moderate conservatives are to reverse the radical course of their party and movement, however, they will need to express their sentiments with much greater force. For too long, political fundamentalists have operated in a rightist echo chamber. They have proffered favored homilies with very little opposition, presenting ideas to fellow partisans as if their concepts represented sacred, unassailable Truths. Vibrant democracy requires much more vigorous debate. Reasonable, open-minded conservatism needs more aggressive champions.

Not surprisingly, partisans of the radical right showed little evidence of questioning their beliefs when conservative fortunes waned in the summer of 2006. At the time, President George W. Bush's approval ratings had dropped into the 30 percent range and ratings for the GOP-controlled Congress were about ten points lower. These low ratings did not necessarily mean that Republicans would face electoral disaster in the years ahead. Rightist leaders often manage to conceal their shortcomings in governance at election time by characterizing Democrats as inadequate warriors against terrorism and weak defenders of Christian and family values. Nevertheless, the news about Washington-based scandals, pork-barrel extravagance, spiraling budget deficits, and a quagmire in Iraq created a serious image problem for the right. Conservatives struggled to come up with explanations for the growing difficulties of the politicians and party that they had energetically supported. Under these circumstances, many radcons produced a rationale similar to the response fundamentalists frequently make when confronting information that clashes with their beliefs. Conservatives remained committed to their faith and complained that their leaders failed to live up to it. The problem, they said, was that some GOP leaders did not give *real* conservatism a fair chance to work.

Quite a few radcons dealt with the Bush administration's declining popularity by turning on their own people. They tried to absolve their movement of responsibility for recent setbacks by attacking the man they had favored enthusiastically just a short time before. Bruce Bartlett, Robert Novak, Peggy Noonan, and Pat Buchanan, among others, complained that George W. Bush had violated conservative values. Bush was not truly in the mold of Ronald Reagan, they lamented.[3] Rightists also lashed out at Republican congressmen for supporting expensive drug benefits and promoting large spending bills that delivered pork to their districts. Government had not shrunk in the Bush era, these rightists griped. Instead, it had grown substantially. The problem, said these critics, was that Bush and many GOP congressmen behaved like wayward conservatives and somewhat like liberals. Enjoying the privileges of political power, they turned into big spenders and supporters of expansive government. Thus, real conservatism had not been tried.

This explanation for problems in governance is unconvincing. It was disingenuous for rightist pundits to characterize the Republican leadership as counter-conservative or quasi-liberal. Many radcon ideas had been tried or implemented under the leadership of George W. Bush and the Republican-dominated Congress. Leaders on the right had demanded giant tax cuts that benefited the rich, attempted to privatize social security, voted for huge increases in defense budgets, and promoted extensive intervention in Iraq. They had appointed lots of ideological colleagues to the federal courts and the federal regulatory agencies. Those appointees vigorously promoted deregulation. Radcon leaders had also encouraged agitation over abortion, gay marriage, and other emotion-laden "social" issues. America's Culture Warriors, Stealth Libertarians, and Hawkish Nationalists had no reason to complain that their interests had been overlooked in recent years. Coveted radcon principles had been put into practice.

Many of the problems that dragged down the popularity of President Bush and the GOP-led Congress were directly related to the application of conservative ideas rather than to departures from them. Large tax cuts (a favorite goal of the radcons) along with gigantic defense budgets (another favorite) and ambitious war-making in Iraq (defended through radcon jingoism) swelled the federal deficit and badly damaged the United States' global image. FEMA, a model of efficiency in the Clinton era, looked like a striking example of bureaucratic incompetence after radcons privatized some of its programs and filled its top ranks with right-wing cronies. The Medicare drug program promoted by the GOP delighted the pharmaceutical industry, because its costly arrangements promised large profits to corporations. The Republican plan did *not* allow the government to negotiate aggressively in order to reduce drug prices. In these programs and several other examples of conservative governance, the handling of public affairs was problematic.

A fundamental reason for this disappointing leadership was that key people in charge of federal programs were hostile toward the basic idea of activist government in America's nonmilitary affairs. Libertarian-minded politicians proved to be poor planners and agency heads in Washington. They were uncomfortable with their basic task of creating broadly effective public agencies of the national government. As devotees of the private sector, these Stealth Libertarians looked suspiciously on programs designed to give the state substantial influence in American society. "Conservatives cannot govern well for the same reason that vegetarians cannot prepare a world-class boeuf bourguignon," suggests Alan

Wolfe. "If you believe that what you are called upon to do is wrong, you are not likely to do it very well."[4]

Governance by the right has been disappointing, too, because it is influenced by people who base their judgments on convictions rather than open-minded analysis of real-world problems. Back in 2004, investigative reporter Ron Suskind gave readers a memorable example of the mindset when he described a comment made to him by a figure in the Bush administration two years before. An aide spoke contemptuously about people like Suskind, describing them as members of the "reality-based community." The aide said confidently: "That's not the way the world works anymore. . . . We're an empire now, and when we act, we create our own reality. And while you're studying that reality—judiciously as you will—we'll act again, creating other new realities, which you can study."[5] Many Americans who read Suskind's report considered the aide's statement a striking example of political hubris. Ron Suskind recognized a larger significance in the statement, one that applies not only to a specific individual in the Bush administration but to radcons generally: that decision-making based on faith and belief rather than questioning and debate can lead to badly mistaken judgments about framing economic and foreign policy. The title of his article identified a fundamentalist outlook: "Without a Doubt."

## Introduction

1. John Micklethwait and Adrian Wooldridge, *The Right Nation: Conservative Power in America* (New York: Penguin Press, 2004), 154.
2. George Packer, *Assassins Gate: America in Iraq* (New York: Farrar, Straus and Giroux, 2005), 52.
3. See Fred Barnes, *Rebel-in-Chief: Inside the Bold and Controversial Presidency of George W. Bush* (New York: Crown Forum, 2006).
4. Barnes defended a war effort that his magazine had been promoting vigorously since the 9/11 tragedy. For a critical view of that role that appeared in a conservative publication, see Scott McConnell, "The Weekly Standard's War: Murdoch's Magazine Stands Athwart History Yelling 'Attack,'" *American Conservative*, November 21, 2005.
5. Steven Tanner, *The Wars of the Bushes: The Father and Son as Military Leaders* (Philadelphia: Casemate, 2004), 240.
6. Francis Fukuyama reports on a related negative reaction to a public address by Charles Krauthammer. When seeing that applause greeted a Krauthammer address in defense of the Bush administration's invasion and occupation of Iraq at the American Enterprise Institute, Fukuyama wondered why more critical judgment had not been registered. Krauthammer's presentation came a year after the problems of U.S. occupation had become acute. See Francis Fukuyama, *America at the Crossroads: Democracy, Power, and the Neoconservative Legacy* (New Haven, Conn.: Yale University Press, 2006), x–xi.
7. Jimmy Carter, *Our Endangered Values: America's Moral Crisis* (New York: Simon and Schuster, 2005), 31–35.
8. Robert Reich, *Reason: Why Liberals Will Win the Battle for America* (New York: Alfred A. Knopf, 2004), 17.
9. Ibid., 113.

## Chapter 1. Politics as Religion

1. Thomas Frank, *What's the Matter with Kansas? How Conservatives Won the Heart of America* (New York: Henry Holt, 2004), 226.
2. Ibid., 175.
3. Ibid., 122.
4. Ibid., 172.
5. Ibid., 221.
6. Michael Lind, *Up from Conservatism: Why the Right Is Wrong for America* (New York: Free Press, 1996), 252.
7. David Brock, *Blinded by the Right: The Conscience of an Ex-Conservative* (New York: Crown, 2002), 285.

8. Daniel J. Balz and Ronald Brownstein, *Storming the Gates: Protest Politics and the Republican Revival* (Boston: Little, Brown, 1995), 52.

9. Sidney Blumenthal, *The Rise of the Counter-Establishment: From Conservative Ideology to Political Power* (New York: Times Books, 1986), 328–329.

10. Fareed Zakaria, "How We Could Have Done It Right, Like It's 1999," *New Republic Online.* Posted June 23, 2004; issue date June 28, 2004.

11. Fareed Zakaria, *The Future of Freedom: Illiberal Democracy at Home and Abroad* (New York: W. W. Norton, 2003), 142.

12. Frank, *What's the Matter with Kansas?* 172.

13. The broadly encompassing term "enthusiastic religionists" is suggested by Robert William Fogel in *The Fourth Great Awakening and the Future of Egalitarianism* (Chicago: University of Chicago Press, 2000).

14. Jonathan M. Schoenwald identifies this important strain within conservatism as essentially a libertarian tradition in *A Time for Choosing: The Rise of Modern American Conservatism* (New York: Oxford University Press, 2001), 12.

15. Kevin Phillips says conservatives with business interests often get their way because religiously inclined people on the right are preoccupied with cultural issues. "With much of the GOP's low-and middle-income electorate listening to conservative preachers," argues Phillips, "the corporate and financial agenda not only prevails but often runs riot." See Kevin Phillips, *American Theocracy: The Peril and Politics of Radical Religion, Oil, and Borrowed Money in the Twenty-first Century* (New York: Viking, 2006), 394.

16. Evidence of important differences and divisions among conservatism appears in Gregory L. Schneider, ed., *Conservatism in America since 1930: A Reader* (New York: New York University Press, 2003), 376–378, 383–391, 415–417; Gary Dorrien, "Inventing an American Conservatism," in Amy E. Ansell, ed., *Unraveling the Right: The New Conservatism in American Thought and Politics* (Boulder, Colo.: Westview Press, 1998), 65–68; Nina Easton, *Gang of Five: Leaders at the Center of the Conservative Crusade* (New York: Simon and Schuster, 2000), 359–364, 279, 282; John A. Andrew III, *The Other Side of the Sixties: Young Americans for Freedom and the Rise of Conservative Politics* (New Brunswick, N.J.: Rutgers University Press, 1997), 62, 103–108; David Frum, *Dead Right* (New York: Basic Books, 1994), 142–143; Mark Gerson, *The Neoconservative Vision: From the Cold War to the Culture Wars* (Lanham, Md.: Madison Books, 1996), 271; Sara Diamond, *Roads to Dominion: Right-Wing Movements and Political Power in the United States* (New York: Guilford Press, 1995), 30–33; Lee Edwards, *The Conservative Revolution: The Movement That Remade America* (New York: Free Press, 1999), 291, 328; Alan Crawford, *Thunder on the Right: The "New Right" and the Politics of Resentment* (New York: Pantheon Books, 1980), 176–178; David Brooks, "A House Divided, and Strong," *New York Times,* April 5, 2005, A27.

17. A brief but useful review of the way various conservative intellectuals dealt with their conflicting viewpoints and tried to bring disparate groups together under a big tent can be found in Jennifer Burns, "In Retrospect: George Nash's *The Conservative Intellectual Movement in America since 1945," Reviews in American History* (September 2004), 447–459.

18. Lou Cannon, *Reagan* (New York: G. P. Putnam's Sons, 1982), 154–160.

19. Rodney Ho, "Rush: I'm Addicted; Talk Show Host to Check into Drug Rehabilitation," *Atlanta Journal-Constitution,* October 11, 2003.

20. Corky Siemaszko, "Rush Back, Still a Pill to Liberals," *Daily News* (New York City), November 18, 2003.

21. "Limbaugh Might Want to Try Compassionate Conservatism" (editorial), *Chicago Sun-Times,* October 14, 2003, 27.

22. Frank Rich employed the term "cultural commissar." See his column "Tupac's Revenge on Bennett," *New York Times,* May 18, 2003; Mimi Hall, "Bennett Says He Set Bad Example: Will Quit Gambling," *USA Today,* May 6, 2003; Cathy Grossman, "Bennett's Gambling Admission Puts a Morality Debate on the Table," *USA Today,* May 7, 2003.

23. Andrew Ward, "Gambling Links Hinder the Rise of a Christian Republican in Georgia," *Financial Times* (London), January 21, 2006, 8.

24. Nina J. Easton, *Gang of Five: Leaders at the Center of the Conservative Crusade* (New York: Simon and Schuster, 2000), 135–142.

25. Thomas B. Edsall, "In Georgia, Abramoff Scandal Threatens a Political Ascendancy," *Washington Post,* January 16, 2006.

26. Judi Enda, "Judiciary Chairman Admits He Had Affair," *Pittsburgh Post-Gazette,* September 17, 1998.

27. Ellen Goodman, "Starr Probe Has Triggered a Sexual Meltdown," *Buffalo News,* September 15, 1998.

28. "Second Lawmaker Who Criticized Clinton Admits to Affair," *St. Louis Post-Dispatch,* September 11, 1998.

29. Tom Teepen, "No Tears for Targets among G.O.P.," *Atlanta Journal-Constitution,* September 13, 1998.

30. John Lang, "Lawmakers Tear Lid Off Pandora's Box," *Chicago Sun-Times,* December 20, 1998; Enda, "Judiciary Chairman Admits He Had Affair."

31. Tabassum Zakaria, "Washington Braces for Sex Scandals: Porn Publisher Threatens to Expose More Politicians," *Toronto Star,* December 23, 1998.

32. Robert Scheer, "Republicans Will Rue the Day They Decided to Use Sex as a Weapon," *Pittsburgh Post-Gazette,* December 24, 1998.

33. Buckley made the contributions in numerous publications, including *Up from Liberalism* (New York: McDowell, Obolensky, 1949). Nash's work *The Conservative Intellectual Movement in America since 1945* (New York: Basic Books, 1976) was also significant.

34. Packer, The *Assassins' Gate,* 16.

35. Ibid., 23.

36. Richard Hofstadter, *The Paranoid Style in American Politics and Other Essays* (New York: Vintage Books, 1964), 3–5. Reference to the "spiritual wrestling match" appears on page 35. Hofstadter maintained that these individuals showed signs of a restless dissatisfaction with American life that was unlike the view of traditional conservatives: "They have little in common with the temperate and compromising spirit of true conservatism in the classical sense of the word, and they are far from pleased with the dominant practical conservatism of the moment as it is represented by the Eisenhower administration" (44). Hence, he called them "pseudo-conservatives." For Hofstadter's view on the demonic "enemy," see 31–35.

37. Ibid., 35.

## Chapter 2. Fundamentalism

1. George M. Marsden, "Defining American Fundamentalism," in Norman J. Cohen, ed., *The Fundamentalist Phenomenon: A View from Within, a Response from Without* (Grand Rapids, Mich.: William B. Eerdman, 1990), 22. For related views of militant anger, see David Edwin Harrell Jr., "American Revivalism from Graham to Robertson," in Edith L. Blumhofer and Randall Balmer, eds., *Modern Christian Revivals* (Champaign-Urbana: University of Illinois Press, 1993), 197; and Joel A. Carpenter, *Revive Us Again: The Reawakening of American Fundamentalism* (New York: Oxford University Press, 1996), 5.
2. Martin E. Marty and R. Scott Appleby, *The Glory and the Power: The Fundamentalist Challenge to the Modern World* (Boston: Beacon Press, 1992); Gabriel A. Almond, R. Scott Appleby, and Emmanuel Sivan, *Strong Religion: The Rise of Fundamentalisms around the World* (Chicago: University of Chicago Press, 2003).
3. Karen Armstrong, *The Battle for God* (New York: Alfred A. Knopf, 2000), x–xi.
4. Ibid., xi.
5. George M. Marsden, *Understanding Fundamentalism and Evangelicalism* (Grand Rapids, Mich.: William B. Eerdmans, 1991), 117; Almond, Appleby, and Sivan, *Strong Religion*, 19, 26,
6. Marty and Appleby, *The Glory and the Power*, 5, 16, 25–26, 34.
7. Armstrong, *The Battle for God*, 270–272.
8. Although Almond, Appleby, Sivan, and others observe a related characteristic of orthodoxy in the three groups, there are, of course, significant differences in the ways these religious groups deal with ideas. For instance, Orthodox Jews fit into Almond, Appleby, and Sivan's definition of fundamentalism in some important ways, yet these Jews often engage in lively disputes with each other when interpreting the meaning of the sacred works.
9. Almond, Appleby, and Sivan, *Strong Religion*, 148.
10. Ibid., 18, 97; Marty and Appleby, *The Glory and the Power*, 5, 16, 25–26, 34.
11. Cass R. Sunstein, *Radicals in Robes: Why Right-Wing Courts Are Wrong for America* (New York: Perseus, 2005), xiv.
12. Jacob S. Hacker and Paul Pierson, *Off-Center: The Republican Revolution and the Erosion of American Democracy* (New Haven, Conn.: Yale University Press, 2005), 30. For upbeat stories about Reagan's character and leadership, see Lee Edwards, *The Essential Ronald Reagan: A Profile in Courage, Justice, and Wisdom* (Lanham, Md.: Rowman and Littlefield, 2005); Steven F. Hayward, *Greatness: Reagan, Churchill, and the Making of Extraordinary Leaders* (New York: Crown Forum, 2005).
13. Almond, Appleby, and Sivan, *Strong Religion*, 103–105.
14. Ibid., 157.
15. Marty and Appleby, *The Glory and the Power*, 30–33.
16. Ibid., 65, 80, 82.
17. Marsden, *Understanding Fundamentalism and Evangelicalism*, 2–6; Marsden, "Defining American Fundamentalism," 22–37; George M. Marsden, *Religion and American Culture*, 2nd ed. (Fort Worth, Tex.: Harcourt College, 2001), 268–271. Also see Carpenter, *Revive Us Again*, 8. For a good overview of the early fundamentalists, see George M. Marsden, *Fundamentalism and American Culture: The Shaping of Twentieth-Century Evangelism, 1870–1925* (New York: Oxford University Press, 1980).

18. Lionel Trilling, *The Liberal Imagination: Essays on Literature and Society* (New York: Viking Press, 1951), ix.

## Chapter 3. Right-Wing Fundamentalists

1. Robert Dallek, *Ronald Reagan: The Politics of Symbolism* (Cambridge, Mass.: Harvard University Press, 1984), 21–23; Stephen Vaughn, *Ronald Reagan in Hollywood* (New York: Cambridge University Press, 1994), 146–185. For Reagan's own descriptions of the conditions that led him to change, see Kiron K. Skinner, Annelise Anderson, and Martin Anderson, eds., *Reagan: A Life in Letters* (New York: Free Press, 2003), 147–149. One of the best overviews of Reagan's political ideas and actions is Lou Cannon, *President Reagan: The Role of a Lifetime* (New York: Simon and Schuster, 1991).
2. Ronald Reagan, with Richard G. Hubler, *Where's the Rest of Me?* (New York: Duell, Sloan, and Pearce, 1965), 138–139.
3. Ibid., 141.
4. Ibid., 169.
5. Ibid., 176.
6. Edmund Morris, *Dutch: A Memoir of Ronald Reagan* (New York: Random House, 1999), 447.
7. Ibid., 458.
8. Irving Kristol, *Neoconservatism, The Autobiography of an Idea* (New York: Free Press, 1995), 3.
9. Peter Steinfels, *The Neoconservatives: The Men Who Are Changing American Politics* (New York: Simon and Schuster, 1979), 81–82.
10. For details on Irving Kristol's transformation toward conservatism, see Murray Friedman, *The Neoconservative Revolution: Jewish Intellectuals and the Shaping of Public Policy* (New York: Cambridge University Press, 2005), 77–79.
11. Kristol, *Neoconservatism*, 4, 6.
12. Ibid., 6.
13. Ibid., 7–8.
14. Anne Norton, *Leo Strauss and the Politics of American Empire* (New Haven and London: Yale University Press, 2004), 25, 28, 51.
15. Ibid., 30.
16. Ibid., 32.
17. Kristol, *Neoconservatism*, 4–5.
18. Michael Lind, *Up from Conservatism: Why the Right Is Wrong for America* (New York: Free Press, 1996), 70.
19. Ethan Bronner, *Battle for Justice: How the Bork Nomination Shook America* (New York: W. W. Norton, 1989), 62.
20. Easton, *Gang of Five*, 142.
21. Ibid., 141.
22. Ibid., 128.
23. Frank, *What's the Matter with Kansas?* 122.
24. Blumenthal, *Rise of the Counter-Establishment*, 46.
25. Russell Kirk, *The Conservative Mind: From Burke to Eliot*, rev. ed. (Chicago: Henry Regnery, 1953), 1, 4–5.

26. Easton, *Gang of Five*, 79–80.
27. George N. Nash, *The Conservative Intellectual Movement in the United States since 1945* (New York: Basic Books, 1976), 105–106.
28. Brad Miner, *The Concise Conservative Encyclopedia: 200 of the Most Important Ideas, Incitements, and Institutions That Have Shaped the Movement—A Personal View* (New York: Free Press, 1996), 228–229.
29. Kristol, *Neoconservatism*, 7, 106, 161.
30. J. David Hoeveler Jr., *Watch on the Right: Conservative Intellectuals in the Reagan Era* (Madison: University of Wisconsin Press, 1991), 18.
31. Nash, *The Conservative Intellectual Movement in the United States*, 15.
32. Gerson, *The Neoconservative Vision*, 42.
33. Andrew, *The Other Side of the Sixties*, 17.
34. Dorrien, "Inventing an American Conservatism," 61–62; Miner, *Concise Conservative Encyclopedia*, 156–157; Nash, *The Conservative Intellectual Movement in the United States*, 90–91; Andrew, *The Other Side of the Sixties*, 12.
35. R. Emmett Tyrrell Jr., *The Conservative Crack-Up* (New York: Simon and Schuster, 1992), 35.
36. Nash, *The Conservative Intellectual Movement in the United States*, 145; Godfrey Hodgson, *The World Turned Right-side Up: A History of the Conservative Ascendancy in America* (Boston: Houghton Mifflin, 1996), 70.
37. Hoeveler, *Watch on the Right*, 281.
38. Ronald Radosh, *Prophets on the Right: Profiles of Conservative Critics of American Globalism* (New York: Simon and Schuster, 1975), 11. Ann Coulter defends Radosh in *Treason: Liberal Treachery from the Cold War to the War on Terrorism* (New York: Crown Forum, 2003), 5.
39. Quoted in Bronner, *Battle for Justice*, 58.
40. Others who dabbled with socialism include Seymour Martin Lipset, Nathan Glazer, and Melvin Lasky. See Gerson, *The Neoconservative Vision*, 20.
41. Damon Linker, "The Christianizing of America: Without a Doubt," *New Republic Online*, March 24, 2006.
42. Richard John Neuhaus, *Catholic Matters: Confusion, Controversy, and the Splendor of Truth* (New York: Basic Books, 2006).
43. David Horowitz, *The Politics of Bad Faith: The Radical Assault on America's Future* (New York: Free Press, 1998), 54, 57.
44. Ibid., 57.
45. Ibid., 66.
46. Ibid., 71.
47. Michael Medved, *Right Turns: Unconventional Lessons from a Controversial Life* (New York: Crown Forum, 2004), 1–5.
48. Milton and Rose D. Friedman, *Two Lucky People* (Chicago: University of Chicago Press, 1998), 23.
49. Blumenthal, *Rise of the Counter-Establishment*, 92.
50. Brock, *Blinded by the Right*, 287.
51. Ibid., 288.
52. Quoted in ibid., 290.
53. Easton, *Gang of Five*, 70–85.
54. Crawford, *Thunder on the Right*, 112–113.

## Chapter 4. Stealth Libertarians

1. Richard Armey, *The Freedom Revolution: The New House Majority Leader Tells Why Big Government Failed, Why Freedom Works, and How We Will Rebuild America* (Washington, D.C.: Regnery, 1995), 7, 13.
2. Ibid., 171.
3. Ibid., 165.
4. David Boaz, *Libertarianism: A Primer* (New York: Free Press, 1997), 2.
5. Ibid., xiv.
6. Friedrich A. von Hayek, *Road to Serfdom* (Chicago: University of Chicago Press, 1944), 122–123. Hayek suggested a distinction between forms of security that government could legitimately attempt and the kinds that seemed inappropriate. "Limited security," such as protection against severe deprivation, could be achieved for all and, therefore, was an "object of desire." With appropriate caution, the government could help to establish a minimum of food, shelter, and clothing sufficient to preserve health and the capacity to work, he said. On the other hand, "absolute security" that promised "a given standard of life" could not be provided for all. An effort to achieve that degree of economic comfort would require control of business or abolition of the market. Governmental programs designed to guarantee absolute security would endanger "general freedom." The state could not legitimately work in that direction. Thus, Hayek's promarket argument in *The Road to Serfdom* did not advance the extreme, antigovernment position promoted today by many libertarian-oriented conservatives in the United States. See page 120.
7. For a description of Rothbard's numerous political switches, see Llewellyn H. Rockwell Jr., *The Irrepressible Rothbard* (Burlingame, Calif.: Center for Libertarian Studies, 2000), xv–xvi.
8. Murray Rothbard, *For a New Liberty: A Libertarian Manifesto*, rev. ed. (New York: Collier Books, 1978) 2–7.
9. Ibid., 10, 12, 14, 16.
10. Ibid., 50–51.
11. Ibid., 162.
12. Ibid., 165.
13. Ibid., 120.
14. Ibid., 119–120.
15. Ibid., 103–104.
16. Ibid., 105.
17. Ibid., 105–114.
18. Ibid., 247.
19. Ibid., 265.
20. Ibid., 266–271.
21. Ibid., 272.
22. Friedman, *The Neoconservative Revolution*, 51–53.
23. Milton Friedman, with the assistance of Rose Friedman, *Capitalism and Freedom* (Chicago: University of Chicago Press, 1962), 25–27.
24. Milton and Rose Friedman, *Free to Choose: A Personal Statement* (New York: Harcourt Brace Jovanovich, 1980), 205.
25. Friedman and Friedman, *Capitalism and Freedom*, 28.

26. Friedman and Friedman, *Free to Choose,* 205.
27. Ibid., 211.
28. Ibid., 214.
29. Ibid., 215.
30. Ibid., 243.
31. Milton Friedman, *Bright Promises, Dismal Performance: An Economist's Protest* (New York: Harcourt Brace Jovanovich, 1983), 16.
32. Friedman and Friedman, *Free to Choose,* 212.
33. Ibid., 223.
34. Ibid.
35. Ibid.
36. Friedman, *Bright Promises, Dismal Performance,* 21.
37. Ibid., 26.
38. Joel Miller, "Milton Friedman at 90," *Ottawa Citizen,* July 30, 2002.
39. Jane Zhang, "Major Changes Set for Food Labels," *Wall Street Journal,* December 28, 2005, D1, D6.
40. "Urinary Catheter System Recalled Due to Sterility Risk," *Biomedical Safety & Standards* 35, 22 (December 15, 2005), 175; "Syringes Recalled; Air Aspiration Possible," ibid., 174–175.
41. "Vioxx," *World Almanac & Book of Facts,* 2006, 00841382.
42. Barton Reppert, "States, Congress, Environmental Groups Oppose New EPA Regulation," *Bioscience* 55, 6 (June 2005), 0063568; "FDA to Probe Report of Higher-Mercury Tuna," *Los Angeles Times,* January 1, 2006.
43. Reppert, "States, Congress, Environmental Groups Oppose New EPA Regulation"; "Breathing Difficulties," *Scientific American* 291, 4 (October 2004), 8
44. "Beefing Up Product Recalls," *Consumer Reports,* 64, 7 (July 1999), 9–11.
45. Sheridan Prasso, "Toy Troubles at Fast-Food Outlets," *Business Week,* March 26, 2001, 14.
46. Kara Sissell, "EWG Seeks Warning Labels for Teflon Cookware, *Chemical Week* 165, 19 (May 21, 2003), 67.
47. See the comments by William W. Robertson Jr. in *Clinical Orthopaedics & Related Research* 1, 409 (April 2003), 37–42.
48. William E. Simon, *A Time for Truth* (New York: McGraw-Hill, 1978), xi.
49. David Brock identifies the ghost-writer in *The Republican Noise Machine: Right-Wing Media and How It Corrupts Democracy* (New York: Crown, 2004), 42.
50. Simon, *A Time for Truth,* 3.
51. Ibid., 66.
52. Ibid., 48–56.
53. William E. Simon, *A Time for Action* (New York: McGraw-Hill, 1980), 85.
54. Ibid., 86.
55. Information about these FDA activities is available at the Web site of the Food and Drug Administration (www.fda.gov).
56. Simon, *A Time for Action,* 12.
57. Ibid., 11.
58. Ibid., 52.
59. Ibid., 86.
60. Blumenthal, *Rise of the Counter-Establishment,* 64.

61. Murray gave hint of his libertarian leanings without announcing them as such in his book *In Pursuit: Of Happiness and Good Government* (New York: Touchstone, 1989). The ideas appear especially at the end in sections titled "Inventing Utopia: A Fantasy" and "Inventing Utopia: A Reality." See 300–303.

62. Charles Murray, *Losing Ground: American Social Policy, 1950–1980* (New York: Basic Books, 1984), ix–xi.

63. Ibid., 279.

64. Christopher Jencks, *Inequality: A Reassessment of the Effect of Family and Schooling in America* (Basic Books: New York, 1972).

65. Christopher Jencks, "How Poor Are the Poor?" *New York Review of Books* (May 9, 1985), 41–43.

66. Nicholas Lemann, "The Bell Curve Flattened: Subsequent Research Has Seriously Undercut the Claims of the Controversial Best-Seller," *Slate,* January 19, 1997.

67. Charles Lane, "The Tainted Sources of 'The Bell Curve,'" *New York Review of Books,* December 1, 1994, 14–15.

68. Murray, *Losing Ground,* 224–230.

69. Charles Murray, *What It Means to Be a Libertarian: A Personal Interpretation* (New York: Broadway Books, 1997), 60.

70. Ibid., 62.

71. Ibid., 76.

72. Ibid., 57–58.

73. Ibid., 62.

74. "B. P. Agrees to Safety Overhaul," *Professional Engineering* 18, 18 (October 5, 2005), 13.

75. Murray, *What It Means to Be a Libertarian,* 77.

76. Ibid., 38.

77. Ibid., 37.

78. Jonathan Barnes, "Labor Department Claims Pike Electric Is a Repeat Violator," *ENR: Engineering News-Record* 255, 16 (October 25, 2005).

79. Murray, *What It Means to Be a Libertarian,* 98–100.

80. Ibid., 93.

81. Ibid., 81–88.

82. Ibid., 38.

83. Ibid., 40.

84. Ibid., 116.

85. Ibid., 114–115.

86. Ibid., 105.

87. Ibid., 104.

88. Ibid., 102.

89. Balz and Brownstein, *Storming the Gates,* 55.

90. Edwards, *The Conservative Revolution,* 83.

91. Helms, *When Free Men Shall Stand,* 55–56.

92. Richard Viguerie, *The Establishment vs. the People* (Chicago: Regnery, 1983), 7.

93. Simon, *A Time for Truth,* 3, 96.

94. Watt, *The Courage of a Conservative,* 55.

95. Ibid., 56.

96. Balz and Brownstein, *Storming the Gates,* 126.
97. Edwards, *The Conservative Revolution,* 284.
98. As the Heritage Foundation's Daniel J. Mitchell argued in May 1990, the problem was government spending, not the deficit. Edwards, *The Conservative Revolution,* 284.
99. Sheryl Gay Stolberg, "Shrink Government, the Right Tells the Right," *New York Times,* January 1, 2004, sec. 4: 1.

## Chapter 5. Culture Warriors

1. James Davison Hunter, *Culture Wars: The Struggle to Define America* (New York: Basic Books, 1991). An example of Hunter's influence can be seen in Jonathan Zimmerman's discussion of the application of Hunter's concepts to disputes about public education. See Jonathan Zimmerman, *Whose America? Culture Wars in the Public Schools* (Cambridge, Mass.: Harvard University Press, 2002), 213, 216–217.
2. Hunter, *Culture Wars,* 214.
3. Ibid., 45–46.
4. Ibid., 152.
5. Ibid., 156.
6. Ibid., 157.
7. Lisa McGirr, *Suburban Warriors: The Origins of the New American Right* (Princeton, N.J.: Princeton University Press, 2001), 69.
8. *Interpretation: A Journal of Political Philosophy* 16, 1 (Fall 1988), 145–156, 52–53; Michael W. Hirschorn, "A Professor Decries Closing of the American Mind," *Chronicle of Higher Education,* May 3, 1987, 3, reprinted in Robert L. Stone, *Essays on The Closing of the American Mind* (Chicago: Chicago Review Press, 1989), 47–50.
9. *Wall Street Journal,* April 22, 1987, 30.
10. Robert Pattison, *Nation,* May 30, 1987, 710; Richard Rorty, "The Old-Time Philosophy," *New Republic,* April 4, 1988, 28–33.
11. Allan Bloom, *The Closing of the American Mind* (New York: Simon and Schuster, 1987), 68–75.
12. Ibid., 51.
13. Ibid., 28.
14. Ibid., 26.
15. Ibid., 34.
16. Ibid., 67.
17. Ibid., 141.
18. Ibid., 51–52.
19. Ibid., 164–167.
20. Ibid., 56–57.
21. Ibid., 51.
22. Ibid., 322.
23. Ibid., 314.
24. Ibid., 30, 149–151.
25. Ibid., 150–151.
26. Ibid., 128–131.
27. Ibid., 98–106, 118.

28. Ibid., 313–320.
29. Ibid., 354.
30. Ibid., 354–355.
31. Christopher Lehmann-Haupt, "The Closing of the American Mind," *New York Times,* March 23, 1987, 13. For a reproduction of numerous essays written in reaction to *The Closing of the American Mind,* see Robert L. Stone, *Essays on the Closing of the American Mind* (Chicago: Chicago Review Press, 1989).
32. Paul Weyrich, "An Open Letter to Conservatives," in Schneider, *American Conservatism since 1930,* 428.
33. Ibid., 428.
34. Ibid., 429.
35. James G. Watt, with Doug Wead, *The Courage of a Conservative* (New York: Simon and Schuster, 1985), 29, 32.
36. Brock, *Blinded by the Right,* 123.
37. Gregory Wolfe, "Of What Use Is Tradition?" in Schneider, *Conservatism in America since 1930,* 380–381. Watt presents a similar picture of liberal responsibility for wide-ranging social ills. See Watt, *The Courage of a Conservative,* 121.
38. Jesse Helms, *When Free Men Shall Stand* (Grand Rapids, Mich.: Zondervan, 1976), 16–17, 107–108.
39. Limbaugh, *See, I Told You So,* 82. Criticism of Limbaugh's massaging of facts can be found in Steve Rendall, *The Way Things Aren't: Rush Limbaugh's Reign of Error—Over 100 Outrageously False and Foolish Statements from America's Most Powerful Radio and TV Commentator* (New York: New Press, 1995).
40. Brock, *Blinded by the Right,* 25–30.
41. Ibid., 60.
42. Ibid., 47.
43. Pat Robertson, *The Turning Tide: The Fall of Liberalism and the Rise of Common Sense* (Dallas: Word Publishing, 1993), 267.
44. Ibid., 13.
45. Helms, *When Free Men Shall Stand,* 16.
46. Ibid., 26.
47. Alan Wolfe, *One Nation, After All* (New York: Viking, 1998), 16–22, 319–322; also see Jonathan Rauch, "Bipolar Disorder: A Funny Thing Happened to Many of the Scholars Who Went Out into the Country to Investigate the Red-Blue Divide. They Couldn't Find It," *Atlantic* 295, 1 (January/February 2005).
48. Morris P. Fiorina with Samuel J. Abrams and Jeremy Pope, *Culture War? The Myth of a Polarized America* (New York: Pearson, Longman, 2004).
49. Tyrrell, *The Conservative Crack-Up,* 32; Nash, *The Conservative Intellectual Movement in the United States,* 39.
50. Richard Weaver, *Ideas Have Consequences* (Chicago: University of Chicago Press, 1948/1976), 2.
51. Ibid., 2, 4, 13.
52. Ibid., 5, 6, 185.
53. William F. Buckley Jr., *Up from Liberalism* (Obolensky, N.Y.: McDowell, 1959), 110.
54. Ibid., 109.
55. Ibid., 154.
56. Hunter, *Culture Wars,* 145.

57. James L. Noland Jr., *The Culture Wars: Current Contests and Future Prospects* (Charlottesville: University Press of Virginia, 1996), 44–49.
58. Helms, *When Free Men Shall Stand,* 26–27.
59. Paul Weyrich in Howard Phillips, ed., *The New Right at Harvard* (Vienna, Va.: Conservative Caucus, 1983), 35–36.
60. Watt, *Courage of a Conservative,* 113.
61. Ibid., 179.
62. Ibid., 113.
63. Gerson, *The Neoconservative Vision,* 295.
64. Ibid., 296.
65. James Q. Wilson, *The Moral Sense* (New York: Free Press, 1993), viii–xiii.
66. Dinesh D'Souza, *Letters to a Young Conservative* (New York: Basic Books, 2002), 111.
67. Ibid., 110–111.
68. Quoted in William J. Bennett, *Why We Fight: Moral Clarity and the War on Terrorism* (New York: Doubleday, 2002), 141.
69. George Lakoff, *Moral Politics: How Liberals and Conservatives Think* (Chicago: University of Chicago Press, 2002). Lakoff offers a brief and more partisan guide to "progressives" in *Don't Think of an Elephant! Know Your Values and Frame the Debate: The Essential Guide for Progressives* (White River Junction, Vt.: Chelsea Green, 2004).
70. Jim Wallis, *God's Politics: Why the Right Gets It Wrong and the Left Doesn't Get It* (San Francisco: HarperSanFrancisco, 2005); "Prayer Center," *New Republic* 232, 19 (May 23, 2005), 21–25.
71. Paul Singer, "Roberts and the Religious Right—and Left," *National Journal* 37, 33–35 (August 13, 2005), 2610.
72. "Spirited Progressives Move toward Working Together," *Network News* 25, 3 (Summer 2005), 16–20.
73. Tyrrell, *The Liberal Crack-Up,* 11.
74. Ibid., 36.
75. Ibid., 33.
76. Ibid., 73.
77. Ibid., 33.
78. Robert Bork, *Slouching toward Gomorrah: Modern Liberalism and American Decline* (New York: Regan Books, 1996), 2.
79. Ibid., 4.
80. Ibid., 4.
81. Ibid., 19.
82. Ibid., 102–104, 193.
83. Ibid., 2, 131, 276.
84. Nash, *The Conservative Intellectual Movement in the United States,* 297–298, 301–302; Mark Gerson, ed., *The Essential Neoconservative Reader* (Reading, Mass.: Addison-Wesley, 1996), 59–61.
85. *New Criterion* 17 (March 1999), 1.
86. Limbaugh, *See, I Told You So,* 86.
87. Balz and Brownstein, *Storming the Gates,* 32.
88. Blumenthal, *The Rise of the Counter-Establishment,* 163.

89. Maurice Isserman and Michael Kazin, *America Divided: The Civil War of the 1960s* (New York: Oxford University Press, 2000), 297.

90. Ibid., 294–295, 299.

91. David Farber and Jeff Roche, eds., *The Conservative Sixties* (New York: Peter Lang, 2003), 1–2.

92. Mary C. Brennan, *Turning Right in the Sixties: The Conservative Capture of the GOP* (Chapel Hill: University of North Carolina Press, 1995); Rick Perlstein, *Before the Storm: Barry Goldwater and the Unmaking of the American Consensus* (New York: Hill and Wang, 2001).

93. Lisa McGirr, *Suburban Warriors: The Origins of the New American Right* (Princeton, N.J.: Princeton University Press, 2001).

94. Roger Kimball, *Tenured Radicals: How Politics Has Corrupted Our Higher Education* (New York: Harper and Row, 1990), xvii.

95. Ibid., xii–xiv.

96. Ibid., xii–xiii.

97. Ibid., xi.

98. William J. Bennett, *The Devaluing of America: The Fight for Our Culture and Our Children* (New York: Summit Books, 1992), 157–158.

99. Ibid., 34.

100. D'Souza, *Letters to a Young Conservative,* 39–41.

101. Ibid., 41.

102. John P. Diggins, *The Rise and Fall of the American Left* (New York: W. W. Norton, 1973/1992), 16–19, 313–314, 379, 382.

103. James Glanz, "Scientists Say Administration Distorts Facts," *New York Times,* February 19, 2004, A4.

104. Paul Krugman, "An Academic Question," *New York Times,* April 5, 2005, A27. Additional discussion of the issues appears in Chris Mooney, *The Republican War on Science* (New York: Basic Books, 2005).

105. Bloom, *The Closing of the American Mind,* 315.

106. Ibid., 316.

107. Ibid., 131.

108. "Introduction" in Hilton Kramer and Roger Kimball, eds., *The Betrayal of Liberalism: How the Disciples of Freedom and Equality Helped Foster the Illiberal Policies of Coercion and Control* (Chicago: Ivan R. Dees, 1999), 5.

109. Ibid., 8.

110. Ibid., 8, 13–15.

111. Ibid., 15.

112. Ibid., 17.

113. Kramer and Kimball, *The Betrayal of Liberalism,* 41–42, 119.

114. John Silber, "Procedure or Dogma: The Core of Liberalism," in Kramer and Kimball, *The Betrayal of Liberalism,* 197–203.

115. Ibid., 203.

116. D'Souza, *Letters to a Young Conservative,* 1–3.

117. Ibid., 38.

118. Ibid.

119. Dinesh D'Souza, *What's So Great about America* (Lanham, Md.: Regnery, 2002), 101–130.

120. Ibid., 124–125.
121. Ibid., 128–129.
122. Useful discussions of the conservatives' efforts to capitalize on racial fears can be found in Dan T. Carter, *From George Wallace to Newt Gingrich: Race in the Conservative Counterrevolution, 1963–1994* (Baton Rouge: Louisiana State University Press, 1996); Donald R. Kinder, *Divided by Color: Racial Politics and Democratic Ideals* (Chicago: University of Chicago Press, 1996); Kevin Michael Kruse, *White Flight: Atlanta and the Making of Modern Conservatism* (Princeton, N.J.: Princeton University Press, 2005).
123. George F. Gilder, *Sexual Suicide* (New York: Quadrangle/New York Times Book Company, 1973), 6.
124. Ibid., 6.
125. Ibid., 7–8.
126. Limbaugh, *See, I Told You So,* 79.
127. Rush Limbaugh, *The Way Things Ought to Be* (New York: Pocket Books, 1992), 190, 192.
128. Limbaugh, *See, I Told You So,* 202.
129. Ibid., 203.
130. Ibid., 206.
131. Ibid., 213.
132. Phyllis Schlafly, *Feminist Fantasies* (Dallas: Spence, 2003), 40.
133. Ibid., 42.
134. Ibid., 43, 77–78.
135. Ibid., 223.
136. Ibid., 181.
137. For related attitudes, see Ralph Reed, *Active Faith: How Christians Are Changing the Soul of American Politics* (New York: Free Press, 1996), 77.
138. Cathy Young, "Feminism Revisited," *Boston Globe,* December 19, 2005, A17.
139. Patricia Cohen, "Today, Some Feminists Hate the Word 'Choice,'" *New York Times,* January 15, 2006, sec. 4: 3. Cohen was referring to Linda Hirshman as the feminist who criticized choice.
140. Louise Story, "Many Women at Elite Colleges Set Career Path to Motherhood," *New York Times,* September 20, 2005, A1.
141. Linda Hirshman, "Homeward Bound," *American Prospect,* December 2005, 20.
142. Cohen, "Today, Some Feminists Hate the Word 'Choice,'" sec. 4: 3.
143. Thomas Frank, "Failure Is Not an Option: It's Mandatory," *New York Times,* July 16, 2004, A27.
144. Ibid.; see also Frank, *What's the Matter with Kansas?* 157–161.

## Chapter 6. Hawkish Nationalists

1. For criticisms of this policy, see Arthur Schlesinger Jr., *War and the American Presidency* (New York: W. W. Norton, 2004); Stefan Halper and Jonathan Clarke, *America Alone: The Neo-Conservatives and the Global Order* (New York: Cambridge University Press, 2004); Richard A. Clarke, *Against All Enemies: Inside America's War on Terrorism* (New York: Free Press, 2004); Maureen Dowd, *Bush World: Enter at Your Own Risk* (New York: G. P. Putnam's Sons, 2004); Joseph Wilson, *The Poli-*

*tics of Truth: Inside the Lies That Led to War and Betrayal of My Wife's CIA Identity* (New York: Carroll and Graf, 2004); Seymour M. Hersh, *Chain of Command: The Road from 9/11 to Abu Ghraib* (New York: HarperCollins, 2004); James Bamford, *A Pretext for War: 9/11, Iraq, and the Abuse of America's Intelligence Agencies* (New York: Doubleday, 2004); Michael R. Gordon and General Bernard E. Trainor, *Cobra II: The Inside Story of the Invasion and Occupation of Iraq* (New York: Pantheon, 2006); Mark Danner, *The Secret Way to War: The Downing Street Memo and the Iraq War's Buried History* (New York: New York Review of Books, 2006).

2. Interestingly, the Fox News Channel's John Gibson claims that Bush administration officials "have taken pains to emphasize that they have made no connection between Saddam Hussein and the 9/11 attacks" (recorded commentaries from Bush administration officials contradict Gibson's assertion). Despite this reference in his book, Gibson asserts that he stands with the 69 percent of Americans who believed as late as the second anniversary of the attacks that "Saddam had a hand in the atrocity." See John Gibson, *Hating America: The New World Sport* (New York: Regan Books, 2004), 9.

3. Jacob Hacker and Paul Pierson show that Republican leaders are often able to force their members in the House and Senate to take cohesive positions on key issues. They manage to snuff out internal dissent with impressive ease. See *Off-Center: The Republican Revolution and the Erosion of Democracy* (New Haven, Conn.: Yale University Press, 2005). Also see the author's interview on Terry Gross's radio program on NPR, *Fresh Air,* December 1, 2005.

4. David Horowitz, *Unholy Alliance: Radical Islam and the American Left* (Washington, D.C.: Regnery, 2004), 4.

5. Stefan Halper and Jonathan Clarke, *America Alone: The Neo-Conservatives and the Global Order* (Cambridge: Cambridge University Press, 2004), 4.

6. Ibid., 154.

7. Norman Podhoretz, *Why We Were in Vietnam* (New York: Simon and Schuster, 1982), 14.

8. Ibid., 196.

9. George F. Will, *The Pursuit of Virtue and Other Tory Notions* (New York: Simon and Schuster, 1982), 155.

10. Ibid., 155.

11. Ibid., 153.

12. Watt, *Courage of a Conservative,* 154.

13. Nathan Glazer, "The Campus Crucible: Student Politics and the University," in Gerson, *The Essential Neoconservative Reader,* 112–114.

14. Ibid., 115.

15. Ibid.

16. Charles DeBenedetti, *An American Ordeal: The Antiwar Movement of the Vietnam Era* (Syracuse, N.Y.: Syracuse University Press, 1990), 25–26.

17. Kenneth J. Heineman, *Campus Wars: The Peace Movement at American State Universities in the Vietnam Era* (New York: New York University Press, 1993), 182, 208–209.

18. The fragmentation of liberalism in connection with the Vietnam War is discussed in Allen J. Matusow, *The Unraveling of America: A History of Liberalism in the 1960s* (New York: Harper and Row, 1984), 377–394.

19. Tom Wells, *The War Within: America's Battle over Vietnam* (Berkeley: University of California Press, 1994), 135–137.

20. Matusow, *The Unraveling of America,* 389–393.
21. George C. Herring, *LBJ and Vietnam: A Different Kind of War* (Austin: University of Texas Press, 1994), 179–184. Quote on 183–184.
22. Philip Gold, *Take Back the Right: How the Neocons and the Religious Right Have Betrayed the Conservative Movement* (New York: Carroll and Graf, 2004), 108, 111–112.
23. Kevin J. Smant, *Principles and Heresies: Frank S. Meyer and the Shaping of the American Conservative Movement* (Wilmington, Del.: ISI Books, 2002), 233.
24. Norman Podhoretz, *The Present Danger: Do We Have the Will to Reverse the Decline of American Power?* (New York: Simon and Schuster, 1980), 12.
25. Ibid., 37–38.
26. Ibid., 37.
27. Ibid., 51.
28. Ibid., 40.
29. Ibid., 44.
30. Ibid., 76, 79.
31. Ibid., 77–82.
32. Blumenthal, *The Rise of the Counter-Establishment,* 308.
33. Packer, *The Assassin's Gate,* 21–22.
34. Quote from Lawrence J. Korb, "It's Time to Bench 'Team B,'" *American Progress,* August 18, 2004, http://www.americanprogress.org. Anne Hessing Cahn discusses this history in "Team B: The Trillion Dollar Experiment," *Bulletin of the Atomic Scientists* (April 1993), and her longer analysis appears in *Killing Détente: The Right Attacks the CIA* (College Station, Pa.: Penn State University Press, 1998).
35. Viguerie, *The Establishment vs. the People,* 7.
36. Phillips, *The New Right at Harvard,* 44.
37. Ibid., 49.
38. Ibid., 45.
39. Schneider, *Conservatism in America since 1930,* 196.
40. Phillips, *The New Right at Harvard,* 10.
41. Helms, *When Free Men Shall Stand,* 95.
42. Ibid., 94.
43. Simon, *A Time for Action,* 15–16.
44. Ibid., 127.
45. Ibid., 119.
46. Ibid., 140.
47. Ibid., 120.
48. Ibid., 120–121.
49. Walter Isaacson, *Kissinger: A Biography* (New York: Simon and Schuster, 1992), 608–609.
50. Henry Kissinger, *Years of Upheaval* (Boston: Little, Brown, 1982), 236.
51. Ibid., 982–984.
52. Phyllis Schlafly and Chester Ward, *Kissinger on the Couch* (New Rochelle, N.Y.: Arlington House, 1975), 11–13.
53. Edwards, *The Conservative Revolution,* 242.
54. Ibid., 243.
55. Ibid., 254–257, 273.
56. Peter Schweizer, *Reagan's War: The Epic Story of His Struggle and Final Triumph over Communism* (New York: Random House, 2003).

57. Jay Winik, *On the Brink: The Dramatic behind the Scenes Saga of the Reagan Era and the Men and Women Who Won the Cold War* (New York: Simon and Schuster, 1996). Information about Winik's popularity with President Bush and Vice President Cheney appears on the Web site of the Center for International and Security Studies at the University of Maryland and on Chautauqua's Web site, http://www.chautauqua-inst.org/winik.html. Nuanced interpretations of related issues can be found in books by authors who also praise Reagan's achievements in the Cold War but recognize that the causes of the Soviet Union's fall are, nevertheless, complex. See Paul Lettow, *Ronald Reagan and His Quest to Abolish Nuclear Weapons* (New York: Random House, 2005); and John Lewis Gaddis, *The Cold War: A New History* (New York: Penguin Press, 2005). A brief version of Gaddis's argument can be found in his speech at the Elliott School of International Affairs. See "Strategies of Containment: Post–Cold War Reconsiderations" at http://gwu.edu/~elliott/news/transcripts/gaddis.html.

58. Armey, *The Freedom Revolution*, 49–50.

59. Limbaugh, *The Way Things Ought To Be*, 234.

60. Ibid., 233.

61. Frances Fitzgerald raises diverse questions about the Star Wars program in *Way out There in the Blue: Reagan, Star Wars, and the End of the Cold War* (New York: Random House, 2000).

62. Susan McCaffray, "Charting the Demise of the Soviet Empire," *National Guard Review: Special Issue* (1998), 22.

63. Don Oberdorfer, "The Reagan-Gorbachev Summits," in Brian Lamb, ed., *Booknotes: Stories from American History* (New York: Penguin Books, 2001), 460.

64. For an intriguing and extensive discussion of Gorbachev's contributions as well as Reagan's, see Jack F. Matlock Jr., *Reagan and Gorbachev: How the Cold War Ended* (New York: Random House, 2004).

65. Jack F. Matlock praises both Reagan and Gorbachev, as well as their key aides, for flexibility in the negotiations in *Reagan and Gorbachev*, 319–323.

66. Strobe Talbott, "Shutting the Cold War Down," *New York Times Book Reviews*, August 1, 2004, 7.

67. Raymond L. Garthoff, *The Great Transition: American-Soviet Relations and the End of the Cold War* (Washington, D.C.: Brookings Institution, 1994), 753–754.

68. Don Oberdorfer, *From the Cold War to the New Era: The United States and the Soviet Union, 1983–1991* (Baltimore: Johns Hopkins University Press, 1998), 479.

69. Ibid., 478.

70. Ibid., 479.

71. Ibid., 480.

72. Bennett, *Why We Fight*, 141.

73. Ibid.

74. Ibid., 142.

75. Ibid., 8.

76. Ibid., 147.

77. Ibid., 32.

78. Ibid., 2, 40.

79. Ibid., 17.

80. Ibid., 40.

81. Ibid., 9.

82. Sean Hannity, *Deliver Us from Evil: Defeating Terrorism, Despotism, and Liberalism* (New York: Regan Books, 2004), 7.
83. Ibid., 9.
84. Ibid., 165–169.
85. Ibid., 2.
86. Ibid., 3–4.
87. Ibid., 2–3.
88. Ibid.
89. Ibid., 2–3, 9.
90. Ibid., 8.
91. Lenore Skenazy, "A Savaging for MSNBC & Fired Host," *Daily News* (New York), July 9, 2003.
92. Michael Savage, *The Enemy Within: Saving America from the Assault on Our Schools, Faith, and Military* (Nashville: WND Books, 2003), xi–xiv.
93. Ibid., 3.
94. Ibid., 74.
95. Ibid.
96. Ann Coulter, *Treason: Liberal Treachery from the Cold War to the War on Terror* (New York: Crown Forum, 2003), 203.
97. Ibid., 1.
98. Ibid., 5.
99. Richard A. Clarke, *Against All Enemies: Inside America's War on Terror* (New York: Free Press, 2004), 32.
100. Ron Suskind, *The Price of Loyalty: George W. Bush, the White House, and the Education of Paul O'Neill* (New York: Simon and Schuster, 2004), 72–75.
101. Packer, *The Assassins' Gate*, 29
102. Ibid., 117.
103. Ibid., 137. Also see 114.
104. Ibid., 214.
105. "The 12-Year War," *Wall Street Journal*, March 18, 2003, A16.
106. Ibid.
107. "Review and Outlook," *Wall Street Journal*, March 10, 2003, A18.
108. Ibid.
109. *Wall Street Journal*, March 12, 2003, A18.
110. Oriana Fallaci, "The Rage, the Pride, and the Doubt," *Wall Street Journal*, March 13, 2003, A12.
111. Winston S. Churchill, "My Grandfather Invented Iraq," *Wall Street Journal*, March 10, 2003, A18.
112. Daniel Henninger, "U.S. to World: Take This Job and Shove It," *Wall Street Journal*, March 7, 2003, A10; also see Daniel Henninger, "Terror's Truth: Saddam Will Shop 'Till He Drops,'" *Wall Street Journal*, March 13, 2003, A10.
113. Joshua Muravchik, "We're Better Off without That UN Resolution," *Wall Street Journal*, March 18, 2003, A16.
114. George Melloan, "Chirac's Errant Course Raises Fears in His Party," *Wall Street Journal*, March 4, 2003, A15.
115. Kofi A. Annan, "Keep the UN United," *Wall Street Journal*, March 11, 2003, A14.
116. Albert R. Hunt, "A Just But Worrisome War," *Wall Street Journal*, March 13, 2003, A13.

117. "The Worst-Case Scenario Arrives," *New York Times*, March 6, 2003, A30.

118. "Saying No to War," *New York Times*, March 9, 2003, sec. 4: 12.

119. "President Bush Prepares for War," *New York Times*, March 17, 2003, A22. Also see "War in the Ruins of Diplomacy," *New York Times*, March 18, 2003, A32.

120. Paul Krugman, "Let Them Hate Us as Long as They Fear," *New York Times*, March 7, 2003, A27.

121. Maureen Dowd, "What Would Genghis Do?" *New York Times*, March 5, 2003, A 23.

122. Bob Herbert, "Bombs and Blood," *New York Times*, March 13, 2003, A26.

123. William Safire, "Give Freedom a Chance," *New York Times*, March 6, 2003, A31.

124. Thomas L. Friedman in *New York Times*, March 2, 2003, 13.

125. Jimmy Carter, "Just War—Or a Just War?" *New York Times*, March 9, 2003, sec. 4: 13.

126. John McCain, "The Right War for the Wrong Reasons," *New York Times*, March 12, 2003, A25.

127. This appeared in "*The Times* and Iraq," http://www.NYTimes.com/critique. Also see Daniel Okrent, "Weapons of Mass Destruction? Or Mass Distraction?" *New York Times*, May 30, 2004, sec. 4: 2.

128. The quote is from former *Wall Street Journal* editor Robert Bartley, who is citing Thomas Sowell. "Pessimistic Liberalism," *Wall Street Journal*, April 16, 2003, A18.

129. Norman Podhoretz, *Why We Were in Vietnam* (New York: Simon and Schuster, 1982), 83.

130. "Gallup Poll Shows Tight Race for Presidency," CNN.com, May 6, 2004.

## Chapter 7. Media Wars

1. Peter Steinfels, *The Neoconservatives: The Men Who Are Changing America's Politics* (New York: Simon and Schuster, 1979), 56–58.

2. The term is in the title of one of C. Wright Mills's most influential books, *The Power Elite* (New York: Oxford University Press, 1956).

3. Steinfels, *The Neoconservatives*, 199.

4. Samuel Francis, "Message from Mars," in Schneider, *Conservatism in America since 1930*, 305.

5. Bork, *Slouching toward Gomorrah*, 84.

6. Hoeveler, *Watch on the Right*, 11.

7. Ibid., 6–7.

8. Crawford, *Thunder on the Right*, 168–172, 179.

9. Steinfels, *The Neoconservatives*, 57.

10. Francis, "Message from Mars," in Schneider, *Conservatism in America since 1930*, 308.

11. Crawford, *Thunder on the Right*, 172.

12. Gerson, *The Neoconservative Vision*, 108; Blumenthal, *Rise of the Counter-Establishment*, 14.

13. Eric Alterman, *What Liberal Media? The Truth about Bias and the News* (New York: Basic Books, 2003), 1. David Brock adds a great deal of useful information about the controversies over media bias in *The Republican Noise Machine: Right-Wing Media and How It Corrupts Democracy* (New York: Crown, 2004).

14. Edwards, *The Conservative Revolution*, 167–168.

15. Bill O'Reilly speaking on "Book TV," C-SPAN 2, May 31, 2003.

16. Bernard Goldberg, *Bias: A CBS Insider Exposes How the Media Distorts the News* (Chicago: Regnery, 2002), 8–11.

17. Ibid., 188–189.

18. Bernard Goldberg, *Arrogance: Rescuing America from the Media Elite* (New York: Warner Books, 2003).

19. Robertson, *The Turning Tide,* 133–136.

20. Sean Hannity, *Let Freedom Ring: Winning the War of Liberty over Liberalism* (New York: Regan Books, 2002), 256–257.

21. Ibid., 258.

22. Ann Coulter, *Slander: Liberal Lies about the American Right* (New York: Crown, 2002), 76.

23. Goldberg, *Bias,* 190.

24. Robert S. Boynton, "How to Make a Guerilla Documentary," *New York Times Magazine,* July 11, 2004, 20–23 (quote on 22).

25. Andrew Kohut, "More News Is Not Necessarily Good News," *New York Times,* July 11, 2004, sec. 4: 5.

26. Alterman, *What Liberal Media?* 27.

27. Brock, *The Republican Noise Machine,* 53.

28. Alterman, *What Liberal Media?* 83

29. Brock, *Blinded by the Right,* 72–73.

30. Blumenthal, *Rise of the Counter-Establishment,* 53–54.

31. Goldberg, *Bias,* 216.

32. Blumenthal, *Rise of the Counter-Establishment,* 38.

33. Alterman, *What Liberal Media?* 85.

34. Brock, *Blinded by the Right,* 189.

35. Blumenthal, *Rise of the Counter-Establishment,* 159.

36. Alterman, *What Liberal Media?* 86–87; Hodgson, *The World Turned Right-side Up,* 195.

37. Steinfels, *The Neoconservatives,* 13.

38. Alterman, *What Liberal Media?* 86.

39. John R. Lott Jr., *More Guns, Less Crime: Understanding Crime and Gun Control,* 2nd ed. (Chicago: University of Chicago Press, 2000), x, 124.

40. Ibid., 125.

41. Ibid., 126.

42. Simon, *A Time for Truth,* 228, 240.

43. Ibid., 240.

44. Ibid., 227–228.

45. Ibid., 230.

46. Ibid.

47. Ibid., 234, 240.

48. Clarence Page, "*Fahrenheit 9/11* Prompting Discussion, Praise Its Critics," *San Gabriel Valley* (Calif.) *Tribune,* June 28, 2004.

49. I explore this matter in detail in Robert Brent Toplin, *Michael Moore's* Fahrenheit 9/11: *How One Film Divided the Nation* (Lawrence: University Press of Kansas, 2006).

50. David Segal, "Dixie Chicks Bare Their, Uh, Souls: Ban Counters Critics of Anti-War Remarks," *Washington Post,* April 25, 2003; Paul Krugman, "Channels of Influence," *New York Times,* March 25, 2003.

51. "Speaking Out," *Pittsburgh Post-Gazette,* April 17, 2003.
52. Frank Rich, "The Nascar Nightly News: Anchorman Get Your Gun," *New York Times,* December 5, 2004, sec. 2: 1, 21.

## Chapter 8. The Closing of the Conservative Mind

1. Chris Weinkopf, "The People Speak (Beat the Press)," *American Enterprise* 15, 1 (January–February 2004), 49.
2. Matthew Continetti, "Brave New Academic Freedom: Phi Beta Kappa Goes to Bat for Michael Moore," *Weekly Standard* 10, 24 (March 14, 2005), 10–11.
3. Alan Wolfe, "Why Conservatives Can't Govern," *Washington Monthly* (July/August 2006) Also, see Jonathan Chait, "Binge and Purge: The Right Expels Bush," *New Republic,* June 1, 2006.
4. Wolfe, "Why Conservatives Can't Govern."
5. Ron Suskind, "Without a Doubt," *New York Times,* October 17, 2004, Sec. 6, 44.